Ascent to Heaven in Jewish and
Christian Apocalypses

Ascent to Heaven in Jewish and Christian Apocalypses

MARTHA HIMMELFARB

New York   Oxford
OXFORD UNIVERSITY PRESS
1993

Oxford University Press

Oxford   New York   Toronto
Delhi   Bombay   Calcutta   Madras   Karachi
Kuala Lumpur   Singapore   Hong Kong   Tokyo
Nairobi   Dar es Salaam   Cape Town
Melbourne   Auckland   Madrid

and associated companies in
Berlin   Ibadan

Copyright © 1993 by Martha Himmelfarb

Published by Oxford Unversity Press Inc.
200 Madison Avenue, New York, New York 10016

Library of Congress Cataloging-in-Publication Data
Himmelfarb, Martha, 1952–
Ascent to heaven in Jewish and Christian apocalypses/
Martha Himmelfarb.   p.   cm.
Includes bibliographical references and index.
ISBN 0-19-508203-6
1. Apocalyptic literature.   2. Voyages to the otherworld.
3. Heaven.   4. Angels in literature.
I. Title. BS1705.H56   1993   229'.913—dc20   92-35748

Scriptural quotations are from the Revised Standard Version of the Bible, copyright 1946, 1952, 1971 by the Division of Christian Education of the National Council of the Churches of Christ in the USA. Used with permission.

The quotation from "Revelation and Rapture" by Martha Himmelfarb, which appeared in the issue of the *Journal for the Study of Pseudepigrapha* entitled *Mysteries and Revelations*, is reprinted by permission of the publisher.

The quotation from *The Book of Enoch* by Matthew Black (1985) is reprinted by permission of the publisher, E. J. Brill, the Netherlands.

2 4 6 8 9 7 5 3 1

Printed in the United States of America
on acid-free paper

For my parents,
Judith and Milton Himmelfarb

Preface

This book is a study of the early Jewish and Christian apocalypses involving ascent to heaven: the Book of the Watchers (1 Enoch 1–36), the Testament of Levi, 2 Enoch, the Similitudes of Enoch (1 Enoch 37–71), the Apocalypse of Zephaniah, the Apocalypse of Abraham, the Ascension of Isaiah, and 3 Baruch. These works, which span the third century B.C.E. to the second century C.E., have recently assumed a more prominent role in scholarly discussion because of the early dates of the Qumran fragments of the Book of the Watchers, on the one hand, and the interest in questions of genre, on the other.

Beginning with the Book of the Watchers, these works envision heaven as a temple, and I argue that this conception determines the way they describe ascent. The most striking example is the depiction of the visionary's achievement of equality with the angels through the language of priestly investiture. Some of the ascent apocalypses make secrets of nature an important part of the revelation to the visionary in the course of the ascent, with implications for the origins of evil in the universe and God's accessibility in this world.

The final chapter of this book considers the nature of authorship in these pseudepigraphic apocalypses and the related problem of the status of the visions and ascents. Did the authors themselves experience something like the ascents they describe? Why did they use ancient heroes to put forward their messages? I argue that the apocalypses are best understood not as literary adaptations of personal experiences but as imaginative literature.

The ascent apocalypses are deeply indebted to the later prophetic books of the Hebrew Bible, especially Ezekiel, which had a profound influence on the Book of the Watchers and, through it, on the other ascent apocalypses. But they must also be understood as part of Greco-Roman thought about ascent and divinization. I try to place them in both contexts. I believe that careful attention to the ascent apocalypses will enlarge our understanding of ancient Judaism and Christianity.

Since the manuscript for this book was completed in November 1991, I was unable to take into account literature published after that date except occasionally to note its existence.

I am delighted to thank those colleagues and friends who helped me in the preparation of this book. I have tried to acknowledge debts for specific points in the notes, but there are several people to whom I owe thanks of a more general kind. George W. E. Nickelsburg offered many helpful comments, especially on chapter 1. John Gager, my colleague at Princeton, read drafts of several chapters and encouraged me throughout. My teacher Michael Stone, whose work has had a lasting influence on my own, graciously commented at some length on chapter 5, where I chose to disagree with him. His criticism helped me sharpen and, I hope, improve my arguments.

I am grateful to several students who served as research assistants on this project. Three former Princeton graduate students—A. G. Miller, Judith Weisenfeld, and Timothy Fulop—provided able assistance (despite the fact that their own field is American religious history), as did Charles Bott, formerly an undergraduate in the department and now embarked on graduate studies in the area of early Christianity. My student Gideon Bohak, still at Princeton, served as an assistant toward the end of the project and made many helpful suggestions. Jennifer Herdt, a departmental graduate student in the field of religion, ethics, and politics, prepared the bibliography with great efficiency. None of these assistants would have come my way without the guiding hand of Lorraine Fuhrmann, the department administrator. I thank her and the department's secretaries, Harriet Stuart and Lynn Maselli, for help at so many moments along the way.

My husband, Steven L. Weiss, read the whole manuscript and offered help at many points. That is only the smallest part of my debt to him. My father, Milton Himmelfarb, came out of retirement to advise me on editorial matters. I am grateful for his advice about style and for his comments on many issues of substance. I dedicate the book to him and to my mother, Judith Himmelfarb, with love.

Princeton, N.J.   M.H.
November 1992

Contents

Abbreviations

Bible and Pseudepigrapha

Apoc. Zeph.	Apocalypse of Zephaniah
Asc. Is.	Ascension of Isaiah
2 Bar.	2 Baruch
3 Bar.	3 Baruch
Cor.	Corinthians
Chron.	Chronicles
Dan.	Daniel
Deut.	Deuteronomy
Ex.	Exodus
Ez.	Ezra
4 Ez.	4 Ezra
Ezek.	Ezekiel
Gen.	Genesis
Hag.	Haggai
Isa.	Isaiah
Jer.	Jeremiah
Judg.	Judges
Lev.	Leviticus
Mal.	Malachi
Neh.	Nehemiah
Num.	Numbers
Ps.	Psalm
Rev.	Revelation
Sam.	Samuel

Sir.	Sirach
T. Levi	Testament of Levi
Zech.	Zechariah

Rabbinic Texts

m.	Mishnah
b.	Babylonian Talmud

Journals, Reference Works, and Serials

ANRW	*Aufstieg und Niedergang der römischen Welt*
APOT	R. H. Charles, ed., *Apocrypha and Pseudepigrapha of the Old Testament*
CBQ	*Catholic Biblical Quarterly*
FJB	*Frankfurter Judaistische Beiträge*
HUCA	*Hebrew Union College Annual*
JBL	*Journal of Biblical Literature*
JJS	*Journal of Jewish Studies*
JNES	*Journal of Near Eastern Studies*
JSJ	*Journal for the Study of Judaism in the Persian, Hellenistic and Roman Period*
JTS	*Journal of Theological Studies*
PGM	K. Preisendanz, ed., *Papyri graecae magicae*
RB	*Revue biblique*
RSV	Revised Standard Version translation of the Bible
SVTP	Studia in Veteris Testamenti Pseudepigrapha
VT	*Vetus Testamentum*

Ascent to Heaven in Jewish and
Christian Apocalypses

Introduction

As the patriarch Enoch stands before the divine throne in 2 (Slavonic) Enoch, he undergoes a wonderful transformation:

> And the Lord said to Michael, Take Enoch and take off his earthly garments, and anoint *him* with good oil, and clothe *him* in glorious garments. And Michael took off from me my garments and anointed me with good oil. And the appearance of the oil *was* more *resplendent* than a great light, and its richness like sweet dew, and its fragrance like myrrh, **shining like a ray of the sun**. And I looked at myself, and I was like one of the glorious ones, and there was no apparent difference (9:17–19).[1]

The claim made in such striking terms in this passage, that a human being can become the equal of the angels, stands at the center of a group of eight early Jewish and Christian apocalypses in which ascent to heaven is the mode of revelation.[2] In other ways there are considerable differences among these apocalypses. Some come from Palestine, others from Egypt. They span almost four hundred years, from the early third century B.C.E. to the mid-second century C.E. Some were written by Jews, others by Christians, and there is some debate about which are which. Some of the apocalypses are clearly sectarian in outlook, but others take a rather inclusive view of the righteous. Several are dependent on the earliest of the ascent apocalypses, the Book of the Watchers (1 Enoch 1–36); others give no indication of a literary relationship to any other work. In some, the end of the world and the last judgment are major concerns, while in others they remain in the background or are altogether absent.

3

Yet despite these differences, these apocalypses are all shaped in important ways by the belief that human beings can become the equals of angels. For the implications of achieving angelic status go far beyond the visionary himself. In some texts the visionary's experience serves to reassure readers of their place in God's plan by demonstrating the exalted potential of humanity. In others equality with the angels is represented as the fate of all the righteous dead, and thus an experience that any reader of the apocalypse can some day hope to achieve.

The process by which Enoch becomes an angel in the passage quoted above is a sort of priestly investiture: Enoch dons special garments, and Michael anoints him with oil. Here I shall argue that the depiction of the transformation of the visionary in the apocalypses depends on an understanding of heaven as a temple with angels as heavenly priests, and that the emergence of the idea of heavenly ascent in the apocalypses is closely related to the development of this picture of heaven (chs. 1 and 2).

The belief that the boundary between humanity and the divine is permeable was widespread in the Mediterranean world in the centuries around the turn of the era. It takes a variety of forms, from accounts of wonder-working "divine men" like Apollonius of Tyana and Jesus to the allusions to the "descents" to the chariot of the hekhalot texts, and, as the example of Apollonius shows, it is by no means restricted to Jews and Christians. The apocalypses express this belief in a distinctive way, but they need to be considered in relation to this larger context. I shall argue that the apocalypses are a response to problems in the relationship between human beings and the divine that were widely perceived in the Greco-Roman world, as well as to developments within Judaism of the Second Temple period (ch. 3).

Prominent among the secrets revealed to the visionaries of the apocalypses, often after they have taken their place among the angels, are accounts of creation and the phenomena of the created world. I argue that the revelation of these secrets represents the apocalypses' development of the wisdom tradition's claim that the created world testifies to its creator. These secrets appear in the Book of the Watchers, with its story of the fallen angels, who introduce humanity to various forms of evil, and apocalypses that draw on it. In several cases the secrets are associated with an implicit reinterpretation of the earliest history of the human race, which runs counter to the dominant view of the Book of Genesis.

The primeval history (Genesis 1–11) represents the beginnings of human history as a series of attempts to cross the boundary between humanity and the divine, always with disastrous results. In the Garden of Eden and at the Tower of Babel, at the beginning and end of the primeval history, it is human beings who presume to usurp divine privileges. Between these two moments of human transgression there appears the enigmatic fragment that provides the plot for the Enoch apocalypses, the story of the sons of god who take human wives, divinities who cross the boundary from the other direction, apparently causing the troubles that lead to the flood (Gen. 6:1-4). Thus this story, which is taken up in several of the apocalypses, implies an understanding of the cause of evil in the world quite different from the dominant biblical understanding expressed in the story of Adam and Eve's disobedience in the Garden of Eden and reiterated in the other instances of disobedience in the primeval history, from Cain to the Tower of Babel (ch. 4).[3]

Some interesting recent work reads the pseudonymous visions of apocalyptic literature as reflecting actual experiences of their authors. The concluding chapter of this study explores this question for the ascent apocalypses. I argue against the view that techniques designed to produce ascent were widespread in the ancient Mediterranean world; some recent scholarship suggests that even the hekhalot literature, apparently a promising source for somewhat later Jewish techniques for ascent, allows the mystic to achieve his aims not through ecstatic ascent but through recitation of the ascents of the rabbis of the past who are its heroes. I suggest that the ascents of the apocalypses are in any case best understood as instances of "rapture," that is, ascent to heaven at the initiative not of the visionary, but of God. Further, after consideration of the literary qualities of the ascent apocalypses, I argue that they are best understood not as mystical diaries, however reworked, but as literary creations (ch. 5).

This is a particularly appropriate time to undertake a study of the ascent apocalypses. In the decades since the discovery of the Dead Sea Scrolls there has been no more important publication for the study of apocalyptic literature than J. T. Milik's edition of the Aramaic Enoch fragments from Qumran (1976).[4] Milik's extensive reconstruction of an Aramaic text based on tiny fragments aroused considerable controversy, and his eccentric claims about the history of the Enoch traditions were not widely accepted.[5] Yet one thing became quite clear with the appearance of his book. The paleographical evidence showed that the Astronomical Book of Enoch (1 Enoch 72–82) and the Book of the Watchers (1 Enoch 1–36) are the two oldest apocalypses extant. The Astronomical Book, the oldest of all, turns out to be no later than the early third century B.C.E., while the Book of the Watchers, by far the more influential, dates to the third century or at latest the first quarter of the second century B.C.E.

The significance of these new dates cannot be overstated. Most scholarship had assumed that the apocalypses as a group shared the interests of the two canonical apocalypses—Daniel in the Hebrew Bible and Revelation in the New Testament—which are devoted to revelations about the imminent end of the world. The influence of these two works on the scholarly imagination derived to a considerable extent from their canonicity and from the importance of collective eschatology, their central concern, for the emergence of Christianity.

But of course canonicity should not grant a work special status in scholarly deliberations, nor should the nexus between collective eschatology and early Christianity lead to the dismissal of other aspects of the apocalypses. Still, the scholarly preoccupation with collective eschatology could be justified at least in part by appealing to Daniel's date. Composed during the Maccabean revolt, it is contemporary with the Book of Dreams (1 Enoch 83–90), which is also concerned primarily with collective eschatology. With the Book of Dreams, Daniel was understood to be the earliest of the apocalypses. Thus it could be treated implicitly or explicitly as the apocalypse that defined the entire corpus. In light of the new dates, the subject matter of the Book of the Watchers, with its considerable differences from Daniel and Revelation, including its lack of emphasis on the imminent end, took on a new importance.

As scholars were attempting to absorb the implications of the Aramaic Enoch fragments, the participants in the Apocalypses Group of the Society of Biblical Literature published a volume entitled *Apocalypse: The Morphology of a Genre* (1979), which defined the genre apocalypse on the basis of form as well as content.[6] Coming shortly after the publication of the Aramaic Enoch fragments, its thorough survey of all the early Jewish and Christian apocalypses led to some salutary observations. For example, "The 'historical' apocalypses which give prominence to reviews of history followed by cosmic transformation and on which many generalizations about 'apocalyptic' are based, constitute only about one-third of the Jewish apocalypses and are extremely rare elsewhere."[7] Further, the emphasis on the form of the apocalypses encouraged the reading of the Book of the Watchers and other ascent apocalypses in their own terms rather than through the lenses of Daniel and similar apocalypses.

Another factor that converges to make the past decade and a half so significant for the study of the ascent apocalypses is the remarkable development in the study of the hekhalot literature in this period. The work of Peter Schäfer and David Halperin in particular has opened up new ways of understanding the hekhalot literature, with important implications for the ascent apocalypses.[8]

Yet despite the growth of interest in the apocalypses in the last decades and the fertile soil for a reconsideration of the ascent apocalypses, relatively little attention has been paid to them as a group. Alan F. Segal's article "Heavenly Ascent in Hellenistic Judaism, Early Christianity and Their Environment" (1980)[9] offers a useful survey of the ancient ascent literature, both its pre-Hellenistic roots and its growth and development in the Hellenistic and Roman periods. Apart from a structural interpretation painted with broad strokes, however, it makes no attempt to break new ground in the study of the apocalypses. Christopher Rowland's *Open Heaven: A Study of Apocalyptic in Judaism and Early Christianity* (1982)[10] pays special attention to some of the ascent apocalypses because of Rowland's interest in visions of the divine throne. John J. Collins's *Apocalyptic Imagination: An Introduction to the Jewish Matrix of Chris-*

tianity (1984)[11] carries forward the consideration of the apocalypses as a genre begun in the *Semeia* volume and thus takes account of the role of heavenly ascent in apocalyptic literature.

To my knowledge the only book-length study devoted to the ascent apocalypses as a body of literature in their own right is Mary Dean-Otting's *Heavenly Journeys: A Study of the Motif in Hellenistic Jewish Literature* (1984).[12] Dean-Otting provides a detailed analysis of the ascents that survive in Greek—1 Enoch (primarily chs. 14 and 71, despite the fact that there is no Greek extant for the Similitudes [1 Enoch 37–71]), the Testament of Levi, 3 Baruch, and the Testament of Abraham— as well as much briefer discussions of works that do not survive in Greek but that she considers to be Jewish—2 Enoch, aspects of 4 Ezra (which does not actually contain an ascent), and the Apocalypse of Abraham. Dean-Otting makes an important contribution, particularly in her discussion of 3 Baruch, but I think she has overemphasized the continuity among the apocalypses, which she treats as a tradition. The major drawback to her work is her insistence on the contrast between these apocalypses and their non-Jewish environment. Her reluctance to recognize points of contact makes aspects of her readings of the apocalypses problematic and prevents her from offering a satisfying account of their meaning.[13] Thus the need for a comprehensive study of the ascent apocalypses remains.

Because the visionary's achievement of angelic status is so central to these apocalypses, my study touches on themes treated by such scholars as Jarl E. Fossum, Segal, and, most recently, C. R. A. Morray-Jones, in their work on principal angels, the divine Glory, and associated themes in ancient Judaism and Christianity.[14] I have learned a great deal from their work. But my approach, in which these themes are treated in the course of the examination of a particular body of texts, indicates my uneasiness with their assumption that similar motifs in apocalyptic, rabbinic, hekhalot, early Christian, and gnostic texts demonstrate a continuous tradition of speculation or mystical practice.

I consider here the entire body of Jewish and Christian ascent apocalypses through the second century: the Book of the Watchers, the Testament of Levi, 2 Enoch, the Similitudes of Enoch (1 Enoch 37–71), the Apocalypse of Zephaniah, the Apocalypse of Abraham, the Ascension of Isaiah, and 3 Baruch. The second century marks a natural divide between the works considered here and later Jewish and Christian texts involving ascent. Despite certain points of continuity with the earlier apocalypses, the Christian tours of hell and paradise dating from the third century on are a distinctive tradition with quite different concerns. This is true even of their second-century ancestor, the Apocalypse of Peter, which includes with its vision of hell a brief vision of paradise, but no actual ascent. Similarly the hekhalot texts with their instructions for heavenly ascent must be taken into consideration in a discussion of the ascent apocalypses, but they clearly constitute a separate corpus.

There is one omission from my list of ascent apocalypses that may require some defense, for Dean-Otting and others treat the Testament of Abraham as an Egyptian Jewish ascent apocalypse of the first century. I am far less certain than they about Jewish provenance and first-century date, but more important, despite its formal features, which allow it to be classified as an apocalypse, and its subject matter, which includes a visit to heaven for a glimpse of the judgment of souls, I do not think that the Testament of Abraham is best understood as an apocalypse.[15] The apocalypses considered here, with all their differences, share certain assumptions; read alongside them, the Testament of Abraham stands apart. When George Nickelsburg describes the Testament not as an apocalypse, but as "a didactic but entertaining story,"[16] he is responding to this difference.

I hope that this study of the ascent apocalypses will meet the challenge of the developments of the last decades not only for the history of apocalyptic literature, but also for the history of ancient Judaism and Christianity. For I believe that our understanding of the ascent apocalypses has important implications for ancient Judaism and Christianity and their place in the Greco-Roman world.

1

From Ezekiel to the Book of the Watchers

The vision of 1 Enoch 14 marks a crucial departure in the history of ancient Jewish literature. To a certain extent Enoch's vision stands in the tradition of prophecy. From one angle it can be seen as a dramatic call vision, like Ezekiel's vision of the chariot throne, to which it has some striking parallels. In the culmination of the vision, God commissions Enoch to perform a prophetic task, to deliver a message of judgment to the fallen Watchers. But there is one central difference between Enoch's vision and the visions of the prophets, including Ezekiel's: unlike any of the prophets, Enoch ascends to heaven.[1]

> 8. And it was shown to me thus in a vision: Behold! clouds were calling me in my vision, and dark clouds were crying out to me; fire-balls and lightnings were hastening me on and driving me, and winds, in my vision, were bearing me aloft, and they raised me upwards and carried and brought me into the heavens. 9. And I went in till I drew near to a wall, built of hailstones, with tongues of fire surrounding it on all sides; and it began to terrify me. 10. And I entered into the tongues of fire and drew near to a large house built of hailstones; and the walls of the house were like tesselated paving stones, all of snow, and its floor was of snow. 11. Its upper storeys were, as it were, fireballs and lightnings, and in the midst of them (were) fiery Cherubim, *celestial watchers*. 12. And a flaming fire was around *all* its walls, and its doors were ablaze with fire. 13. And I entered into that house, and it was hot as fire and cold as snow; and there were no delights in it; horror overwhelmed me, and trembling took hold of me. 14. And shaking and trembling, I fell on my face. And I in a vision, 15. and behold! another house greater than that one and its door was completely opened opposite me; and it (the second house) was all

constructed of tongues of fire. 16. And in every respect it excelled in glory
and honour and grandeur that I am unable to describe to you its glory and
grandeur. 17. Its floor was of fire, and its upper chambers were lightnings and
fire-balls, and its roof was of blazing fire. 18. And I beheld and saw therein a
lofty throne; and its appearance was like crystals of ice and the wheels thereof
were like the shining sun, and (I saw) *watchers, Cherubim*. 19. And from underneath the throne came forth streams of blazing fire, and I was unable to look
on it. 20. And the glory of the Great One sat thereon, and his raiment was
brighter than the sun, and whiter than any snow. 21. And no angel was able
to enter this house, or to look on his face, by reason of its splendour and
glory; and no flesh was able to look on him. 22. A blazing fire encircled him,
and a great fire stood in front of him, so that none who surrounded him could
draw near to him; ten thousand times ten thousand stood before him. He had
no need of counsel; in his every word was a deed. 23. And *the watchers and
holy ones* who draw near to him turn not away from him, by night or by day,
nor do they depart from him. 24. As for me, till then I had been prostrate on
my face, trembling, and the Lord called me with his own mouth and said to
me: 'Come hither, Enoch, and hear my word'. 25. And there came to me one
of the holy angels, and he raised me up and brought me to the door, and I
bowed my face low. (1 Enoch 14)[2]

Enoch's ascent belongs to the Book of the Watchers, one of the five
originally independent works contained in 1 Enoch. Milik's publication
of the Aramaic fragments from Qumran places the composition of the
Book of the Watchers in the third century B.C.E., making the Book of
the Watchers the earliest extant apocalypse after another Enochic work,
the Astronomical Book.[3] The Astronomical Book is concerned almost
exclusively with calculations of the paths of sun and moon in the service
of a 364-day solar year. It is thus of far less importance for the development of apocalyptic literature than the Book of the Watchers with its
interest in the divine throne and the entourage of angels that surrounds
it, the fate of souls after death, and cosmology, as well as the last judgment.

Although ascent is a new development, the debt of 1 Enoch 14 to
Ezekiel is profound. The source for the picture of the throne of cherubim[4] Enoch sees in the heavenly sanctuary is not the Second Temple,
which no longer contained these central symbols of the First Temple,[5]
nor the instructions for constructing the tabernacle in the priestly document of the Torah, nor the description of Solomon's temple in 1 Kings
(and 2 Chronicles), but rather, Ezekiel's visions of the chariot that carries God's glory (Ezekiel 1, 8–11, 43). The line of descent is made clear
by the wheels of the throne, which appear only in Ezekiel among biblical works and which no longer have a function in Enoch's ascent, where
the throne sits fixed in heaven. This throne, on which God is seated, is
the counterpart of the cherubim without a rider that stood as a throne
for the invisible God in the holy of holies in the Jerusalem temple. The
earthly cherubim in turn were intended to represent the winged crea-

tures on which the God of Israel, like other ancient Near Eastern deities, was sometimes said to ride.[6]

As the text of the Book of Ezekiel now stands, Ezekiel himself notes the correspondence between the chariot he sees and the furniture of the temple. The term "cherubim" does not appear in the elaborate description of the chariot in Ezekiel 1, where the mysterious four-faced beings that bear the glory of God are called "living creatures."[7] But in chapters 8–11, as the prophet stands in the temple watching the movements of the creatures carrying the glory of God as God prepares to depart from the temple before turning it over to the Babylonians for destruction, he realizes the identity of the living creatures from his first vision: "These were the living creatures that I saw underneath the God of Israel by the river Chebar; and I knew that they were cherubim" (10:20). The text suggests that Ezekiel is able to recognize the creatures as cherubim because of his proximity to the sculpted cherubim of the temple. Clearly the heavenly originals are more awesome and wonderful than their earthly representations.[8]

Ezekiel's visions of the chariot throne mark the beginning of a trend to dissociate God's heavenly abode from the temple in Jerusalem. A century and a half before Ezekiel, the prophet Isaiah saw his vision of God seated on his throne, surrounded by the heavenly host, in the Jerusalem temple. For Isaiah the temple was truly God's earthly home, the place where heaven and earth come together. Isaiah's vision reflects the belief current among Israel's neighbors in Canaan and Mesopotamia that the god actually dwelt in the temple human beings built for him. Sometimes the earthly temple was understood to be modeled on the god's house in heaven or on a sacred mountain.[9] Sometimes, as in the Bible, the god is depicted giving instructions for building the temple,[10] and ceremonies mark the moment when the god takes up residence in the temple.[11]

Recent scholarship has rejected the view so popular with earlier historians of religion that a cosmic mountain played a central role in ancient Mesopotamian cosmology.[12] A cosmic mountain, a place where heaven and earth come together and the divine is present on earth, does, however, appear prominently in the Ugaritic texts, where the mountains on which the gods live and assemble are understood in these terms.[13] Some strands of biblical literature treat Mount Sinai as a cosmic mountain, but it is primarily Mount Zion to which the imagery associated with the mountain of the gods in Ugaritic literature is applied.[14] The view that Zion is inviolable, immune from conquest, which shows up especially in the Zion psalms, has its background in these myths about the mountains of the gods.[15]

According to the biblical narrative (Isaiah 36–37, and the parallel in 2 Kings 18:13–19:37), when Jerusalem was under siege by the Assyrians, Isaiah counseled King Hezekiah not to surrender. Hezekiah listened to Isaiah, and the Assyrians returned home without taking the city. Modern critics differ about whether such a retreat ever took place, and Isaiah's role in the events is also unclear. While Isaiah may have counseled resistance as an act of trust in God, it seems unlikely that he believed in the absolute inviolability of Jerusalem. He certainly did not hesitate to liken the sinful Jerusalem to Sodom and Gomorrah (1:9–10) and to threaten destruction if its people continued to sin.[16]

What the narrative does show, however, is that people who held that Zion was inviolable understood the events in light of their own convictions and represented the great prophet of their time as the heroic spokesman for these views. For them the Assyrian retreat guaranteed the correctness of their position. This understanding was clearly popular, for more than half a century after the Assyrian siege, Jeremiah argued against the belief that the temple could save Jerusalem from the Babylonians despite its sins: "Do not trust in these deceptive words: 'This is the temple of the LORD, the temple of the LORD, the temple of the LORD'" (Jer. 7:4).[17]

The Deuteronomic school too rejected the popular view of the cosmic significance of the temple and Zion. God's true home is in heaven. It is not because Mount Zion is inherently holy that God chooses to be present there; rather its holiness is a result of God's choice. This view finds expression in Deuteronomy's way of speaking of Jerusalem and the temple, which, according to its narrative framework are still in the future. They are "the place which the LORD your God will choose . . . to put his name" (12:5, etc., with variations).[18]

If for Isaiah in the mid-eighth century the temple was the natural place to encounter God, by the beginning of the sixth century Ezekiel had come to understand the temple as so defiled that it was no longer a fit resting place for the glory of God. From the point of view of history, Ezekiel's charges are grossly exaggerated. Greenberg calls the vision of idolatry in the temple in chapter 8 "a montage of whatever pagan rites were ever conducted at the Jerusalem temple." But the vision's very lack of historicity indicates the depth of Ezekiel's conviction of the temple's defilement.[19]

For Ezekiel it is God himself who commands the destruction, ordering angels to begin the job that the Babylonians finish (Ezek. 9:3–8). The temple's doom is God's fitting reaction to the terrible pollution Ezekiel perceives. Thus even before the destruction God has abandoned the temple for a chariot.[20] His return to a fixed dwelling awaits the temple of the eschatological future; only then will the people of Israel finally be purified. The Book of Ezekiel concludes with a vision of this temple (chs. 40–48), and in the vision Ezekiel falls on his face as he witnesses the return of God's glory to the temple, "like the vision which I had seen when he came to destroy the city and like the vision which I had seen by the river Chebar" (43:3).

The Second Temple is never able to emerge from the shadow of the disengagement of the glory of God. The ark and the cherubim are gone. In the period of the Second Temple, under the influence of Ezekiel, those who are unhappy with the behavior of the people and especially its priests come to see the temple not as God's proper dwelling, the place where heaven and earth meet, but rather as a mere copy of the true temple located in heaven. It is this desacralization of the earthly temple in favor of the heavenly that opens the way for Enoch's ascent in the Book of the Watchers. The first ascent in Jewish literature is thus a journey to the true temple.

Ascent to the Divine Council

The debt of the Book of the Watchers to the Book of Ezekiel is not limited to the impetus for the development of the picture of a heavenly temple. Through its innovations in form, Ezekiel also provides a model for the process of ascent. The series of verbs of motion of which Enoch is the subject in the course of his ascent find their only prophetic precedent in Ezekiel's perambulations in the Jerusalem temple as he watches the departure of the glory of God (chs. 8–11) and his guided tour of the eschatological temple at the end of the book (chs. 40–48).[21]

In content, Enoch's ascent must be understood against the background of an aspect of prophetic thought not limited to Ezekiel, the idea of the prophet's participation in the divine council. As he progresses toward God's throne, Enoch sees a host of angels: "Ten thousand times ten thouand stood before him. He had no need of counsel; in his every word was a deed" (1 Enoch 14:22).[22] This picture is clearly related to the picture of God surrounded by angels described in Isaiah's vision in the temple (ch. 6) and in the narrative of Micaiah b. Imlah's prophecy (1 Kings 22:19–22) and alluded to elsewhere in biblical literature.[23]

The Israelites' understanding of the divine council is indebted to that of their neighbors in the ancient Near East. The council of El plays an important role in Ugaritic literature. The members of El's council are gods, yet unlike the gods of the Mesopotamian myths, who assert themselves as individuals in the proceedings of the council, the gods of the council in Ugaritic literature show no independence, but simply confirm El's decrees. So too the members of Yahweh's council exist only to do his will. With the exception of the accuser, who emerges relatively late, these demoted gods have no individuality.[24]

In Ugaritic literature divine messengers convey the decision of the council. In ancient Israel the prophets claim for themselves the role of messengers alongside the regular members of the council. When Isaiah finds himself in the midst of a session of the council in the Jerusalem temple, he volunteers to carry God's message of judgment to the people of Israel. The prophecy of Second Isaiah begins with a report of the proceedings in the council, during which the prophet undertakes to deliver a message of comfort.[25]

The prophets' participation in the council takes place on earth through visions. Enoch's participation also takes place in a vision (vv. 8, 14) while Enoch is asleep (v. 2), but in the course of the vision he ascends to heaven, where the council is located. Upon his arrival before God's throne, Enoch is commissioned to deliver a message of judgment to the Watchers.

The dominant imagery of the divine council in biblical literature is of the royal court. In those texts in which the prophet actually sees the council, God is seated on a throne (1 Kings 22:19, Isa. 6:1), and the purpose of the deliberations of the council is always judgment (in addition to the passages just cited, Psalm 82, Zech. 3:1–10, Job 1:6–12, 2:1–6).[26] In 1 Enoch 14, however, the dominant understanding is of heaven as temple, and it is in the heavenly temple that the divine council meets.

In biblical Hebrew *hekhal* serves for both the king's palace and the temple. In relation to a god, temple and palace are two aspects of the same dwelling place. Thus even in those texts where the idea of temple dominates, the imagery associated with the royal palace never disappears. The purpose of Enoch's ascent is still participation in the deliberations of the heavenly court, but a shift in emphasis in the description of the council and its setting has begun.

The Heavenly Temple

The Book of the Watchers was an extremely influential work, and one aspect of its influence is the picture of heaven as temple that explains so many features of the other ascent apocalypses, whether it stands in the foreground or in the background. Here I would like to consider briefly the weight of architectural detail pointing to the understanding of heaven as temple in the Book of the Watchers and then to turn to the way in which that understanding affects the encounter between Enoch and God.

The two houses through which Enoch must pass according to the Ethiopic (vv. 10–14, 15–17) to reach the throne of God have been treated by some critics as the *hekhal*, or sanctuary ("nave" in RSV), and *devir*, or holy of holies ("inner sanctuary" in RSV), of a temple.[27] But the correspondence is more exact than that. Both the First and Second Temples contained a third, outer, chamber, the *'ulam*, or vestibule (First Temple: 1 Kings 6:3; Second Temple: Josephus, *Jewish War* 5.207–19, m. Middot 4:7).[28]

In fact the text of 1 Enoch 14 does mention a third structure (14:9). In the Ethiopic it is simply a wall. In the Greek, however, Enoch passes through a *building* of hailstones and fire. The Greek text, then, provides a heavenly structure that matches a three-chambered temple quite nicely.[29]

The heavenly temple creates an impression of awesome glitter. It is built from fire, lightning, and fire-balls or shooting stars,[30] and forms of water, including hailstones, snow, and ice. These opposing elements of fire and water can coexist only in heaven.[31] And yet it appears that the earthly temple was described in similar terms.[32] Josephus offers a striking description of the Second Temple that contains many of the same elements:

> The exterior of the building wanted nothing that could astound either mind or eye. For, being covered on all sides with massive plates of gold, the sun was no sooner up than it radiated so fiery a flash that persons straining to look at it were compelled to avert their eyes, as from the solar rays. To approaching strangers it appeared from a distance like a snow-clad mountain; for all that was not overlaid with gold was of purest white.[33]

Reading this description we cannot fail to be reminded of the heavenly temple of 1 Enoch 14. Of course Josephus, who is here describing Herod's temple, wrote perhaps three centuries after the Book of the Watchers. But the cosmological symbolism of Josephus's account has ancient roots, and it may be that his description draws on earlier praise of the temple.[34]

The furnishings of the heavenly temple, too, reflect the earthly. Between the floor of snow (14:10) and the upper stories, or, as Nickelsburg translates, ceiling,[35] of fire-balls and lightnings (14:11) of the middle building of the Greek text, there appear fiery cherubim (14:11). These are not the cherubim of the divine throne discussed earlier, which are mentioned later in the course of the description of the inner temple (14:18), but the heavenly counterpart of the images of cherubim woven into the hangings that form the walls of the tabernacle (Ex. 26:1, 31; 36:8, 35) or engraved on the walls of the temple (1 Kings 6:29, 2 Chron. 3:7, Ezek. 41:15–26).[36]

While it is clear that the heavenly temple of 1 Enoch 14 corresponds to the earthly temple, it does not seem to correspond in detail to any particular temple described in the Hebrew Bible. The only instance of technical terminology is the description of the activities of the angelic priests to be discussed later. The heavenly temples of later apocalypses are also characterized by an absence of technical terminology and by an even more limited correspondence of detail between the earthly and the heavenly temples.

The same limited correspondence is found even in the elaborate description of the Sabbath Songs, which in Newsom's view come close to picturing a particular biblical temple, the eschatological temple of Ezekiel 40–48.[37] The terminology of the songs is eclectic, and the description of the heavenly temple in fact reproduces only the broad outlines of the earthly.[38]

I doubt that this lack of correspondence between the heavenly temple and its earthly counterparts in the apocalypses and the Qumran Sabbath Songs is the result simply of dissatisfaction with the Second Temple. Dissatisfaction is an important motive for interest in heavenly temples.

But our authors surely felt no such dissatisfaction with the tabernacle, Solomon's temple, or Ezekiel's eschatological temple, which, unlike the Second Temple, are described in the Bible.

Rather, the loose correspondence of heavenly temple to earthly seems to reflect the belief that the heavenly temple so transcends the earthly that the correspondence cannot be exact. This is Newsom's understanding of the Sabbath Songs' frequent references to the heavenly temple or its components as seven-fold. The usage is not consistent; singulars stand alongside the plurals in "an attempt to communicate something of the elusive transcendence of heavenly reality."[39]

Finally, it is worth considering Enoch's reaction to the sight of the heavenly temple. Upon entering the outer house, the one built of hailstones, Enoch is overcome by fear and falls on his face (vv. 13–14). Prostration before God hardly requires comment; it is an adaptation of the etiquette of greeting human monarchs, and its meaning is readily apparent. But Enoch is surely drawing on the model of Ezekiel, who regularly falls on his face before the Glory of God.[40] Like Enoch, the heroes of many other apocalypses follow Ezekiel's lead in this, as in so much else.[41]

The fear and trembling that Enoch describes, however, are quite foreign to Ezekiel. When Isaiah stands before God in the Jerusalem temple, he exclaims, "Woe is me! For I am lost!" (6:5). He is afraid that the corruption of his people makes him unfit to stand in God's presence. But Ezekiel's prostrations are never attributed to fear; they are reported each time in the same words, without any mention of emotion, as almost ritual acknowledgments of the majesty of God. The Book of the Watchers, on the other hand, emphasizes the intensity of the visionary's reaction to the manifestation of the divine.

Enoch's prostration stands apart from Ezekiel's in another important respect. Although Enoch catches sight of God on his throne of cherubim from his prostrate position, it is not the sight of God that causes his terror. Rather it is the fearsome experience of standing inside the house of hailstones that makes Enoch tremble and quake and finally fall on his face: "And I entered into that house, and it was hot as fire and cold as snow; and there were no delights in it; horror overwhelmed me, and trembling took hold of me. And shaking and trembling, I fell on my face" (14:13–14). Thus the Book of the Watchers emphasizes the glory of God's heavenly temple by making it, rather than the vision of God himself, the cause of Enoch's fear.

God on His Throne

The description of God seated on his throne in 1 Enoch 14 is also related to the understanding of the heavenly throne room as temple. To be more precise, it is not God himself who is described, but his garment:[42]

And I beheld and saw therein a lofty throne; and its appearance was like the crystals of ice and the wheels thereof were like the shining sun, and (I saw) *watchers, Cherubim*. And from underneath the throne came forth streams of blazing fire, and I was unable to look on it. And the glory of the Great One sat thereon, and his raiment was brighter than the sun, and whiter than any snow. (14:18–20)

The description of the enthroned deity in Ezekiel 1 and 8 shares with this description the mention of radiance. But there is no garment in Ezekiel, and in Ezekiel 1 the radiance around the figure is rainbowlike rather than white.

A much closer parallel to the picture of 1 Enoch 14:20 appears in Dan. 7:9–10: "As I looked, thrones were placed and one that was ancient of days took his seat; his raiment was white as snow, and the hair of his head like pure wool; his throne was fiery flames, its wheels were burning fire. A stream of fire issued and came forth from before him. . . ."

The shining thrones with wheels that appear in both visions are a sign of their debt to Ezekiel. But the fiery streams do not appear in Ezekiel, although they are similar in visual effect to elements of Ezekiel's vision. They have their origins in the ancient traditions of the divine council. The mountain of El at which the council meets in Ugaritic literature has two rivers at its base. The rivers of Canaanite myth are not fiery, but Israelite (and Canaanite) traditions of fiery theophanies could easily suggest fiery rivers.[43] Like other features of the Canaanite traditions of the abode of the gods, the rivers at the base of the cosmic mountain have been transferred in biblical literature to the temple mount, as in the concluding vision of the Book of Ezekiel (47:1–12).[44] On the throne, according to both Daniel and Enoch, God sits, dressed in white. In Daniel God's hair is also described, and it too is white. Daniel 7 maintains the association of the heavenly council with judgment that appears in 1 Kings 22, Isaiah 6, and Psalm 82. It explicitly treats the divine council as a court: "The court sat in judgment and the books were opened" (v. 10).

The scene described in Dan. 7:9–14 has given rise to a large corpus of scholarly literature. It is now widely accepted that the proper background for this vision is Canaanite mythology; the one like a son of man (v. 13) is described with the attributes of Ba'al, while the Ancient of Days resembles El, the patriarch of the Canaanite pantheon, who sits enthroned in the council of the gods to render judgment.[45]

Many scholars have drawn attention to the mentions of El's hoary hair and beard in the texts from Ugarit, which surely account for the white hair of the Ancient of Days.[46] But what of the white robe that appears in Daniel and the Book of the Watchers? To my knowledge the published Ugaritic texts contain no references to a white robe worn by El, although Pope describes a limestone stela in low relief that depicts El enthroned, wearing a crown with bull horns and a long robe.[47] A robe is implied in Isaiah's vision in the temple, ("I saw the LORD sitting upon a throne, high and lifted up; and his train filled the temple" [6:1]), but there is no description of the robe.[48]

Lacocque relates the whiteness of the robe and hair of the Ancient of Days to the symbolism of white in judgment,[49] and it is true that 1 Enoch 14 is also concerned with judgment by the heavenly court. Enoch ascends to plead before the divine judge on behalf of the Watchers, and at the end of the vision the sentence of the Watchers is read out once more.

I suggest a somewhat different explanation for the robe and its whiteness in 1 Enoch 14, an explanation related to the picture of heaven as temple. In the regulations for the garments of the priests and the curtains of the tabernacle in P, the priestly document of the Torah, the general principle is "the more important the object, the more expensive and magnificent it has to be." The high priest dresses daily in four elaborate garments of wool and linen adorned with gold and gems. But there is an exception to this general rule: the one set of plain linen (*bad*) garments that the high priest wears once a year to enter the holy of holies (Lev. 16:4).[50]

The linen of these plain linen garments is plain indeed. The linen used for the garments of the ordinary priests and the undergarments of the high priest is fine linen (*šeš*) (Ex. 39:27–28).[51] Only the breeches of the ordinary priests (Ex. 28:42) and the garments they wear when removing the ashes from the altar (Lev. 6:3) are to be of plain linen (*bad*). And yet the "plain linen vestments [of the high priest on the Day of Atonement] reflect a holiness transcending that of gold and wool-linen mixture. . . . These garments serve to indicate a kind of dialectical elevation into that sphere which is beyond even the material, contagious holiness characterizing the tabernacle and its accessories." Not coincidentally, in Ezekiel (9:2–3, 11; 10:2) and Daniel (10:5, 12:6–7) angels wear garments of linen (*bad*).[52]

Plain linen is more or less white, but the Bible does not comment on the color of the high priest's once-a-year garments. The Mishnah, however, explicitly describes them as white (Yoma 3:6). That white is the color of innocence and purity, especially suited to the judge of all the world, is surely not irrelevant to the white garment of the one seated on the throne in 1 Enoch 14. But here, as opposed to Daniel, the garment alone is mentioned without reference to hair or beard, and this emphasis on the garment may indicate that the plain linen garment that the high priest wore when he entered the holy of holies, the earthly counterpart of the spot where God sits enthroned in the heavenly temple, contributed to the whiteness of the garment in 1 Enoch 14.[53] If this type of projection seems extreme, it should be remembered that the author of 1 Enoch 14 is far more restrained than the rabbis, who did not hesitate to describe God's prayer shawl and phylacteries.[54]

At this point I would like to return to the picture of God in Ezek. 1:26–28, where the aura around the deity is "like the appearance of the bow that is in the cloud on the day of rain . . ." (v. 28). This mode of describing the glory of God appears also in Rev. 4:3, which seems to be drawing directly on Ezekiel. Appropriately enough, Revelation also describes an angel in these terms, "a mighty angel . . . with a rainbow over his head" (Rev. 10:1). Some have seen this glow as a transformation of the rainbow's original purpose as a weapon of the warrior god.[55] Whatever the origins of this image, it comes to be understood in relation to the wardrobe of the high priest, this time the glorious garments he wears daily when he officiates in the sanctuary.

In the period of the Second Temple the high priest's vestments were the object of considerable interest. Their symbolism was discussed in some detail by Philo and Josephus.[56] The Letter of Aristeas offers a fairly straightforward description of the high priest in full dress that may nonetheless suggest something like Ezekiel's glow:

> He was girded with a girdle of conspicuous beauty, woven in the most beautiful colours. On his breast he wore the oracle of God, as it is called, on which twelve stones, of different kinds, were inset, fastened together with gold, containing the names of the leaders of the tribes, according to their original order, each one flashing forth in an indescribable way in its own particular colour. On his head he wore a tiara, as it is called, and upon this in the middle of his forehead an inimitable turban, the royal diadem full of glory with the name of God inscribed in sacred letters on a plate of gold . . . having been judged worthy to wear these *emblems* in the ministrations. Their appearance created such awe and confusion *of mind* as to make one feel that one had come into the presence of a man who belonged to a different world. (Letter of Aristeas 97–99)[57]

That at least one author of the Second Temple period saw a relationship between Ezekiel's description of God and the garments of the high priest is clear from one of the similes Joshua ben Sira applies to the high priest Simeon in his praise of the fathers: "How glorious he was in the midst of the people when he came out of the house of the veil . . . like the rainbow shining in clouds of glory . . ." (50:5, 7; my tr.).[58]

The Songs of the Sabbath Sacrifice suggest that the Qumran community too saw a relationship between priestly garments and the appearance of God. In the thirteenth and last of the Sabbath Songs, the garments of the angelic high priests are described in what Newsom views as the climax of the Songs.[59] The variegated colors of the garments are described using the language of the biblical instructions for the dress of the high priest:[60]

> In their wondrous stations are spirits (clothed with) many colors, like woven work, engraved with figures of splendor. In the midst of the glorious appearance of scarlet, the colors of most holy spiritual light, they stand firm in their holy station before the [K]ing, spirits in garments of [*purest*] color in the midst of the appearance of whiteness. And this glorious spiritual substance is

like fine gold work, shedding [lig]ht. And all their crafted (garments) are purely blended, an *artistry* of woven work. (4Q405 23 ii, lines 7–10)[61]

A description of the glory of God seated on the chariot throne in heaven appears in the twelfth of the Sabbath Songs. "And *there is* a radiant substance with glorious colors, wondrously hued, purely blended . . ." (4Q405 22, lines 10–11).[62] The glory is described in terms associated with the angelic priests, which in turn are drawn from biblical instructions for the clothing of human priests.

The description of the glory of God in the Sabbath Songs, then, is surely influenced by priestly dress. It may also have been influenced by the comparison of the glory of God to a rainbow by the prophet Ezekiel, whose vision of the temple is so important for the Songs. But does Ezekiel's description of the glory of God draw on an understanding of the garment of the high priest as rainbowlike? Ezekiel is certainly the most priestly of prophets, and I do not think that it would be at all surprising to find him depiciting God as priest. The problem is that there is no consensus about Ezekiel's relationship to P or about P's relationship to conditions of the period before the exile. Ezekiel's vision of the restored temple provides only for linen (*pištim*) garments for the priests (44:17–19), and no high priest is mentioned. The omissions of Ezekiel 40–48 relative to P have been interpreted in very different ways,[63] but if Ezekiel knew the institution of high priest and the associated garments and preferred not to place them in his temple of the future, it would not be surprising to find them transferred to God.[64]

The Heavenly Priesthood

Every temple needs priests, and the priests of the heavenly temple in 1 Enoch 14 are angels:

> A blazing fire encircled him, and a great fire stood in front of him, so that none who surrounded could draw near to him; ten thousand times ten thousand stood before him. He had no need of counsel; his every word was a deed. And *the watchers and holy ones* who draw near to him turn not away from him, by night or by day, nor do they depart from him. (14:22–23)[65]

The negative language, "none who surrounded him could draw near to him," "he had no need of counsel," points to God's greatness, his utter self-sufficiency. Despite the negatives, the role of the angels as members of the divine council is clear.

The depiction of the angels as priests is perhaps more subtle, but it is also clear. *Engizō*, the Greek verb translated "draw near," is used in the Bible of priests serving in the sanctuary.[66] The priestly role of the angels is implicit in the language of God's response to the petition of the fallen Watchers: "It is you who should be petitioning on behalf of men, and not men on your behalf" (15:2). Intercession is a task for priests.

Next God accuses the Watchers of having defiled themselves through contact with women:

> Why have you left the high heaven and the eternal Holy One,[67] and lain with the women, and defiled yourselves with the daughters of men and taken to yourselves wives, and acted like the children of earth and begotten giants for sons. And you were holy, spirits that live forever, yet you have defiled yourselves with the blood of women, and have begotten (children) by the blood of flesh; and you lusted after the daughters of men and have produced flesh and blood, just as they do who die and perish. (1 Enoch 15:3–4)

The blood of women with which the Watchers are defiled must be the blood of virginity rather than menstrual blood.[68] For the very fact of marriage is defiling to the Watchers, who as spiritual beings should have no such physical needs. Both the Damascus Covenant (col. 5, lines 6–7) and the Psalms of Solomon (8:12 [13]) claim that defilement with menstrual blood causes pollution of the temple, but in neither text are the sinners said to be priests. Ordinary Jews might pollute the temple if, while themselves defiled, they brought sacrifices for the priests to offer.

The charge that the Watchers married improperly echoes accusations against priests of the Second Temple, who come under attack for marriage to foreign women as far back as the time of Ezra and Nehemiah. Priestly families made up a large part of the Jerusalem aristocracy from the period of the return, and thus they were more likely than common people to intermarry as a means of cementing cordial relations with neighbors who were political allies or trading partners. The marriage of any Jew to a foreign woman is a subject of concern to Ezra and Nehemiah, but when such marriages involve priests they are a threat not only to the definition of the holy people but also to the sanctity of the temple. Indeed, even the native women permitted to a priest are more carefully regulated in the Bible than the women permitted to an ordinary Israelite.[69]

Charges of fornication and improper marriages continue to figure prominently in condemnations of the people in the later Second Temple period as in the Damascus Covenant (col. 4, lines 12–19)[70] and the Psalms of Solomon (2:11–13 [13–15]; 8:9–13 [9–14]). Such charges are also directed specifically against priests. The Testament of Levi 14–16 is a diatribe against descendents of Levi for a variety of sins, including sexual sins. It mentions specifically marriage to gentile women purified "with a *form of* purification contrary to the law" (14:6).[71]

At the start of his condemnation of the future sins of his descendents, Levi claims to have learned about them from the "writing of Enoch" (T. Levi 14:1). In a fragment of the Aramaic Levi document that seems to correspond to the Testament of Levi 14, Levi claims that Enoch had already accused the priests of the sins he inveighs against. Since such accusations are not to be found elsewhere in the extant Enoch literature, it seems likely that the author of Aramaic Levi understood the

Book of the Watchers as a polemic against the priesthood.[72] Thus the sins attributed to the Watchers point to an understanding of angels as priests of the heavenly temple.

We have seen that the origins of the development of an elaborate picture of the heavenly temple lie in the feeling that the Jerusalem temple is defiled. If the earthly temple is polluted, the true temple must be found in heaven. This is the picture of the Testament of Levi; the surviving fragments suggest that it was also the picture of Aramaic Levi, but it is impossible to be certain. Such a picture is implicit in the attention given the heavenly temple in the Sabbath Songs from Qumran.

In the Testament of Levi and the Sabbath Songs the heavenly temple functions perfectly. Priests on earth may be corrupt, but their angelic counterparts are not. In the Book of the Watchers the relation between heaven and earth is quite different. If the heavenly temple remains undefiled, it is only because the Watchers had to leave it to go astray. The very feature that calls into question the sanctity of the earthly temple is projected onto the heavenly: some of the priests of the heavenly temple are defiled!

The absence of an absolute dichotomy between heaven and earth in the Book of the Watchers suggests an attitude toward the Jerusalem temple and its priests somewhat different from that of the Testament of Levi or the Qumran literature. The picture of heaven in the Book of the Watchers implies that not all earthly priests are bad. The fallen Watchers, condemned to eternal damnation, are the counterparts of the polluted priests. But the fact that other priests persevere in the service of the heavenly temple implies that some priests on earth continue to serve as they should. So the presence of evil in heaven in the Book of the Watchers is the result of a more positive view of the situation on earth.

The milder condemnation of the Jerusalem priesthood in the Book of the Watchers fits its third-century date well. At least as early as Ezra, the priests of the Second Temple were not without blemish in the eyes of the pious, but nowhere in Ezra or Nehemiah is there a blanket condemnation of priests. As late as 180 B.C.E., a traditionalist like Joshua b. Elazar b. Sira could sing the praises of a high priest. Simeon the Righteous was righteous in the eyes of the pious. But just at this time priests without any respect for the old ways were coming to prominence; their intrigues, recounted at length at the beginning of 2 Maccabees, provide the background for the revolt. Indeed ben Sira may have used the example of Simeon as an admonition to Simeon's sons to preserve the ways of their father, which they appeared to be in danger of deserting.[73] So the Jerusalem priesthood of the late third and early second centuries was not all of a piece; a pious man like the author of the Book of the Watchers might not have wished to condemn all priests. Only later do the Hasmonean usurpation of the high priesthood and the rapid loss of traditional values by the new high priestly family and the priestly aristocracy generally lead to a view of the Jerusalem priesthood as utterly corrupt, a view that precipitated the emergence of the Qumran community.

Enoch as Priest and Scribe

Enoch enters the narrative of the Book of the Watchers in his professional capacity, as scribe.[74] The Watchers who remain in heaven ask Enoch to deliver a message of doom to their fallen brethren (12:3–6), who in turn request that Enoch draw up a petition on their behalf to read to God (13:4). It is not clear why the message of doom requires Enoch's professional expertise, but his scribal skills are surely needed for the proper drafting of a petition.

But Enoch's title is not simply scribe, as Enoch refers to himself (12:3). First the Watchers who remain in heaven (12:4) and then God himself (15:1) address Enoch as "scribe of righteousness."[75] The title suggests the exalted role Enoch plays: as scribe he mediates not between man and man or even God and man, but between God and the angels.[76]

The history of Judaism in the Second Temple period is often written as the tale of tension between two types of religious leaders, priests and scribes. Priestly leadership represents a certain continuity with the preexilic period; the institution of the temple bridges the two periods. But it also represents a change, for the power of priests before the destruction was limited to their own arena, the cult, while in the period of the return the high priest emerges as the political head of the Jewish community in Palestine in relation to its imperial rulers.

A scribe is a professional writer in a society in which literacy is rare. In the ancient Near East scribes served their kings by composing diplomatic correspondence and decrees.[77] The covenant form that shapes Deuteronomy has suggested to some scholars that it is the work of court scribes, the only group likely to be familiar with the form.[78] Scribes also offered counsel to their kings, a function derived not so much from the ability to write as from the learning and experience that go with that ability.[79]

The scribal profession, then, was well established in the period before the exile, but, like the priests, scribes came to occupy more important political roles with the return. Their increased importance has to do in large part with the needs of the Persian empire, and the Hellenistic empires that succeeded it, for civil servants to administer their territories. The codification of the Torah as the constitution of the Jewish polity is in large part a consequence of that same need.[80]

It is the emergence of a written legal corpus that makes conflict between scribe and priest possible. As long as priestly practice was passed on orally within families, it was impossible for outsiders to hold opinions about it. But with a written code non-priests are in a position to offer interpretations of the code that compete with those of priests.

We find a striking example of such conflict in the career of Nehemiah, a high-ranking Jewish official in the Persian civil service.[81] In his memoirs Nehemiah tells us that he drove Tobiah the Ammonite from the rooms in the temple that the high priest himself had given him and then purified the rooms of the uncleanness caused by the presence of a foreigner (Neh. 13:1–9). Nehemiah was able to expel Tobiah from the temple because he was the Persian governor with the might of the Persian empire behind him, and his motives were surely in part political, since Tobiah's priestly friends opposed Nehemiah's reforms. But he justified his action by appealing to his interpretation of the Torah: "On that day they read from the book of Moses in the hearing of the people; and in it was found written that no Ammonite or Moabite should ever enter the assembly of God . . ." (Neh. 13:1).[82]

The implications of Nehemiah's action must be stressed:

> By all traditions of ancient religion the High Priest was the final authority on cult law, especially on purity law, and above all on purity law as it applied to his own temple. Yet here is Nehemiah, not a priest at all, a layman who could not even enter the holy area reserved to the priests (6.10 f.), not only declaring unclean and forbidden what the High Priest had declared clean and permitted, but also overriding the High Priest's ruling and cleansing the temple of the pollution which he said the High Priest had introduced into it.[83]

This potential for conflict between priests, who actually practice in the temple, and skilled interpreters of the law, who respect the priesthood but not always the priests, believing that they know better than many priests how to run the temple, comes to an end only with the destruction of the Second Temple.[84]

Yet in Egypt and in Babylonia scribes and priests were regularly one and the same. And indeed many of the men of the Second Temple period who are known to us as scribes were also priests by heredity. Ezra, "a scribe skilled in the Torah of Moses" (Ez. 7:6), is often regarded as the founding father of Second Temple scribes. But Ezra was a priest as well as a scribe; the Book of Ezra introduces him as "Ezra the son of Seraiah, son of Azariah . . . son of Phineas, son of Eleazar, son of Aaron the chief priest" (Ez. 7:1–5). Michael Fishbane discerns scribal activity in the transmission of priestly regulations and suggests the existence of scribes trained at the temple.[85] Indeed, Steven Fraade has recently argued against the existence of a class of scribes independent of the priesthood in the Second Temple period. Rather, he claims, teaching and interpretation of scripture were seen as part of the biblical mandate for priests.[86] Teaching is a priestly duty in many places in the Hebrew Bible (e.g., Lev. 10:11, Deut. 17:10, Mal. 2:7, Hag. 2:11–13). Scribes are among the groups of Levites listed in Chronicles (2 Chron. 34:13). Later Antiochus III refers to the temple scribes of Jerusalem in an edict preserved in Josephus (*Antiquities* 12.142). Ben Sira writes of Aaron, "In his commandments [God] gave him authority in statutes and judgments, to teach Jacob the testimonies, and to enlighten Israel with his law" (45:17).

Like Ezra, Enoch is priest as well as scribe.[87] While Enoch is actually designated "scribe" in the Book of the Watchers, his priestly role is implicit in the narrative. Enoch's intercession on behalf of the Watchers is a traditional priestly task,[88] and in order to intercede, Enoch enters the heavenly temple and gains access to the sanctuary, a place reserved for priests.

The understanding of Enoch as priest becomes explicit in the Book of Jubilees, written some time in the middle of the second century B.C.E. According to Jubilees, when Enoch is taken off to the Garden of Eden he serves not only as scribe, recording the judgment of all humanity (4:23), but also as priest, "burn[ing] the incense of the sanctuary" (4:25).[89] It seems probable that the author of the Aramaic Levi document, who took from 1 Enoch 12–16 traditions about Enoch's ascent for his account of the commissioning of the ancestor of the priestly line, also understood Enoch as priest.[90] As we shall see, Enoch is considered priest as well as scribe in 2 Enoch also.

Finally, there is a strong prophetic element in the way Enoch is pictured in 1 Enoch 12–16.[91] Like the biblical prophets Enoch participates in the proceedings of the heavenly council, although with a priestly overlay to this prophetic activity since heaven is a temple.

The claims made for Enoch in the Book of the Watchers are powerful indeed. He is a human being who mediates between angels and angels and then between God and angels. He ascends to the heavenly temple, passes through the court to the sanctuary, and looks in to the holy of holies. The God enthroned within speaks to Enoch "with his own mouth" (14:24). For our author the three roles of prophet, priest, and scribe coexisted as ideals, and only by bringing them together could he define the role of the most exalted of men.

The Heavenly Temple and the Origins of Apocalyptic Literature

The fact that the heaven to which Enoch ascends is understood as a temple has implications that go beyond the Book of the Watchers. In the next chapters I hope to show how the picture of heaven as temple influences later apocalypses, even those not particularly interested in temples, and shapes their understanding of the experience of the visionary and the righteous after death. Here I would like to consider the implications of this picture for the emergence of apocalyptic literature.

The publication of the Aramaic fragments of Enoch from Qumran has forced a reassessment of some of the old assumptions about apocalyptic literature. The Astronomical Book and the Book of the Watchers are quite different in content from the once standard description of an apocalypse, for they are far less concerned with the eschatology that dominates a work like Daniel. As a result of the reassessment, more attention has been focused on features of apocalyptic literature particularly prominent in the Book of the Watchers and the Astronomical Book, such as secrets of nature.[92] In addition, greater care has been taken to distinguish apocalyptic eschatology from the genre apocalypse as such.[93] The Book of the Watchers clearly belongs to the genre apocalypse, and it contains some apocalyptic eschatology, although the center of its interests lies elsewhere. Nonetheless, because of its early date and wide influence it is of considerable interest even for the discussion of apocalyptic eschatology.

For one influential school of thought, the origins of apocalyptic eschatology lie in intracommunual tensions of the period of the return from Babylonia.[94] On the one hand, the argument goes, there emerges a "hierocratic"[95] group that finds the fulfillment of its hopes in the rebuilding of the temple and the political power of priests, recognized as the leaders of the Jewish community by the imperial rulers. On the other hand, a "visionary" group remains loyal to the traditions of the prophets and refuses to find in the reality of the present the fulfillment of the prophetic visions. The visionary group, powerless against the priestly establishment, becomes progressively more alienated from it. This alienation leads to the divorce of prophecy from history and the emergence of an eschatology that can now be characterized as apocalyptic.

For Paul Hanson, Ezekiel 40–48 plays a particularly important role in the dialectic out of which apocalyptic eschatology emerges.[96] He admits that the vision comes from a priest "who [has] been denied [his] temple."[97] Since the chapters employ visionary forms, in the context of Ezekiel's own time they might be considered truly visionary. Yet in the end Hanson insists that Ezekiel's vision of the new temple is "the fountainhead of the hierocratic tradition"[98] and that even without regard to later use it is essentially hierocratic:

> The ultimate goal of Ezekiel's prophecy seems to be the promulgation of a program of restoration which is dedicated to the preservation of the institutions of the immediate past and which thus stands in marked contrast to the themes of later apocalyptic such as the absolute break with structures of the past and the imminent judgment followed by a new creation. The priestly interests of Ezekiel are thus very visible beneath the visionary forms, and they determine the use to which those forms are put: the temple would be rebuilt according to the traditional patterns of the era immediately preceding the Babylonian destruction, and the Glory of Yahweh would then return to a cultic setting emulating that which existed prior to the exile.[99]

There can be no doubt that Ezekiel's temple is in accord with "traditional patterns" if by that we mean that Ezekiel worries about the issues involved in the proper maintenance of the sacred that have always concerned priests. But the relationship between the details of his plan—and for priests details are all-important—and the preexilic reality is far from straightforward.[100] Hanson's claim that Ezekiel's plan calls for rebuilding "according to the traditional patterns" might be paraphrased, "If you've seen one temple, you've seen them all." For Hanson it settles the argument to say that Ezekiel's "priestly interests" are visible beneath the visionary forms, because Hanson sees priestly interests as incompatible with visionary concerns.

In a much less extended discussion, Hanson reaches conclusions about the background of 1 Enoch 6–11 in line with his views of the visionary group in *The Dawn of Apocalyptic*. In the account of the punishment of Asael, Hanson sees a "mythologization and eschatologization" of the ritual of the Day of Atonement described in Leviticus 16, in which a scapegoat is sent into the wilderness to Azazel. This process must have taken place in circles that stand "outside the mainstream of temple praxis" because only there "the *textus classicus* of the holiest festival of the cultic calendar could be dealt with so freely." The Asael story, then, represents "a harsh indictment against the temple cult," involving a rejection of the efficacy of the ritual for the Day of Atonement.[101] But why mythologization and eschatologization of a ritual should imply rejection of the ritual as practiced in the present is far from clear, unless you assume, as Hanson does, that apocalyptic eschatology entails rejection of the temple.[102]

Hanson nowhere considers the Book of the Watchers as a whole. 1 Enoch 12–16, usually taken as a development of and comment on 1 Enoch 6–11, certainly makes the work a problematic case for Hanson. We have seen that chapters 12–16 involve a critique of the Jerusalem priestly establishment that takes seriously the priesthood's claims for itself and the importance of priestly duties and categories. This attitude is at once critical of the reality it sees in the temple and deeply devoted to the ideal of the temple understood in a quite concrete way.

This stance toward the temple and the conduct of affairs there is one that Hanson seems unable to imagine. For Hanson there is no midground between the dismissal of priestly rules in favor of an ideal future of utter equality in 3 Isaiah (a reading of 3 Isaiah that is itself not unproblematic)[103] and the practical agenda for priests he finds in Ezekiel.

Hanson is in good scholarly company in his view of Ezekiel 40–48 as "hierocratic" rather than visionary. Indeed, many scholars have reduced Ezekiel's own contribution to chapters 40–48 to a very small portion since such pedantic concern with the temple is not fit for a prophet's vision.[104] But others have insisted on the continuity between these chapters and the extravagant visions at once priestly and prophetic that characterize the rest of Ezekiel.[105] Susan Niditch has recently made a strong case that Ezekiel's model of the temple is of cosmological significance (like all temples), and thus entirely appropriate for a prophetic vision.[106]

Our reading of 1 Enoch 12–16 lends support to a view of Ezekiel 40–48 as visionary hope rather than "pragmatic" building instructions. In 1 Enoch 12–16 the heavenly temple is the appropriate abode for the deity, but it also serves as a vehicle for criticizing the conduct of affairs in the temple on earth. Ezekiel's critique is directed at a temple already in the past, which Ezekiel saw as having been polluted by idolatry. A temple untainted by idolatry means the dawn of a new era. For Ezekiel, as for the author of 1 Enoch 12–16, a deep concern with the proper conduct of affairs in the temple is not only not in conflict with eschatological hope; it represents the very essence of eschatological hope.

Ezekiel himself was not responsible for ordering the material in his book, but his followers showed real insight in their arrangement. The vision of the return of the glory to the restored temple (43:1–4), in a sense the culmination of the book, answers the vision on the River Chebar at the beginning of the book, to which it is explicitly compared. Further it cannot be accidental that the vision of a restored temple follows the eschatological wars of Gog and Magog.[107] Hanson might have considered this placement in his comment quoted earlier about apocalyptic eschatology requiring a break with the past to be followed by new creation. Proper conduct of affairs in the temple and proper regulation of the holy and the profane: without divine intervention these can be a reality only in heaven. It is worth remembering that Ezekiel is the prophet who looked forward to having God replace Israel's hearts of stone with hearts of flesh (11:19). Human beings have it in their power to fulfill God's will, yet only God's intervention will make human beings truly human. So too a properly functioning temple is at once within human reach and miraculous.

I suspect that the real basis for the view that apocalyptic groups are inherently antitemple, of which Hanson is one of the most prominent representatives, is to be found in Christian theology. Like so many scholars before him, Hanson takes it as given that prophecy and cult—read gospel and law—are entirely separate spheres.[108] Significantly, although Hanson mentions Qumran in his book as a place where alienated priests have become an apocalyptic community, he never develops this point.[109] Even for priests more accepting of the status quo than those at Qumran, there could surely exist a sense of the disparity between the actual—the Second Temple, under foreign domination—and the ideal.

Johann Maier has argued that it is precisely in priestly speculation about the heavenly correlate of the earthly temple that we find the origins of that strand of apocalyptic literature concerned with the throne of God.[110] The content of 1 Enoch 12–16 makes it difficult to disagree that there is a large priestly component in apocalyptic speculation. Of the great classical prophets before the destruction, Isaiah was deeply devoted to the temple, and Jeremiah, that great opponent of the temple, was a priest by heredity. Hanson himself understands several of the prophets of the Second Temple as hierocratic, and I believe that he is wrong to read 3 Isaiah as antitemple. We have seen too the community of interests between priests and scribes and the remarkable overlap of membership in the two groups. If we ignore priests and their friends in our search for the origins of apocalyptic literature or even apocalyptic eschatology, we are in danger of losing all of our candidates.

2

Heavenly Ascent
and Priestly Investiture

In the centuries that followed its composition, the Book of the Watchers was among the most influential works outside the canon for both Jews and Christians. Several of the later ascent apocalypses are deeply indebted to it. Even those that show no clear signs of dependence take over a central aspect of its legacy, the depiction of the visionary's ascent to heaven in terms drawn from the understanding of heaven as a temple. This is not to suggest that the picture of heaven as temple was restricted to the Book of the Watchers; on the contrary, it is clear that the picture was widely held in early Judaism. But the Book of the Watchers is the first Jewish work to depict an ascent to heaven, and it sets the tone for the entire body of later apocalyptic literature.

In the Book of the Watchers, Enoch is overcome by fear at the awesome majesty of the heavenly temple, yet God welcomes him and speaks to him without requiring any purification or change in his physical being. In most of the later apocalypses the visionary undergoes some kind of physical transformation in order to stand before God, a transformation that is shaped by the understanding of heaven as temple. This chapter examines such transformation in works explicitly indebted to the Enochic tradition, 2 Enoch and 3 Enoch (Sepher Hekhalot). Chapter 3 treats transformation in works that are not directly dependent on this tradition, the Apocalypse of Zephaniah, the Ascension of Isaiah, and the Apocalypse of Abraham, as well as the Similitudes of Enoch (1 Enoch 37–71), which, despite its debt to the Book of the Watchers, is better treated with those works for reasons to be discussed there.

The Testament of Levi

Although the subject of this chapter is transformation, it is useful to begin the discussion with the Testament of Levi, a work in which there is no transformation, but rather a vision of Levi's investiture as priest on earth following his ascent to heaven. The process of transformation described in other apocalypses draws on priestly investiture for its imagery; the Testament of Levi is helpful because there the purpose of the process of investiture is explicit.

The Testament of Levi forms part of the Testaments of the Twelve Patriarchs. The Testaments is a Christian work, although it clearly draws on Jewish sources.[1] The nature and extent of the Jewish sources is the subject of continued debate.[2] But for the Testament of Levi, these questions can be answered with a greater degree of certainty than for most of the other testaments. The major source on which the Testament of Levi draws is an Aramaic document about Levi only partially preserved in fragments from Qumran and the Cairo geniza, and in translation in a passage in a Greek manuscript of the Testaments of the Twelve Patriarchs from Mount Athos (MS e).[3] This work, together with the Enochic fragments found at Qumran, is usually assigned to the pre-Qumranic literature, suggesting a date before the middle of the second century B.C.E., and origins in the same circles as the Book of the Watchers.[4] Like the other works considered in this chapter, the Testament of Levi is also indebted to the Book of the Watchers, probably not directly, but rather through the influence of the Book of the Watchers on the Aramaic Levi document.[5]

The central concern of the Testament of Levi is the corruption of the priesthood by Levi's descendants. At the start of the Testament, Levi describes two visions in which he is commissioned to serve as priest. In the first (chs. 2–5), he ascends to the heavenly temple where God himself entrusts him with the priesthood. In the second vision (ch. 8), angels anoint him and clothe him in the vestments of the priesthood. After the visions, Levi exhorts his sons and condemns the future sins of their descendants.

Like the Book of the Watchers, the Testament of Levi glorifies the role of priest while condemning those who actually serve as priests. In the Book of the Watchers, Enoch is explicitly called scribe while the narrative implies a priestly role for him. In the Testament of Levi the situation is reversed. Levi's designation as ancestor of the priestly line is perhaps the central theme of the text. Yet alongside specifically sacerdotal functions, the Testament assigns to Levi and his descendents many duties more obviously associated with scribes (e.g., 8:17, ch. 13, 14:4).

With the Epistle to the Hebrews, the Testament of Levi offers striking evidence for the continuing significance of the priesthood for some early Christians. The prophecy about Levi's descendants in chapter 8 concludes with the establishment of a "new priesthood" (8:14), and the penultimate chapter of the Testament is devoted to a description of the wonders accompanying and accomplished by the eschatological "new priest."[6]

The contents of the Aramaic Levi document would be of tremendous importance to our understanding of the development of the themes discussed here. But while the fragments attest the existence in Aramaic Levi of the two visions discussed here, they are disappointingly incomplete. One fragment breaks off at the start of the first vision, after the mention of a vision of heaven (4QTestLevi[a], col. ii, lines 15–18), while another set of fragments (Bodleian a, 1QTestLevifg3) contains the conclusion of the second vision, with the end of the blessing of Levi's descendants, the departure of the seven angels, and Levi's awaking from the vision. Thus of necessity it is primarily the Testament of Levi, the Greek document that forms part of the Christian Testaments of the Twelve Patriarchs, that will be discussed here.

Levi's Ascent

Levi's vision of the seven heavens comes at the beginning of the testament. While he herds his sheep, Levi contemplates the corruption of humanity and prays to be saved. He falls asleep, the heavens open, and an angel invites him into the heavens (2:3–6). The existence of more than a single heaven constitutes a significant departure from the ascent in the Book of the Watchers,[7] but the patchwork quality of the account of the seven heavens suggests that it represents a reworking of earlier sources. Very little is said about the contents or appearance of the first three heavens as Levi ascends through them (2:7–12). A more detailed description is provided by the angel as he and Levi stand in the third heaven. According to the angel the three lower heavens are associated with the day of judgment: the first heaven sees the sins of humanity, while the second and third contain instruments of vengeance (3:1–3). Next the angel describes the four upper heavens, which constitute the heavenly temple, but he describes them from top to bottom (3:4–10). The highest heaven is the "holy of holies," in which the "Great Glory" dwells.[8] The sixth heaven is the scene of expiatory sacrifice on behalf of the righteous. In the fifth the deeds of humanity are offered to God,[9] and in the fourth angels sing praise.

The description of the heavens is followed by the angel's praise of the priestly office (ch. 4). The centrality of the understanding of heaven as a temple is made clear by Levi's vision of God, only loosely connected to the description of the heavens in chapter 3. "The gates of heaven" open to reveal "the holy temple (*naos*) and the Most High upon a throne of glory" (5:1).[10] As de Jonge notes, the singular "heaven," so out of place in the context of what has come before, may be a remnant of the

Aramaic vision that contained only a single heaven.[11] There is no indication in chapter 5 that the heaven in which God sits is the seventh heaven, nor is Levi said to ascend to him.

Yet despite the emphasis on heaven as temple and the vision of God himself, Levi betrays no emotion nor even an awareness of protocol. He does not shake and tremble, and he neglects to fall on his face. It is possible that the absence of any reaction is intended to emphasize Levi's distinction as founder of the priestly line. Even an ordinary priest is at home in the earthly temple, so perhaps the ancestor of all priests feels at home in the heavenly temple as well, and at ease with the sight of the awesome one who dwells there.

But I think this is unlikely. Rather, Levi's lack of reaction to the sights he sees is the most striking indication of the transformed significance of the priesthood for the author of the Greek Testament of Levi.[12] The author of Aramaic Levi with his intense interest in the earthly priesthood would surely have made his hero react appropriately to the heavenly temple. A good priest is always a little bit nervous, even in the earthly temple, operating in such close proximity to the divine.[13] How much more should he feel awe in the heavenly temple! The author of the Greek Testament found priests and temples extremely important, but their meaning had been transformed so that the mundane details of the cult had lost their power. Later I will point out another example of his insensitivity to the awesomeness of the heavenly temple.

From Heaven to Heavens

The ascent apocalypses that date from the first century C.E. or later contain seven heavens, although the picture of a single heaven continues to appear in a wide variety of texts, including some related to the ascent apocalypses, such as Revelation, the Apocalypse of Peter, and the Apocalypse of Paul.[14] A number of the apocalypses with seven heavens are reworkings of earlier apocalypses with a single heaven. I hope to show that the Testament of Levi recasts the contents of the ascent in the Book of the Watchers and the Aramaic Levi document to fill seven heavens. The seven heavens of 2 Enoch combine and reorder the contents of the two separate journeys Enoch undertakes in the Book of the Watchers, the ascent (1 Enoch 14) and the journey to the ends of the earth (1 Enoch 17–36).[15] Clement of Alexandria's citation of a passage about the fifth heaven from an Apocalypse of Zephaniah suggests that there once existed such a reworking of the extant Apocalypse of Zephaniah with its single heaven.

It is difficult to specify the causes of the emergence of the picture of seven heavens and to explain why it took place at a particular moment in history. Adela Yarbro Collins has recently argued that the seven planetary spheres of Greek cosmology are not the source of this picture; rather she points to the prominence of the number seven for heavens in

Sumerian and Babylonian magic.[16] Indeed, seven plays an important role in the symbolism of the Bible, and it is by no means a surprising number in this context. One of the most revealing clues to the significance of the number may be its use in the Songs of the Sabbath Sacrifice from Qumran to express the multifold perfection of the world of the heavenly temple.[17]

The use of the contents of the ascent in the Book of the Watchers in the description of the heavens in the Testament of Levi is shaped by the requirements of a schema of seven heavens. Some elements of 1 Enoch 14 have been transformed in keeping with this framework. In 1 Enoch 14 the separate chambers of the heavenly temple are described. In the Testament of Levi the heavens themselves seem to provide the chambers, although this is explicit only for the seventh heaven, which is identified as the holy of holies. Heavenly sacrifices are offered in the sixth heaven, just as sacrifices in the earthly temple are offered in the hall outside the holy of holies. This correspondence is not maintained, however. To match the earthly temple's three chambers, we would expect the heavenly temple to be made up of three heavens. But in the Testament of Levi it is the four upper heavens that serve as temple. Of course, loose correspondence to the earthly temple is the rule in depictions of the heavenly temple. The appearance of different classes of angels in each of heavens four through six is probably also the result of the need to fill seven heavens.[18]

The three lower heavens with their connection to the day of judgment provide a link between the ascent and the predictions of eschatological judgment that play so large a role in the later part of the Testament. They also provide a heavenly background for Levi's angelically commanded mission of vengeance against Shechem.

In the second heaven the angel points out snow, fire, and ice, to serve as instruments of punishment on the day of judgment (3:2). The same elements, of course, appear in 1 Enoch 14, among the materials out of which the heavenly temple is built.[19] Thus the author of the Testament transforms the awe-inspiring building materials of the heavenly temple into weapons. I read this transformation, together with Levi's lack of reaction to the heavenly temple, as a sign that the author of the Testament had little appreciation of the awesomeness of temples. This is perhaps one additional piece of evidence in favor of de Jonge's contention that the author was a Christian living in perhaps the second half of the second century rather than a Hellenistic Jew.

Sacrifice in Heaven

In the earthly temple sacrifice was the central ritual. But sacrifice appears in very few descriptions of the heavenly temple.[20] The last of the Songs of the Sabbath Sacrifice from Qumran mentions sacrifices, emphasizing especially their aroma (11QShirShabb 8–7, lines 2–3). I shall return to it. Jubilees mentions first the Feast of Weeks celebrated in heaven until the time of Noah (6:18), and then the sacrifices by which the children of Israel observed the festival (6:22), thus suggesting sacrifice in heaven as well. Like the Aramaic Levi work, Jubilees was not written at Qumran, although it was read there.

Among the apocalypses, only Revelation, which is not really an ascent, and 3 Baruch refer to sacrifice in heaven; in both works the offering is the prayers or good deeds of the righteous. The climax of the Book of Revelation makes it clear that for Christians the temple is obsolete. When the new Jerusalem descended from heaven, John reports, "I saw no temple in the city, for its temple is the Lord God the almighty and the Lamb" (21:22). Yet the city is described in terms that allude to Ezekiel's description of the eschatological temple at the end of the Book of Ezekiel. Revelation's heaven is also described with elaborate temple imagery. The presence of the spiritual temple in heaven makes the physical temple on earth unnecessary. In the single instance of sacrifice in Revelation, an angel mixes incense with the prayers of the saints on an altar that appears when the seventh seal is opened (8:3–5). The inclusion of incense in this representation of heavenly sacrifice is part of a tendency to emphasize the aroma of sacrifice in heaven rather than its more grossly corporeal aspects.

Like Revelation, 3 Baruch has no interest in the restoration of the earthly temple.[21] But Michael, the angelic high priest, offers the prayers or good deeds of men in the heavenly temple (ch. 14).[22] The fact of sacrifice in heaven in 3 Baruch serves to demonstrate its point that the world continues to function properly in the absence of the earthly temple.

This brief survey suggests that depiction of sacrifice in heaven is compatible with a variety of attitudes toward sacrifice on earth. Let us return now to the sixth heaven of the Testament of Levi, where the angels offer "a sweet savor, a reasonable and bloodless offering" (*osmēn euōdias, logikēn kai anaimakton prosphoran*) (3:7). De Jonge takes the "reasonable and bloodless offering" as the work of the Christian author of the Testaments, because the term "bloodless offering" appears in early Christian literature, first for prayer, later for the eucharist. The contexts in which the phrase appears often involve rejection of physical sacrifice. For the passage in the Testament of Levi, de Jonge prefers the meaning "prayer" on grounds of date. Against the claim that the phrase is Christian, Becker points out that Plutarch used it twice and argues for a background in Hellenistic Judaism.[23]

As we have seen, the Book of the Watchers implies the existence of some kind of service in heaven, but it is not interested in the details. My guess is that the picture of angels engaged in the heavenly liturgy in the upper heavens of the Testament of Levi is drawn from the lost description of heaven from the Aramaic Levi document. It seems likely that a work as concerned with proper priestly behavior on earth as the

Aramaic Levi document, with its detailed instructions for sacrifice, would also be concerned to represent priestly behavior in heaven.

With this in mind, the sweet savor that stands in apposition to the reasonable and bloodless offering deserves a little more attention. The Testament of Levi's phrase for sweet savor, *osmē euōdias*, is the Septuagint's standard translation of the Hebrew *reyaḥ niḥoaḥ*, the aroma produced by sacrifice. Suzanne Daniel has suggested that this choice of translation itself represents a movement away from the more concrete sense of the Hebrew toward an understanding of the sweetness of the savor as relational, its sweetness for God.[24] I do not know any other instance of the application of the entire phrase to heavenly sacrifice, but the very fragmentary beginning of the thirteenth Sabbath Song from Qumran refers to "the sacrifices of the holy ones," and then "the odor of their offerings," and "the odor of their drink offerings" (11QShirShabb 8–7, lines 2–3).

Newsom's comment about the phrases involving odor is worth quoting:

> In the OT where *ryḥ* is used in connection with sacrifice, it always occurs in the stereotyped phrase *ryḥ nyḥwḥ*. The Shirot seems intentionally to vary biblical terminology relating to the technical matters of the cult, perhaps as a means of suggesting the difference as well as the correspondence between the heavenly and the earthly service.[25]

In light of the thirteenth Sabbath Song, I am inclined to see the "sweet savor" of the Testament of Levi as a cultic term intended to suggest that heavenly sacrifices are at once like and unlike earthly. The sweet savor is the most ethereal product of the sacrifices performed on earth; in heaven it becomes the sacrifice itself. Remember the incense mixed with the prayers of the righteous as the lone sacrifice of the Book of Revelation. The phrase, I would guess, comes to the Testament of Levi from Aramaic Levi. It is not unlikely that the author of the Sabbath Songs too had read Aramaic Levi, since the work was copied at Qumran.

This understanding of the sweet savor of the sixth heaven leaves us with two possibilities for the "reasonable and bloodless offering." The language of the phrase certainly suggests that it was introduced into the Testament of Levi in Greek by the Christian author. De Jonge may be correct to see in the phrase a polemic against earthly sacrifice, by which the author transforms the sweet savor, separating it from its association with earthly sacrifice. Alternately, it is possible that the juxtaposition with the sweet savor represents not a polemic against earthly sacrifice, but a further statement of the differences between heavenly and earthly sacrifice.

In the Second Temple, according to some accounts, hymns accompanied sacrifice.[26] Angelic hymns are very popular in the ascent apocalypses; all mention them, although only the Similitudes of Enoch and the Apocalypse of Abraham describe the content of the hymns.[27] In the hekhalot texts, the hymns of the angels are the subject of intense interest and are reported in detail, sometimes because they are understood to make possible the ascent of the initiate, but often because of their inherent value.[28] The hymns that the angels sing to praise God turn out to be strikingly similar to the hymns of the earthly liturgy.

Why is so much more attention devoted to angelic song than to heavenly sacrifice? In part it may have to do with the difficulty of imagining heavenly sacrifice. Bullocks and their fat—even the odor of their fat—seem out of place in heaven. But another factor may be more important. The authors of those works in which the heavenly service is a central concern were often people deprived of participation in the earthly temple. For some, like the residents of Qumran, the earthly temple was seen as corrupt and unworthy of allegiance. For others, like the hekhalot mystics, the earthly temple was no longer standing. In the course of communal worship, however, the authors and the members of their communities did recite songs of praise. Thus the description of such songs in heaven would be more effective in creating a feeling of participation in the heavenly service than would the description of sacrifice. Indeed, Peter Schäfer has recently argued that the visionary's discovery that the heavenly liturgy awaits the completion of the earthly, with its implicit claim for the exalted status of the people of Israel at prayer, is at the very center of the concerns of the hekhalot literature.[29]

The picture of the heavenly liturgy in the Testament of Levi suggests that Aramaic Levi's heaven contained both sacrifices and hymns. Despite the danger of speculating about the missing portions of a fragmentary text, I would guess that the later apocalypes are indebted to Aramaic Levi for the conception of heaven as the home of the heavenly liturgy.

Levi's Investiture

Levi's ascent to heaven is followed by a second vision (ch. 8) in which seven angels anoint Levi, dress him in the vestments of priesthood, and prophesy to him about the future of the priestly line. Again Levi betrays no reaction of any kind to his exalted visitors. After this vision of consecration Jacob gives Levi his tithes (9:4), a sign that Levi has begun to serve as priest.

The process of anointing and dressing falls into two parts. First the angels tell Levi to put on seven priestly garments, which they list for him (8:2–3). In the second part of the passage each of the seven angels in turn performs part of the consecration (8:4–10). The first anoints Levi and gives him a staff, the second washes him, feeds him bread and wine, and dresses him in a robe, and so on. The correspondence between the items that the angels list and those in which Levi is actually dressed is not exact.[30]

The priestly garments that the angels list are drawn from the biblical perscriptions for priestly dress.[31] But each article of clothing has attached to it an abstract noun in the genitive: "the robe of the priest-hood / and the crown of righteousness / and the breastplate of under-standing / and the garment of truth / and the plate of faith / and the turban of (giving) a sign / and the ephod of prophecy" (8:2). These genitives shift the focus from priestly garments as required elements of the cult to the larger meaning of priesthood.

Most of the elements of the consecration in the second section of the chapter are drawn from the biblical instructions for the consecration of priests or other priestly activities. But the account also introduces a number of items to Levi's wardrobe that are more clearly associated with kingship than priesthood, such as the staff of judgment and the diadem (*diadēma*). Although it is here called a diadem of priesthood, in the Greek Bible the diadem is the headdress of kings rather than of priests.[32]

Only the very end of the second vision has survived in the Aramaic Levi document, but taken together with the passage that follows, it sug-gests a significant difference between Aramaic Levi and the Testament. At the end of their speech to Levi in the Aramaic text, the angels say, "Now, see how we elevated you above all and how we gave you the anointing of eternal peace."[33] The Aramaic goes on to report that after giving Levi tithes, Jacob dressed him in priestly clothes and "filled his hands," that is, conse-crated him. In the Aramaic, then, the angels begin the process of consecra-tion in the vision, but Jacob completes it on earth. For the Testament of Levi, on the other hand, the consecration takes place through the vision; it is never reenacted on earth.[34] While it is tempting to see the placement of the entire process of consecration in a vision as an aspect of the Christian author's distance from the earthly cult, caution is required since Jubilees also places Levi's consecration in a vision.[35]

What is most significant for our purposes here is something the Testament and the Aramaic document have in common. In both, Levi's ascent to heaven is followed by a process of consecration as priest in which he is anointed and dressed in priestly garments. The purpose of the ascent is God's appointment of Levi as priest, and the consecration is thus the fulfillment of the ascent.

As the Testament of Levi makes clear, there is a heavenly dimen-sion to Levi's priestly role: "For you will stand near the Lord and will be his minister and will declare his mysteries to men . . ." (2:10).[36] In the Testament of Levi priestly investiture follows an ascent to the divine presence for commissioning as priest. In the other apocalypses to be considered, the visionary must first be consecrated as priest in order to be admitted to the heavenly temple in which the divine presence dwells.

2 Enoch

It requires a certain amount of daring to approach 2 Enoch. First, basic textual questions remain to be resolved. In the introduction to his recent translation, F. I. Andersen not only argues against the regnant view that the shorter recension is always to be preferred to the longer, but even calls into question the division of all the manuscripts into two recensions.[37]

Further, the gap between the earliest preserved evidence for 2 Enoch, from a fourteenth-century Slavonic work,[38] and the provenance widely assumed, first-century Egyptian Judaism,[39] is enormous, even for the pseudepigrapha, where assumptions are so often based on rather little evidence. Early in this century A. S. D. Maunders argued that 2 Enoch was the work of Bogomils, medieval dualists who lived in Slavic lands, but this suggestion has been adequately refuted.[40] Still, the process of the transmission of 2 Enoch from its presumed Greek original in the first century to the surviving Slavonic manuscripts of the Middle Ages and later has yet to be explored.

My own guess is that the standard view of the provenance of 2 Enoch, although it was arrived at without adequate grounds, is more or less correct. My view is based on two considerations, one negative and one positive: 2 Enoch does not look like medieval Christian apocalypses, but it shows many similarities to apocalypses that clearly belong to the early centuries of this era. An Egyptian location seems plausible, as I shall argue later in this chapter. There is nothing in 2 Enoch that requires or even suggests particularly Christian concerns. This does not eliminate the possibility of a Christian author, but it makes a Jewish author more likely.

The debt of 2 Enoch to several of the units of 1 Enoch is manifest. At some points there is a clear literary relationship, as in the description of the patriarch's ascent through the seven heavens. The contents of the heavens, as noted above, are drawn from both journeys of the Book of the Watchers, the ascent (1 Enoch 14–16) and tour to the ends of the earth (1 Enoch 17–36), reworked to fit the schema of seven heavens. The question-and-answer form of the tour to the ends of the earth reappears in those heavens of 2 Enoch in which the contents are drawn from the tour to the ends of the earth, but not in the other heavens. Even some of the language used in the description of the heavens in 2 Enoch appears to be drawn from the Book of the Watchers.[41]

In 2 Enoch, Enoch's ascent begins when two angels appear to him as he lies weeping in bed (1:1–3).[42] The influence of the idea of heaven as temple is felt first in the prominence of the angelic liturgy in the heavens. It is clearest in the sixth and seventh heavens (chs. 8–9), where offering praise is the only activity of the various kinds of angels who inhabit them. Only in the first heaven, where various cosmological phenomena are found (ch. 3), and the second, where the fallen Watchers are punished (ch. 4), is there no mention of angelic songs of praise. In the third heaven, where heaven and hell are located (ch. 5), the angels guarding paradise praise God (5:7). In the fourth heaven, where the sun and moon run their courses (ch. 6), an armed troop of angels offers praise with musical accompaniment (6:25).[43] When Enoch arrives in the fifth heaven, the home of the mournful watchers (ch. 7), he does not hear praise being offered. He immediately inquires of his guides, "Why are they *so* very sad, and their faces downcast, and their mouths silent, and *why* is there no service in this heaven?" (7:3). The assumption is clear: the heavens should be the scene of praise.[44]

The Seventh Heaven

God himself dwells in the seventh heaven, worshiped by armies of angels. (The military metaphor is used of the angels in the fourth and fifth heavens as well.) At the sight of the angels of the seventh heaven Enoch feels terror for the first time during the ascent. The angelic guides encourage him and from a safe distance they show him God enthroned (ch. 9).

It is worth taking a moment to consider the words of encouragement spoken by the angelic guides: "Take courage, Enoch, do not be afraid" (9:15). The same words are spoken a little later by the angel Gabriel (9:3) and then by God himself (9:15). They appear to echo God's words to Joshua in the first chapter of the book that bears his name, *ḥazaq ve'emaṣ*, "Be strong and resolute" (New Jewish Publication Society Translation), or "Be strong and very courageous" (RSV).

Words of encouragement based on the words from Joshua appear also in the Apocalypse of Zephaniah (3:1, 6),[45] an apocalypse written in Egypt around the turn of the era that will be considered in the next chapter, and the Apocalypse of Paul (ch. 14), also of Egyptian provenance, but probably from the third century.[46]

The Apocalypse of Zephaniah is preserved in Coptic, the Apocalypse of Paul in several languages of which the Latin is the best witness, and 2 Enoch in Slavonic. This makes caution essential in comparing each apocalypse's version of the words of encouragement to the others' and to the biblical text. Still, I think it is clear that the Apocalypse of Paul borrows these words from the Apocalypse of Zephaniah, as it borrows so much else.[47] It seems unlikely that their presence in 2 Enoch is the result of direct borrowing from the Apocalypse of Zephaniah, since the two works otherwise have very little in common. But in light of the undoubted Egyptian origin of the Apocalypse of Zephaniah and the Apocalypse of Paul, the occurrence of the words of encouragment speaks in favor of the Egyptian provenance of 2 Enoch.

After offering encouragement to Enoch, the guides depart. In terror at being left alone, Enoch falls on his face (9:8). When the angel Gabriel comes to him, Enoch answers his words of encouragement by describing the extremity of his distress and begging for the return of the angels who had accompanied him. Gabriel responds by bringing him near God's throne (9:9–11). Upon seeing the face of God, Enoch is overwhelmed and falls on his face a second time (9:12–14). This time it is the angel Michael who raises him (9:15). As in the Book of the Watchers, God speaks to Enoch "with his own mouth" (2 Enoch 9:15, 1 Enoch 14:24).

The scene in the seventh heaven in 2 Enoch is clearly indebted to the account of Enoch's experience before the divine throne in the Book of the Watchers. But the author of 2 Enoch improves on 1 Enoch 14 by making Enoch fall on his face twice. The placement of the two incidents of prostration is significant. The second incident serves to recognize the awesomeness of the sight of God. The first, however, is Enoch's response not to any new sight but to the departure of his guides. The distress he expresses to Gabriel, "Alas, *my* lord, I am paralyzed by fear" (9:10), is a striking contrast to the absence of any emotion in the account of Levi's vision of God in the heavenly temple in the Testament of Levi, and it goes beyond the Book of the Watchers in emphasizing the terror that the visionary feels upon finding himself in the heavens. The intensity of Enoch's fear at being left without his guides serves to emphasize the magnitude of what takes place next.

Transformation by Investiture

After Michael lifts Enoch from his second prostration, God commands him, "Take Enoch, and take off his earthly garments, and anoint *him* with good oil, and clothe *him* in glorious garments . . ." (19:17). Michael does as he is commanded,[48] the wondrous nature of the oil is described in some detail, and then Enoch reports, "I looked at myself, and I was like one of the glorious ones, and there was no apparent difference" (9:19). Enoch has become an angel.

The combination of clothing and anointing suggests that the process by which Enoch becomes an angel is a heavenly version of priestly investiture. The idea that there are special garments for the righteous after death is widespread in this period.[49] Some examples from the ascent apocalypses are discussed in the next chapter, and, as I shall show, donning such a garment can imply equality with the angels (or better!). When Paul speaks of a spiritual body (1 Cor. 15:42–50) for the righteous after death, he seems to have in mind something similar to these heavenly garments. What is distinctive about the glorious garments of 2 Enoch is their association with anointing and the ceremony of priestly consecration invoked.[50]

Elsewhere in 2 Enoch it is clear that Enoch is regarded as a priest.[51] In 16:3 he is referred to as God's chosen who carries away men's sins. Further, the concluding chapters of 2 Enoch (21–23) are devoted to the succession of the priesthood after Enoch's ascension, clearly implying that Enoch himself served as priest.

It is striking that in 2 Enoch, as in the Testament of Levi and Aramaic Levi, anointing precedes dressing in priestly garments, in opposition to the instructions for the consecration of Aaron as high priest in Exodus 29. The Testament of Levi as part of the second-century Testaments of the Twelve Patriarchs is probably too late to have influenced 2 Enoch. Could the author of 2 Enoch have known a Greek version of the Aramaic Levi document? (Egyptian Jews do not appear to have known Hebrew beyond a few key terms; if the Aramaic Levi document influenced the author of 2 Enoch, it was almost surely in Greek.) Perhaps it was a Greek translation rather than the original Aramaic Levi that served as a source for the author/compiler of the Testaments. The existence of such a translation might also help to explain the material drawn from Aramaic Levi that appears only in MS e of the Greek Testament of Levi.

The Melchizedek Section

The last section of 2 Enoch relates Methuselah's assumption of the priesthood after the ascension of his father, Enoch, Methuselah's death, the passing of the priesthood to Methuselah's nephew Nir, and the miraculous birth of Melchizedek to a barren old woman, apparently without the intervention of a father.[52] It concludes with the appearance of an angel to take the child Melchizedek to the Garden of Eden to avoid the flood, after which Melchizedek is to return to serve as high priest. Thus the continuity of the priesthood even through the disaster of the flood is assured.

The role assigned to Melchizedek in this section has led some scholars to view it as influenced by the Epistle to the Hebrews.[53] But the parallels to Hebrews are very general, and the evidence for a well-developed tradition of Jewish Melchizedek speculation at Qumran makes the influence of Hebrews less likely.[54] This is not to suggest that the Qumran traditions influenced 2 Enoch, either. For Qumran and Hebrews, Melchizedek is primarily a heavenly figure. For 2 Enoch, he remains an earthly one, despite his sojourn in the Garden of Eden.

Was the Melchizedek section originally part of 2 Enoch? It is not present in all the manuscripts, but Andersen argues that since it appears only as part of 2 Enoch, it must be an original part of 2 Enoch.[55] The parallel it provides to the concluding chapters of 1 Enoch (chs. 106–7), about the miraculous birth of Noah, also stands in favor of this view.[56]

Priestly garments play a prominent role in this narrative, but anointing is never mentioned. The elders dress Methuselah in a "gorgeous robe" and a "splendid crown" (21:7), so that he can officiate as priest; not unlike ben Sira's high priest, he looks like "the morning star when it rises" as he ascends the altar (21:8). When it is time for Methuselah to die, God speaks with him to instruct him about the arrangements for his successor, including investiture in Methuselah's own robes (22:4–5). The wondrous child Melchizedek is born with "the seal of the priesthood . . . on his breast" (23:18), perhaps the priestly breastplate. But Melchizedek is not born fully attired. Only after washing the child do Noah and Nir dress him in the priestly garments (23:20).

From a literary point of view the three large sections of 2 Enoch—the ascent and revelation (chs. 1–11), the exhortations to pious behavior (chs. 13–20),[57] and the priestly succession to Melchizedek (chs. 21–23)—are only loosely connected to each other. In the ascent, anointing and investiture together constitute consecration as priest. The absence of anointing in the concluding section with its strong interest in priestly dress strengthens the impression that the author of 2 Enoch drew together originally separate sources.[58]

The Earthly Temple

This conclusion receives further support from the absence of any traces of the conception of heaven as temple outside the ascent. Despite the interest in the earthly priesthood in the concluding chapters, the idea of heaven as temple does not appear there. It is even missing from God's account of creation, which is the culmination of the ascent. In Jubilees the angels are said to praise God upon their creation (2:3), but although the heavens of the ascent are filled with angelic praise, there is no mention of such praise when God recounts the creation of the angels to Enoch (10:18). Enoch's report of what was revealed to him in the seventh heaven makes no allusion to heaven as temple either. His exhortations to his sons include some remarks that may refer to sacrifice, although this is not entirely clear.[59] Yet nowhere in these chapters is there an appeal to heavenly practice to justify earthly practice, as in Jubilees. Even earthly sacrifice receives little attention.

The lack of interest of the author of 2 Enoch in the contemporary priesthood is striking because he drew on a work so deeply concerned with the failings of the priests of its own time. The criticism of priests in the Book of the Watchers remains implicit, but it is a central theme of the work. The Testament of Levi, probably reflecting Aramaic Levi,[60] explicitly criticizes the priests, although the criticism is necessarily presented as prophecy. It appears that 2 Enoch is not interested in criticizing priests at all. The ascent includes a visit to the fallen Watchers, who, in the Book of the Watchers, represent the corrupt priests of the Jerusalem temple and are themselves represented as priests, but there is no trace of this identification in 2 Enoch. Enoch's transformation into an angel is not represented as a criticism of angels but rather as praise of Enoch.

Nor does the picture of the pre-Levitical priesthood in the concluding chapters appear to be intended as a polemic against the descendants of Levi, although it could certainly be used for such a purpose. The narrative demonstrates the survival of the priestly line from Enoch's days on earth before the flood to the period after the flood and promises its resumption at the eschaton, but it does not address the question of the relationship between the priesthood of Melchizedek and the Levitical line.

Ulrich Fischer raises the possibility that it is not the Jerusalem temple but the temple at Leontopolis that stands in the background of 2 Enoch, although he offers little argument in favor of this intriguing suggestion.[61]

It has long been assumed that 2 Enoch comes from Egypt, although not on very compelling grounds. True to its fictive setting, it never mentions Jerusalem. But several times it names the place where its pre-Levitical priests practiced, Akhuzan. It is possible that the priests of Leontopolis, though they could claim Aaronic descent, would have found the existence of priests who sacrificed in a place other than Jerusalem useful in justifying their own institution. But if these chapters are intended as propaganda on their behalf, the propaganda is so subtle as to be ineffective.

Shlomo Pines saw in Enoch's exhortation to tie the sacrificial animal by all four legs (15:8) evidence to identify 2 Enoch as the work of a sect known to the rabbis of the Mishnah.[62] On close examination, however, Pines's reading of m. Tamid 4:1 is not without difficulties. The passage contrasts the incorrect and correct ways of tying the lamb for the daily whole offering: "The lamb was not [wholly] bound (*kpt*), but only tied (*'qd*)."[63] The difference between the two verbs the Mishnah contrasts here is not obvious in ordinary usage, and it is not reassuring that the earliest authority who can be cited in favor of Pines's understanding is the eleventh-century commentator Rashi.[64]

The grounds for Pines's identification are further weakened when we look at the question of why the Mishnah forbids the practice of "wholly tying." The basis of Pines's claim is the Venice first edition of the Babylonian Talmud, according to which one amora suggests that it is in order to avoid the practice of the heretics (*minim*). But according to most printed editions, it is to avoid the practice of the gentiles (*goyim*). In his discussion of the passage from m. Tamid, Saul Lieberman notes that the Greeks and Romans do not seem to have bound their sacrifices, although the Egyptians did, and suggests that the discussion in the Talmud refers to the practice of some "Oriental cult."[65] Altogether it is safe to say that m. Tamid 4:1 does not provide a very secure basis for assuming the existence of a sectarian practice of tying together the four legs of the sacrificial animal.[66]

Futhermore, the content of 2 Enoch makes a sectarian provenance extremely unlikely. The absence of any polemic against or condemnation of opposing groups speaks against it, as does the universalism of the hortatory section, so often noted by scholars attempting to identify its origin.[67]

In the end, then, I think it is best to return 2 Enoch to Alexandria. I shall argue in chapter 4 that the account of creation that God reveals to Enoch as the culmination of his ascent shows the influence of popular Platonism, which fits well in Alexandria. The absence of criticism of earthly priests is perhaps another argument in favor of placing 2 Enoch's origins in Egypt. The diaspora's distance from the temple helps to keep the image of that august institution and its personnel untarnished, as the attitudes of the Letter of Aristeas and Philo show.

If this account of the setting of 2 Enoch is correct, it has some important implications for our picture of Egyptian Judaism. First it shows that Egyptian Jews were reading a Greek version of some parts of the Enochic corpus and perhaps of the Aramaic Levi document.[68] This suggests contact not only with the Palestinian establishment, but also with groups on its margins.

The Apocalypse of Zephaniah and 2 Enoch stand apart from other Egyptian Jewish literature in their use of a literary genre that is Jewish rather than Greek in origin. They exhibit none of the concern for relations with non-Jews that is so prominent in other strands of Egyptian Judaism, from the elite philosophical culture of Philo to the nationalistic but also deeply Hellenized outlook of 3 Maccabees and the Hellenized but pro-Egyptian propaganda of the Jewish Sybilline oracles. Our understanding of Egyptian Judaism around the turn of the era would surely be enhanced by giving more attention to these apocalypses.

3 Enoch

The Book of the Watchers sees Enoch as worthy of the companionship of the angels. Second Enoch suggests that Enoch was physically transformed into an angel. In the hekhalot text titled Sepher Hekhalot, or 3 Enoch, Enoch is the hero of an even more impressive success story. According to this work, the patriarch is transformed into the angel Metatron, God's second in command. The only comparable transformation in all of apocalyptic literature is also ascribed to Enoch in a chapter added to the end of the Similitudes of Enoch, which describes Enoch's transformation into the heavenly Son of Man, who, according to the body of the Similitudes, occupies a throne next to God's.[69] (This transformation is discussed in the next chapter.)

Third Enoch is the only hekhalot text to draw extensively on traditions known to us from earlier Jewish apocalyptic literature.[70] Although all of the hekhalot texts are pseudepigraphic, only 3 Enoch takes as its hero a biblical figure; the other hekhalot works use great rabbis of the tannaitic period as their heroes. The debt of 3 Enoch to the traditions found in 1 and 2 Enoch is evident, although there is no clear indication of a literary relationship. It can be seen not only in the use of the story of the exaltation of Enoch to angelic status, which opens the work, but also in the interest in the fate of souls after death and cosmological phenomena in the tour of the concluding chapters (41–48),[71] an interest not typical of the hekhalot literature. The means by which the author of 3 Enoch came to know these Enochic traditions is far from clear, since 3 Enoch appears to have been composed in Babylonia in the fifth or sixth century.[72]

Third Enoch is presented as a revelation by Metatron, the exalted Enoch, to R. Ishmael, the hero of many hekhalot texts. In the opening passages R. Ishmael ascends to heaven and hears from Metatron the story of his own ascent (chs. 1–16). The story is composed of a number of different traditions, which are never entirely unified. Chosen by God because of his piety in an evil generation (4:3), Enoch is taken to heaven, where God gives him divine attributes and enlarges his body until he is the size of the world, makes 72 wings grow on him, and gives him 365,000 eyes (9:2–3). God makes him a throne and proclaims his new status to all the angels who are now under his charge (ch. 10). Then God dresses Metatron in a magnificent robe and crown (ch. 12). Finally the former Enoch describes how the process of transformation felt: "At once my flesh turned to flame, my sinews to blazing fire, my bones to juniper coals, my eyelashes to lightning flames . . ." (15:1).

It is, of course, Metatron's robe and crown that are of most interest for us:

> Out of the love which he had for me, more than for all the denizens of the heights, the Holy One, blessed be he, fashioned for me a majestic robe, in which all kinds of luminaries were set, and he clothed me in it. He fashioned for me a glorious cloak in which brightness, brilliance, splendor, and luster of every kind were fixed, and he wrapped me in it. He fashioned for me a kingly crown in which 49 refulgent stones were placed, each like the sun's orb, and its brilliance shone into the four quarters of the heaven of 'Arabot, into the seven heavens, and into the four quarters of the world. (12:1–4)

Elsewhere in rabbinic tradition Metatron is called the heavenly high priest. This function is not mentioned in 3 Enoch, although a chapter that appears in a single manuscript and is thus relegated by Alexander to the appendix may allude to it.[73] Nonetheless, God completes Enoch's transformation by dressing him in glorious garments. The crown is explicitly a crown of kingship, appropriate to Metatron's function as vice-regent in heaven, and the garments may well be royal garments. But their brilliance also recalls the vestments of the high priest. Here it is the crown that is set with stones, rather than the breastplate of the high priest, and the stones number forty-nine rather than twelve. But the cloak, *me'il*, recalls the cloak of the ephod, *me'il ha'ephod*, one of the garments of the high priest's attire in the account of Aaron's consecration in Exodus 29. Finally, although the crown is called a crown of kingship, in the next chapter (13) we learn that God inscribed on it "the letters by which heaven and earth were created," not unlike the golden diadem of the high priest, the *ṣiṣ*, inscribed, "Holy to the LORD" (Ex. 28:36–38).[74] Thus while priestly investiture is perhaps not the central aspect of Enoch's transformation, it can nevertheless be discerned in the background.

Conclusions

In the Book of the Watchers the implications of the picture of heaven as temple for the visionary's reception in heaven are relatively undeveloped. Enoch displays appropriate fear in the presence of God, and his priestly role is hinted at, but it is only in later works that draw on the

Book of the Watchers that the visionary's ability to stand before God is clearly linked to his membership in the heavenly priesthood. Perhaps influenced also by the Aramaic Levi document, 2 Enoch describes Enoch's transformation into an angel, that is, a heavenly priest, in terms drawn from priestly investiture. Enoch's transformation into Metatron in 3 Enoch also shows traces of the process of priestly investiture.

It is a sign of how deeply the idea of heaven as temple came to inform apocalyptic ascent that it influenced 2 Enoch this way, for unlike the Book of the Watchers and the Testament of Levi (or its Aramaic source), 2 Enoch has little to say about human priests. For 2 Enoch, it is a given that to enter heaven is to enter a temple and that to be an angel is to be a kind of priest.

The transformation of human beings into angels, implicitly or explicitly, after death or before, is not uncommon in the apocalypses, as the texts discussed in the next chapter show. In many of the ascent apocalypses, the idea of angels as heavenly priests plays an important role in the description of transformation. Once again the Book of the Watchers exerts a powerful influence even on works with interests quite distant from its own.

3

Transformation and
the Righteous Dead

The boundaries between gods and mortals were not always clearly marked
in the Greco-Roman world. Wandering prophets such as Apollonius of
Tyana or Alexander of Abonuteichos were considered gods on the basis
of the wonders they performed, and, perhaps, their teachings. The great
philosophers were sometimes considered divine by their followers because
of their wisdom and virtue. Nor are wonder worker and philosopher
entirely separate categories, as the depictions of the mythic figure of
Pythagoras show.[1] The crossing of the boundary between human and
divine was institutionalized in the routine promotion of Roman emper-
ors to godhood on their deaths, although it is clear that this process was
not taken seriously by everyone.

Thus there were several different paths human beings could travel
to earn the epithet "divine." While the examples just offered reserve
divinization for a tiny elite, the ritual found in the Mithras Liturgy (*PGM*
IV.475–829), offered a somewhat more accessible route to godhood.
Anyone who was willing to undertake the elaborate ritual and recite the
words dictated there could become immortal. At the culmination of an
ascent to heaven in which he saw the order of the heavens and the gods,
the initiate could describe himself thus in greeting the beautiful and fiery
god Helios: "Since he has been born again from you today, [he] has
become immortal out of so many myriads in this hour according to the
wish of god the exceedingly good . . ." (*PGM* IV.646–47).[2] The Chaldean
Oracles too offer a ritual for ascent intended to achieve immortality,
although the Oracles' learned combination of Platonism and magic must
have limited their appeal.[3]

Another magical text contained in the same papyrus as the Mithras Liturgy provides a ritual for attaching oneself to Helios. After performing a preliminary ritual and reciting a prayer, the supplicant waits for a sea falcon to strike him with its wings. He then burns incense while reciting these words: "I have been attached to your holy form. / I have been given power by your holy name. / I have acquired your emanation of the goods, / Lord, god of gods, master, daimon" (*PGM* IV.216–19). The spell concludes with a string of magical words. Then the instructions continue, "Having done this, return as lord of a godlike nature which is accomplished through this divine encounter" (*PGM* IV.220–22).[4]

In the last chapter I considered several works that claim in narratives about the patriarch Enoch that it is possible to traverse the distance between human beings and the divine. The Book of the Watchers makes the man Enoch the companion of the angels. In 2 and 3 Enoch, Enoch becomes an angel, and no ordinary angel at that. According to 2 Enoch he is worthy of hearing secrets never before revealed, even to the angels, while 3 Enoch goes so far as to make the transformed Enoch God's second in command.

These Enoch apocalypses are not the only apocalypses to claim for their hero the status of a particularly exalted angel, as we learn from the words of Baraies the Teacher, a third-century disciple of Mani, in the Cologne Mani Codex.[5] In the course of a discussion of Mani's forerunners, Baraies quotes from apocalypses attributed to five of the antediluvian patriarchs. In Baraies's account of an apocalypse attributed to Adam, the first man received a revelation from an angel and then "became more exalted than all the powers and angels of creation" (50). This is a transformation hardly inferior to Enoch's in 3 Enoch. Adam's son Seth, whom Baraies calls Sethel, undergoes a transformation somewhat more modest than his father's, but impressive nonetheless: "When I heard these things, my heart rejoiced, and my understanding was changed, and I became like one of the greatest angels" (51).[6] While there is nothing in these passages to suggest the use of the priestly imagery found in the Enoch apocalypses, they are so brief that it is unwise to draw any conclusions.

Ancient Jewish literature knows a variety of intermediary figures who stand between God and humanity, including angels and hypostasized attributes of God, such as Wisdom and the Glory of God.[7] The apocalypses with transformations of men into angels belong to one strand of a large and diverse body of literature that treats the biblical patriarchs and especially Moses as in some sense divine. The literature comes from both Egypt and Palestine, and includes works ranging from Philo and Ezekiel the Tragedian to the Testament of Moses and passages in rabbinic literature.[8] The structural similarities in the mediating roles of the different kinds of beings are clear, and the categories are far from airtight, as Enoch's transformation into Metatron or the figure of Jesus indicates. Still, the attainment of a place among the angels by a human being seems to me quite different in its implications from the descent of an angel or an aspect of God to humanity, as I shall argue at the end of the chapter.

Perhaps the most extended treatment in Jewish or Christian literature of the divinization of a human being is Philo's treatment of Moses. For example,

> He was named god and king of the whole nation, and entered, we are told, into the darkness where God was, that is into the unseen, invisible, incorporeal and archetypal essence of existing things. Thus he beheld what is hidden from the sight of mortal nature, and, in himself and his life displayed for all to see, he has set before us, like some well-wrought picture, a piece of work beautiful and godlike, a model for those who are willing to copy it. (*On Moses,* 1.158)[9]

Philo's description of Moses uses a vocabulary and concepts drawn from the philosophical discussions of Alexandria. The position of Enoch in 2 Enoch is rather similar to the one Philo gives Moses, but the language of the two works differs dramatically.

Enoch and Moses are exceptional figures, men of such great righteousness that they serve as examples to admire rather than emulate in any practical way, despite Philo's words. They also lived in a safely distant past. In a recently published fragment from Qumran, a speaker who is not identified in the extant portion of the passage claims to have been granted "a mighty throne in the congregation of the gods [*'elim*]" and to be "reckoned with the gods [*'elim*]." He goes on to boast of his ability to endure evil and of the authority of his teachings and legal rulings. Morton Smith has argued convincingly that the content of this song of triumph indicates a human speaker, a member of the sect living around the turn of the era, rather than an ancient hero. The relevance of this extraordinary passage for the claims some early Christians made for Jesus should be apparent.[10]

But at Qumran fellowship with the angels, if less dramatically described, was understood to be more widely available. The sectarians, for whom the very fact of membership in the community was an indication of righteousness, claimed to live in the presence of the angels: "Thou hast cleansed a perverse spirit of great sin that it may stand with the host of Holy Ones, and that it may enter into community with the congregation of the Sons of Heaven" (Thanksgiving Hymns [1QH] col. iii, lines 21–22).[11] The extreme purity demanded in everyday life in the community is related to the belief that angels were present in the camp with the sect.[12] The recitation of the Sabbath Songs with their description of the liturgy in the heavenly temple was intended to create a feeling of participation in the service on high.[13]

A number of apocalypses reserve for the afterlife what the community at Qumran claims for the present.[14] According to these texts, the reward of the righteous after death is membership in the heavenly host. The apocalypses in question, most of which do not contain ascents, date from the middle of the second century B.C.E. on, when the persecution of Antiochus made the fate of the martyrs a subject of great concern. Nickelsburg has shown that this understanding of the fate of the righteous is a development of the theme of the exaltation of the wise courtier found in ancient Near Eastern court tales. In the basic plot of these tales, the wise courtier is unjustly accused of a crime against his king and is deposed. Ultimately, however, he is vindicated and raised to the highest rank in the kingdom. The story of Ahiqar is a good example of this plot; the adventures of Joseph in Egypt represent a still recognizable variation. In the apocalypses the courtier has become the righteous collectively, and the exaltation to authority in the earthly court has become exaltation in heaven after death.[15]

Probably the most famous passage describing this form of exaltation appears at the end of Daniel: "And those who are wise shall shine like the brightness of the firmament; and those who turn many to righteousness, like the stars for ever and ever" (12:3). Notice here that the righteous become not angels but stars. The Hebrew Bible sometimes equates the heavenly host with the stars, as in the Song of Deborah (Judg. 5:20), where stars appear as the heavenly army of the divine warrior, or in Job (38:7), where the morning stars stand parallel to the sons of God, and are said to sing. The widespread use of star terminology and associated language for describing transformation in these apocalypses may be due to the prominence of the idea of astral immortality in the contemporary Greco-Roman world.

The equivalence of angels and stars in this stream of thought is made clear in a passage from one of the exhortations in the Epistle of Enoch (1 Enoch 91–105), where the righteous are promised first that they will shine like stars and then that they will be companions of the heavenly host:

> Be of good courage, for aforetime you were worn down by evils and afflictions, but now you shall shine and appear as the lights of heaven, and the portals of heaven shall be opened unto you. . . . Be of good courage, and do not abandon your hope; for you shall have great joy as the angels of heaven. . . . But now fear not, you righteous, when you see the sinners growing strong and prospering: be not companions with them, but keep afar from all their evil-doings; for you shall become companions of the angels of heaven. (104:2–6)

The Similitudes of Enoch also makes this association when it describes the righteous dead enjoying the company of the angels and shining brightly: "And there I saw another vision of the dwellings of the righteous and the resting-places of the holy. / There my eyes saw their dwellings with the angels / And their resting-places with the holy ones. . . . / And all the righteous and elect were radiant like the brightness of fire before him . . ." (1 Enoch 39:4–7).

At the end of the first or beginning of the second century C.E. 2 Baruch also equates fellowship with the angels with becoming a star: "For in the heights of that world shall they dwell, / And they shall be made like the angels, / And be made equal to the stars . . ." (51:10). Like the Ascension of Isaiah, which I discuss later in this chapter, but more explicitly, 2 Baruch claims that at the eschaton the righteous will be more exalted than the angels: "Then shall the splendour of the righteous exceed even the splendour of the angels" (51:12).[16]

In "Die Himmelsreise der Seele," Wilhelm Bousset's classic essay on the idea of heavenly ascent in the ancient world, he argued that ecstatic ascent to heaven during life was understood in texts from many different cultures as an "anticipation" of the ascent of the soul after death.[17] This is certainly not the understanding of ascent that informs the Enochic works discussed in the last chapter, but it fits somewhat better the ascents of two apocalypses that share a number of features, the Apocalypse of Zephaniah and the Ascension of Isaiah. In these works the visionary's experience is indeed an indication of what the righteous have in store for them after death, although the hero of the Apocalypse of Zephaniah does not anticipate the fate of the righteous after death, but actually experiences it.

These apocalypses offer strong evidence of how the understanding of heaven as temple has become a standard feature of apocalyptic ascents. For despite their lack of interest in earthly temples and priests, the Apocalypse of Zephaniah and the Ascension of Isaiah use the process of investiture and participation in the heavenly liturgy to describe the visionary's transformation as he takes his place among the angels.

The Apocalypse of Zephaniah

The Apocalypse of Zephaniah survives in a single manuscript in the Akhmimic dialect of Coptic; significant portions of the work, including the beginning and the end, are missing.[18] The original language was Greek. Translation into Coptic points to an Egyptian provenance, as does the fact that the clearly Egyptian Apocalypse of Paul is deeply indebted to it. Its single heaven makes a relatively early date likely, probably before the end of the first century C.E. There is no reason to consider the work Christian, except in the sense that any work in Coptic was translated for and transmitted by Christians.

The identity of the hero of the apocalypse is not entirely clear. Without the beginning or end of the manuscript, there is no title, and the visionary is never actually named in the course of the narrative. Some scholars still prefer to refer to the work as the anonymous apocalypse. But it is usually identified with Zephaniah because that name appears in a fragment of a Sahidic manuscript that is bound together with the manuscript of our work.[19]

If the hero of the apocalypse is indeed named Zephaniah, what does the name signify? Zephaniah is of course the name of a prophet, although not one of the more eminent ones in later tradition. While there is no attempt in the extant portion of the apocalypse to provide details that would identify its protagonist with the prophet, the summary of the content of Zephaniah's prophecy in the brief account of his career in the Lives of the Prophets shows that it is possible to read the Book of Zephaniah as suggesting the subjects of the Apocalypse of Zephaniah: "He prophesied concerning the city, also concerning the end of the nations and the confounding of the wicked" (Lives: Zephaniah 2).[20]

"The city," the earthly Jerusalem, does not figure in the extant portion of the apocalypse, but the "beautiful city" so important to Zephaniah's heavenly journey is probably an idealized Jerusalem on the order of Ezekiel's description in chapters 40–48. "The confounding of the wicked" would make a fine motto for the description of the punishments of sinners after death that forms a major part of the apocalypse. "The end of nations" could describe the eschatological prophecies that begin as the manuscript breaks off. I do not mean to suggest that the author of the Apocalypse of Zephaniah drew on the traditions of the Lives of the Prophets,[21] but only to show that it is possible to read the Book of Zephaniah as suggesting topics that an author with an apocalyptic bent might treat as they are treated in the Apocalypse of Zephaniah. On the other hand, a number of other prophetic books might be summarized with some justice in a quite similar way. So we are still left without a clear reason for the choice of Zephaniah.

A further complication in the attempt to resolve the problem of the identity of the hero of the Apocalypse of Zephaniah is that the hero is himself a dead soul, who is personally experiencing the fate of the righteous after death. The fragmentary scene with which the text begins appears to describe a funeral, and the Apocalypse of Paul draws on the experience of the visionary in the Apocalypse of Zephaniah for its picture of the departure of wicked and righteous souls from the body at death.[22] But the most important reason for taking the protagonist of the Apocalypse of Zephaniah as a soul facing judgment, a kind of hero without parallel in the apocalypses, is that this status makes sense of the terrifying ordeal the seer undergoes, also without parallel in the apocalypses.[23]

In the Ascension of Isaiah the prophet is distinguished from the rest of the righteous by the fact that he ascends and experiences their exalted status while still alive. Not so the hero of the Apocalypse of Zephaniah. If an identification with the prophet is intended, it is a little surprising that the hero of the apocalypse is presented as righteous but by no means free of sin, and as rather confused by the other world. Since Zephaniah does not appear to have been a popular name among Egyptian Jews,[24] it is unlikely that we have in this apocalypse a unique instance of a Jewish apocalypse that is not pseudepigraphic. In the end it seems likely that the hero of the work is indeed the prophet Zephaniah, although his name may have been chosen for its very lack of associations, to represent the righteous generally.

In the first complete episode of Zephaniah's tour of heaven, his angelic guide shows him several punishments endured by wicked souls. Then Zephaniah arrives at a beautiful city (ch. 2). Many of the details of the experience in the city are obscure. What is clear is that the visionary misperceives the sights he sees and that the beautiful city turns out to be quite threatening.

> But I walked with the angel of God. I looked in front of me; *and* [25] I saw gates. Then, when I approached them, I found they were gates of copper. The angel touched them *and* they opened before him. I went in with him. I found myself in what seemed to be the main street of ⟨a⟩ beautiful city. I walked down the middle of it. Then the angel of the Lord transformed himself beside me there. And I looked and I saw gates of copper with bolts of copper and bars of iron. And they closed against me there. I saw in front of me the gates of copper breathing out fire *to a distance of* about fifty stades. Again I turned; *and* I saw a great sea. And I thought it was a sea of water. I found it was a whole sea of fire, like a marsh, that breathed out fire continually, and its waves burned with sulphur and pitch. They began to come near me. . . . (2:1–4).

It is worth remarking here on the templelike qualities of the beautiful city. First of all, any heavenly city is likely to be modeled on Jerusalem. The shiny gates of the city have a parallel in the gates of the temple, described by Josephus as covered with gold (*War* 5.208). The sea of Zephaniah's city recalls the enormous laver in Solomon's temple, called the "molten sea" to underscore the cosmic symbolism (1 Kings 7:23).

Zephaniah's misperception continues. As the waves of fire draw near him, he sees a supernatural figure in front of him, and, believing that God has come to save him, prays to be rescued from the danger (2:5–6). The visitor, however, is not God, but a terrible angel, later identified as the accuser (2:7). When he recognizes this, the seer again prays for deliverance (2:8–9).

Even as the seer's prayers are answered, the misperception continues. The terrifying angel is replaced by an angel of splendid appearance, whose face shines like the sun (2:10). The seer proceeds to worship him as God until the angel explains that he is not God but "the great angel Eremiel, whose *place* is *in the world* below, *and* [*who has*] *been appointed* over the abyss and hell . . ." (2:11–12).

If the Apocalypse of Zephaniah were a hekhalot text, Zephaniah would by now have shown himself to be completely unworthy. Misperception, or at least giving voice to misperception, is a dangerous thing in the hekhalot literature. For asking a question that indicates that he has mistaken the glittering marble of the sixth palace for drops of water, a mystic can expect to be attacked by angels armed with iron axes (Schäfer, *Synopse*, #259 [Hekhalot Rabbati], #408–9 [Hekhalot Zuṭarti]).[26] But Zephaniah is rescued rather than punished.

After the rescue, the angel Eremiel takes out a scroll on which are written all the sins Zephaniah has ever committed. No sooner has Zephaniah besought God's mercy than an angel announces his triumph. "Be victorious, be strong; for you have been strong, you have been victorious over the accuser, you have come up from hell and the abyss, you shall now cross at the ferry-place" (3:1). Another scroll is unfurled, but we never find out what it contains because there follows a lacuna of two pages. O. S. Wintermute suggests quite reasonably that the second scroll lists all the seer's good deeds and that the account of the good deeds is followed by another prayer, this time of thanksgiving, and another angelic proclamation of triumph.[27] The determination of the visionary's fate by reference to lists of his deeds again suggests that he is a dead soul.

The ordeal of the visionary in the Apocalypse of Zephaniah is extraordinary for apocalyptic literature. In the other apocalypses, the visionary may feel awe or even terror at the sight of his heavenly surroundings, but he is never in danger. Nowhere else in the apocalypses does the visionary have such a terrifying encounter with a hostile angel without the support of an angelic companion by his side. This scene is perhaps best understood as the description of what befalls all souls, righteous or not, as the prelude to the examination of their record. Wicked souls would not emerge unscathed from the encounter with the accuser.

Having been judged worthy, the visionary undergoes a transformation. He is transported to paradise on a boat: "They were singing praises before me, namely thousands upon thousands and myriads upon myriads of angels. I also put on an angelic garment. I saw all those angels praying. I too prayed together with them: I knew their language that they spoke with me" (3:3–4).

Zephaniah explicitly describes both of the scrolls with which he is confronted as written "in my own language" (2:15, 3:2). But after he has put on the angelic robe, he is able to join the angels in their prayers because he speaks their language. The donning of the angelic garment suggests the priestly investiture that appears in the apocalypses examined in the last chapter. The use of participation in the angelic liturgy as a sign of fellowship with the angels is also an indication that the picture of heaven as temple stands in the background in the Apocalypse of Zephaniah.

Although Zephaniah is now able to join the angels at prayer, he is apparently not fully their equal. Zephaniah reports about an angel who has announced his triumph (3:6–8), "I wanted to exchange greetings with him; *but* I could not, so great was his glory" (3:9). This same angel then goes to join Abraham, Isaac, Jacob, Enoch, Elijah, and David, with whom "he talked . . . like a friend with friends" (3:10). Thus there is a hierarchy among the righteous dead. Zephaniah is again depicted as an ordinary righteous soul, not an extraordinary one; his fellowship with the angels is not as complete as that of the biblical heroes.

The Apocalypse of Zephaniah continues with another vision of the punishment of the wicked and the intercession of the biblical heroes in paradise on their behalf, and finally the beginning of a revelation about the events associated with the last judgment. The manuscript breaks off after a few lines of this revelation.

The Apocalypse of Zephaniah, then, is the story of the triumph of an ordinary soul that can serve as a model for all readers. It is not a soul particularly at home in the other world, as its misperceptions show. Enoch in the Book of the Watchers would never have blundered so foolishly. But in the end Zephaniah's good deeds outweigh his sins, while the sins allow readers a measure of identification with Zephaniah that they could never feel with Enoch.

The Ascension of Isaiah

The Ascension of Isaiah consists of an account of Isaiah's martyrdom (chs. 1–5) and an ascent to heaven that takes place shortly before the martyrdom during which Isaiah has a vision of Christ's descent to earth and subsequent triumphant ascent (chs. 6–11). In some versions the ascent circulates without the martyrdom. This lends support to the internal indications that the two sections are of separate origin.[28]

The martyrdom of Isaiah is usually treated as a Jewish document, and there is reason to believe that the ascent draws on an earlier Jewish source,[29] but the ascent is undoubtedly a Christian work. The ascent fits well in the Christianity of the early second century.[30]

As he prophesies before King Hezekiah and a group of prophets and elders, Isaiah falls into a trance during which he ascends through the heavens in the company of an angelic guide. In each of the first five heavens, he sees an angel seated on a throne with angels on either side offering praise. The arrangement of the angels is probably influenced by the vision of Micaiah b. Imlah in 1 Kings 22. The praise of the angels on the right is superior to the praise of the angels on the left, and the glory of the angel seated on the throne is greater than the glory of the other angels.[31] The angelic praise is directed not at the one on the throne, but at God in the seventh heaven and his Beloved (7:17).

In the second heaven Isaiah is overcome by the glory of what he sees, which is greater than the glory of the first heaven. He tries to worship the angel sitting on the throne, but his guide restrains him, telling him to worship only in the seventh heaven. The progressively greater glory of each successive heaven has a counterpart in the physical transformation Isaiah undergoes as he ascends, which he notices in the third heaven: "The glory of my face was being transformed . . ." in the course of ascent (7:25).[32]

The sixth heaven marks a new stage of holiness and glory. "When I was in the sixth heaven, I thought the light I had seen in the five heavens was darkness" (8:21). When they reach this heaven, the angelic guide insists that Isaiah no longer call him "Lord": "I am not your Lord, but your companion" (8:5). In the sixth and seventh heavens, there is no throne in the middle, and the angels on the left are equal in glory to the angels on the right. When he and the guide join the angels of the sixth heaven in offering praise, Isaiah reports, "Our praises were like theirs" (8:17). His guide tells Isaiah that, although he has seen sights unseen by any other being who has to return to the body, Isaiah must wait until his time on earth is up to remain permanently in heaven (8:23–28). After death, Isaiah will receive a garment, "and then [he] will become equal to the angels of the seventh heaven" (8:15).

When Isaiah tries to enter the seventh heaven, he is challenged by a voice that asks, "How far may anyone go up who lives among aliens?" Isaiah is afraid, but another voice, later identified as the voice of Christ, answers, "The holy Isaiah is permitted to come up here, for here is his garment" (9:1–2). In the seventh heaven Isaiah sees a host of angels and all the righteous from Adam on (9:7). The righteous appear clothed "in their garments of the world above . . . , like angels, standing there in great glory" (9:9). They do not yet sit on their thrones or wear their crowns of glory; this must await the return of Christ (9:10–13). Isaiah also sees a book in which he finds written the deeds of the children of Israel and of others whom he does not know, presumably the nations who will later become Christians. The book, then, is the universal counterpart to the scrolls containing Zephaniah's deeds in the Apocalypse of Zephaniah.

In the seventh heaven Isaiah is so far transformed that he becomes like an angel (9:30).[33] He then joins the angels in worshiping Christ (9:31). Once again joining the angels in praise serves as a sign of equality with the angels. Once again an understanding of heaven as temple stands in the background.

At this point indications of a somewhat different hierarchy from the one presented so far begin to emerge. In the course of his sojourn in the seventh heaven, Isaiah is able to join the righteous in their praise of Christ and the Holy Spirit. It is the righteous who offer praise first, followed by the angels. But Isaiah is not transformed to equal the righteous in glory, and he can only observe while the righteous praise God (9:33).[34] While the angels and Isaiah himself are capable only of glancing at God, Isaiah sees the righteous "gazing intently upon the Glory" (9:37–38).

Thus despite the angel's promise in the sixth heaven that Isaiah can look forward to becoming like one of the angels of the seventh heaven after death, in the seventh heaven it appears that the most exalted place is occupied not by the angels, but by the righteous dead. Apparently Isaiah cannot achieve their status until after death. In the meantime, to judge by his participation in the praise offered in the seventh heaven, he occupies a rung between the angels and the righteous dead. The great prophet's distinction is that he has been able to join the angels while still alive; after death all the righteous share a status higher than that of the angels.

I suspect that the contradiction between the information offered by Isaiah's angelic guide and what actually happens in the seventh heaven is not unintentional. Rather it appears to represent an attempt to tone down the radical claim that the righteous dead stand above the angels in the heavenly hierarchy. It is noteworthy that this claim is never stated outright.

Indeed the angel's misinformation is part of a larger framework that leads us to expect that equality with the angels is the highest status a human being can achieve. In the five lower heavens, it will be remembered, there is an explicit hierarchy of glory. The angel enthroned in the middle is most glorious of all, so glorious that the guide needs to instruct Isaiah not to worship him, while the angels to his right surpass those to his left. In the sixth heaven, however, the throne disappears, and with it the distinction between left and right; all the angels are equal. It is here that the guide tells Isaiah that he is not his superior but his "companion," and that after death he will be the equal of the angels in the seventh heaven. In the highest heavens, then, we find equality among angels, and we are told to expect equality between angels and men. But in the seventh heaven it emerges that the righteous dead have the ability to look upon God with steady gaze, placing them on a higher rung of the heavenly ladder than the angels.

The culmination of Isaiah's ascent is a vision of Christ's descent and ascent. The picture of the heavens in the vision differs significantly from the picture I have just examined. When he has descended to the fifth heaven, Christ assumes a disguise in order to keep his mission on earth secret even from the angels. As he passes through the lower heavens, he appears like one of the angels of the heaven in which he finds himself. The angels fail to recognize him and do not offer him praise. From the third heaven down, Christ gives a password to the angelic guardians of the gates of the heaven. The same picture of angelic gatekeepers at the entrances to the heavens appears in the account of Christ's triumphant ascent, where the angels lament their failure to have recognized him. Angelic guardians at the gate who demand a password from all who seek to enter appear also in hekhalot literature (Schäfer, *Synopse,* #204–51 [Hekhalot Rabbati], #413–16 [Hekhalot Zuṭarti]; 'Ozhayah fragment: *Geniza-Fragmente* 2a/37–38) and in Origen's report about the Ophites (*Contra Celsum* 6.31).[35] The Ascension of Isaiah's picture of Christ's descent in disguise resembles that of the Epistle of the Apostles (chs. 13–14).

Isaiah's ascent alludes to the vision of Christ's descent and ascent that follows, and the two sections share certain features. Both set the sixth and seventh heavens apart from the lower heavens. One might argue that Christ's disguise is the opposite side of Isaiah's transformation: while a human being needs to become more like the dwellers in the highest heavens to ascend, Christ needs to become more like the dwellers in the lower heavens to descend. But the activity of the angels in the heavens is strikingly different in the two sections. There is no hint of the gate-keepers in Isaiah's ascent and no manifestation of hostility toward Isaiah, a human being, until he reaches the highest heavens. Yet Christ in angelic disguise must provide the password to be able to enter the three lowest heavens. These differences suggest different sources for Isaiah's ascent and Christ's descent.[36] There is some reason to believe that there existed in the Second Temple period a Jewish Apocalypse of Isaiah involving ascent to heaven and a vision of hell, and it is possible that Isaiah's ascent in the Ascension of Isaiah is drawn from this apocalypse.[37] But the question whether the earliest form of the ascent was written by a Jew or a Christian is not important for our purposes; what is clear, I think, is that the ascent is deeply indebted to the early Jewish tradition of ascents.

Heaven as Royal Court and Temple

The central theme of the Apocalypse of Zephaniah is the judgment of souls. The righteous judge is of course God himself. We never actually see him presiding over the proceedings, perhaps because of the lacuna after an angel brings forward a second scroll, probably listing Zephaniah's good deeds; in the Apocalypse of Paul, in a section that is clearly indebted to the Apocalypse of Zephaniah, God himself announces the verdict to dead souls (chs. 14–18).[38] Heaven in the Apocalypse of Zephaniah is thus understood as a court, but because the judge is the king of kings, it is a royal court. The angels play an important role in carrying out the judgment, announcing the results and directing the soul to its reward or punishment.

It is clear from the thrones and crowns that await the righteous dead at the eschaton that the Ascension of Isaiah also understands heaven as a royal court. The thrones recall Dan. 7:9 ("As I looked, thrones were placed and one that was ancient of days took his seat . . ."), where the plural thrones are apparently intended for the angelic courtiers who attend the divine monarch. Descriptions of the divine council in Ugaritic texts also speak of "princely thrones" for the gods.[39] The promise of thrones for the righteous in the Ascension of Isaiah derives its particular power from the glory of the enthroned angels of the lower heavens. The crowns are a further development of this imagery, as far as I know without a Canaanite background, but paralleled in Revelation.

While the judgment of souls is a theme implicit in Isaiah's ascent, the Ascension of Isaiah does not show the court sitting in judgment. But the book of deeds that Isaiah sees in heaven (9:21–22) clearly points toward such a scene. The divine council in Dan. 7:10 consults books, which must also contain the deeds of all the nations.[40]

But the understanding of heaven as temple is not absent in these two works. Zephaniah puts on a garment and is then able to join the angels in their praise; Isaiah joins the angels at prayer and is told that a garment is reserved for him after his death. Royal court and temple are simply different aspects of the dwelling place of God. What we learn from the Apocalypse of Zephaniah and the Ascension of Isaiah is that even in relation to the fate of souls after death, where the aspect of royal court might seem more immediately relevant, the authors of these apocalypses draw also on the understanding of heaven as temple.

Similitudes of Enoch

The fate of souls after death is also a central concern of the Similitudes of Enoch (1 Enoch 37–71), although the relationship between the experience of the visionary and the fate of the righteous here is not as explicit as in the Apocalypse of Zephaniah or the Ascension of Isaiah. The language of the work suggests that the righteous are not the people of Israel as a whole, but rather a chosen few; most scholars date the work to the turn of the era.[41]

Because of its importance for the understanding of early Christian use of the title, the figure of the Son of Man has received more attention than other aspects of the Similitudes.[42] The figure in the Similitudes is drawn from Daniel 7, as its association in the Similitudes with a name for God that reflects the Ancient of Days of Daniel 7 makes clear.[43] The Son of Man, who is also known as the Chosen or Elect One, will be enthroned next to God as judge at the end of days (61:8).

But the most important influence on the Similitudes is the Book of the Watchers. The Similitudes in my view is best understood as a retelling of the Book of the Watchers that integrates elements of the story of the fallen angels, the ascent to the heavenly temple, and the journey to the ends of the earth, into three discourses, called parables or similitudes, about the ultimate vindication of the righteous and punishment of the wicked. Because the author assumes that his readers know the Book of the Watchers, he is able to proceed in a highly allusive style. He never actually tells the story of the fall of the Watchers, but knowledge of this story is necessary to the understanding of a considerable portion of the work.[44]

At the very beginning of the Similitudes, Enoch is carried to heaven by clouds and a wind (39:3), an allusion to 1 Enoch 14:8. Like the Book of the Watchers, the Similitudes imagines a single heaven, rather than the seven heavens of many of the later ascents. The first sight Enoch sees in heaven is the dwelling of the righteous. As we have already seen, the Similitudes makes the righteous dead the companions of the angels. Until the last chapter it treats Enoch as one of their company, an associate of the angels but not their superior.

Petitionary prayer and the heavenly liturgy play an important part in the Similitudes. Enoch finds the righteous praying on behalf of humanity (39:5). Soon Enoch offers praise to God (39:9–12) and watches as angels praise him (39:13). The sight is apparently too glorious for Enoch to behold: "My countenance was changed until I was unable to look" (39:14). The continuation of this vision describes the praise offered by the four archangels (ch. 40). In the next scene (ch. 41) Enoch is shown the secrets of heaven, and he learns that the sun and moon praise God (41:7).

Earthly prayer, too, figures in the Similitudes. In the second parable the prayer and blood of the righteous ascend to heaven, where they are joined by the prayers of the angels in heaven. In response God finally seats himself on the throne of glory and opens the record books in the presence of the divine council so that the judgment of the sinners can begin (ch. 47).

Prayer plays a part in the denouement of the eschatological drama as well. The third parable describes the praise offered to God at the eschaton, first by the righteous, the angels, and the Son of Man (here called the Elect One) (61:10–13), then, as the judgment unfolds, by the sinners, who praise God as they acknowledge their sins (63:1–5).

Like the Apocalypse of Zephaniah and the Ascension of Isaiah, then, the Similitudes uses participation in the heavenly liturgy as a way of expressing the visionary's angelic state (39:9–13), and like them it refers to "garments of glory"—also called "garment[s] of life"—for the righteous when they achieve an angelic state, after death (62:15–16). With its emphasis on the judgment of the righteous and wicked, the Similitudes also shares with the Apocalypse of Zephaniah and the Ascension of Isaiah the double vision of heaven as at once temple and royal court.

The Similitudes originally concluded with a brief account of Enoch's departure from earth to stand in the presence of the Lord of spirits (ch. 70).[45] The author of the chapter that now stands at the end of the work went much farther, suggesting that Enoch ascended to take his place in heaven as the Elect One, an identity he discovers only in the course of this last ascent.[46]

The description of Enoch's transformation into the Elect One draws on the throne vision of 1 Enoch 14 and on an earlier vision in the Similitudes (ch. 46).[47] When Enoch falls on his face before the fiery glory of heaven, described with imagery drawn from 1 Enoch 14 and Daniel 7, the angel Michael raises him and shows him heavenly secrets (71:1–4). Then the spirit carries Enoch off to the highest heaven. This comes as a surprise since so far the Similitudes has revealed only a single heaven.

In the highest heaven Enoch sees a structure reminiscent of the heavenly temple of 1 Enoch 14, with a myriad of angels going in and out of it. At last God himself emerges, accompanied by the four archangels (71:5–10). It is at the sight of God that Enoch undergoes his transformation. "And I fell on my face / And my whole body became weak from fear, / And my spirit was transformed; / And I cried out with a loud voice, / With the spirit of power, / And blessed and glorified and extolled" (71:11). Enoch's first act upon being transformed, then, is to praise God. In his high estimation of the role of praise in heaven, the author of this chapter is of one mind with the rest of the Similitudes.

The body of the Similitudes treats Enoch as Isaiah is treated in the Ascension of Isaiah, worthy in life to join the righteous and the angels in heaven. But the author of the chapter that now concludes the Similitudes takes a quite different approach. An angel informs Enoch after his transformation that Enoch himself is the Son of Man. As Collins points out, the association of the Son of Man with the fate of the righteous throughout the Similitudes provides a starting point for the identification of the heavenly figure with the most conspicuous of the righteous according to the Similitudes.[48] In addition, the author of this chapter seems to have read the Book of the Watchers as the authors of 2 Enoch and 3 Enoch did. All three authors concluded that Enoch's sojourn with the angels meant that he had become not merely an angel, but the most exalted of angels.

The Apocalypse of Abraham

Although it does not share their interest in the fate of the righteous after death, the Apocalypse of Abraham has in common with the Apocalypse of Zephaniah, the Ascension of Isaiah, and the Similitudes of Enoch an understanding of heavenly ascent in which the visionary's participation in the angelic liturgy marks his achievement of angelic status. Unlike the Apocalypse of Zephaniah and the Ascension of Isaiah and at greater length than the Similitudes, the Apocalypse of Abraham actually provides the words to the song sung by the angels. It was in part this song that led Scholem to claim that the Apocalypse of Abraham "more closely resembles a Merkabah text than any other [text] in Jewish apocalyptic literature."[49] The Apocalypse of Abraham is usually treated as a Jewish work, although there is at least one passage (ch. 29) that appears to have undergone revision by Christians in the course of its transmission.[50] The work refers to the destruction of the temple, so a date after 70 is required.

The apocalypse begins with a story containing many comical details of Abraham's rejection of idolatry, similar in broad outline to the traditions that appear in rabbinic sources.[51] After Abraham has arrived by himself at a rejection of idolatry, God speaks to him and orders him to undertake preparations for a revelation (ch. 9). Upon hearing a voice but seeing no one, Abraham faints, and God sends the angel Iaoel to assist him (ch. 10).

Like the angel Eremiel, Iaoel is glorious in appearance. In keeping with the "ineffable name" (10:4)[52] that forms part of Iaoel's name, the description of Iaoel's appearance (11:2) includes elements that elsewhere appear in descriptions of God. (There is of course considerable guesswork involved in this comparison, since the Apocalypse of Abraham survives in Slavonic while the descriptions of God come primarily from the Hebrew Bible.) Iaoel's body of sapphire recalls the sapphire pavement beneath God's feet in Ex. 24:10 and Ezek. 1:26; it is worth noting that two manuscripts make Iaoel's feet sapphire, rather than his body.[53] The hair of Iaoel's head is like snow, like God's hair in Dan. 7:9.[54]

Iaoel's wardrobe has strong priestly associations.[55] The linen band around his head recalls Aaron's headdress of fine linen (Ex. 28:39); the rainbowlike appearance of this linen band brings together the two central color schemes employed elsewhere in the description of God as high priest, whiteness and the multicolored glow. The purple of Iaoel's robe is one of the colors of the high-priestly garments of Exodus 28. The golden staff, like other aspects of the description, is not only obviously royal, but also priestly;[56] Aaron's rod figures prominently in the story of the confrontation with Pharoah (Ex. 7:9, 19–20; 8:1, 12), and in the wilderness after the rebellion of Korah it sprouts to indicate the choice of Aaron and his descendants as priests (Num. 17:16–26).

Thus Abraham's ascent and subsequent vision are presented as the culmination of the story of his rejection of idolatry. They are placed in the framework of the vision of Genesis 15, the covenant between the pieces, and some elements of the ascent are inspired by the biblical text.[57] But the account in the Apocalypse of Abraham implicitly compares Abraham's ascent to Moses' experience at Sinai. Thus, for example, Abraham performs the sacrifice described in Genesis 15 at Mount Horeb (the name for Mount Sinai in some biblical sources) after forty days of fasting in the wilderness. The exegetical occasion for the association of Genesis 15 and Exodus 19–20 is the manifestation of the presence of God in smoke and fire in both passages.[58]

The connection between the ascent and the preceding story of Abraham's rejection of idolatry is made by Iaoel himself, when in his introduction to Abraham before the ascent he includes the information that he was the angel who set Terah's house on fire (10:13). But there are clear structural indications of unity as well. Idolatry, which is the central problem in the first section, plays a crucial role in the vision of the ascent, where it appears as the cause of the destruction of the temple. The burning of Terah's house, where idols are made and worshiped, precedes Abraham's ascent; it is matched in the vision by the burning of the temple, which has become the scene of idolatry. Sacrifice plays a central role in both sections. In the narrative, sacrifice to idols serves as the occasion for Abraham's discovery of the one God. Sacrifice to God later provides the means for Abraham's ascent; he and the angel travel to heaven on the backs of the birds they have sacrificed. Idolatrous sacrifices lead to the destruction of the temple, and God promises the restoration of the temple and its cult after the last judgment.

Although the Apocalypse of Abraham subscribes to a seven-heaven schema,[59] there is no mention of the lower heavens in the course of the ascent. Rather, Abraham and his angelic companion ascend directly to the throne of God, a journey quite frightening for Abraham:

> And [Iaoel] took me up to the edge of a fiery flame. And we went up as if *borne aloft* by many winds, to the heaven established on the expanses. And I saw in the air, on the height to which we went up, a great light, which is indescribable. And behold, by that light *I saw* a burning fire of people—many people, males all of them, changing *their* appearance and *their* form, running *hither and thither* as they changed their form, and worshipping and crying out in a language I did not know.
>
> And I said to the angel, Why have you brought me now to this place; for I cannot now see, my strength is gone, and I am at the point of death. And he said to me, Stay by me, and do not be afraid: he whom you will see coming straight towards us with a great and holy voice, he is the Eternal One, who has set his love on you. (But you will not actually see him). Do not let your spirit fail, for I am with you to strengthen you. (15:4–16:4)[60]

Abraham is not the only visionary to be terrified at first by the sights he sees in the heavens, though his problem is different from Zephaniah's. Zephaniah misperceives, mistakes the accuser for God; Abraham is merely overwhelmed. Zephaniah faces a truly hostile angel; Abraham is afraid, but no one threatens him. The fiery melee that so distresses Abraham when he first arrives in the midst of the heavenly host is a form of angelic worship. In two of the manuscripts the angel's response to Abraham's expression of fear singles out the noise as a cause: "Do not let your spirit fail *for the shouting*."[61] This is followed by his instruction to Abraham to sing a song of praise that turns out to be the song of the angels, including the creatures of the throne. In other words, the remedy for fear of the angelic worship is to become part of it.

The instructions for ascent from the Mithras Liturgy provide an interesting parallel to Abraham's experience. During the ascent, according to the Mithras Liturgy, "You will see the gods staring intently at you and rushing at you. So at once put your right finger on your mouth and say: 'Silence! Silence! Silence! Symbol of the living, incorruptible god . . .'" (*PGM* IV.555–60).[62] The instructions continue with magical names and sounds to ward off the gods. After reciting them, "You will see the gods looking graciously upon you and no longer rushing at you, but rather going about in their own order of affairs" (*PGM* IV.565–70). Here the heavenly beings are not only noisy but also genuinely hostile to the initiate; but here, as opposed to the Apocalypse of Zephaniah, steps can be taken to deal with their hostility.

We return to Abraham as he joins the angelic liturgy:

> And while he was speaking, behold a fire round about, *and it was* coming towards us; and there was a voice in the fire like the sound of rushing waters, like the roaring of the sea. And the angel with me bowed *his head and* wor-

shipped. And I would have fallen prostrate on the ground; but the place on the height, where we were standing, at one moment lifted itself up *and* at the next sank back *again*. And he said, Only worship, Abraham, and sing the song I have taught you (for there was no ground to fall on). And I worshipped only, and I sang the song he had taught me. And he said, Sing without stopping; and I sang, and he himself also sang the song. (17:1–6)

Unlike the Apocalypse of Zephaniah, the Ascension of Isaiah, or the Similitudes of Enoch, the Apocalypse of Abraham treats the song sung by the visionary as part of the means of achieving ascent rather than simply as a sign of having achieved angelic status after ascent. In this it stands close to some of the hekhalot texts, and like them it provides the words of the song. In the other apocalypses the hymns are rarely quoted; when they are, as in the Similitudes of Enoch or Revelation, they are rather brief, and none contains the elaborate piling up of adjectives found in the Apocalypse of Abraham. This style is close to that of one type of hymn preserved in the hekhalot literature.[63]

After his initial moment of terror Abraham shows no fear, even when confronted with sights that might be expected to produce fear. As he arrives before the divine throne, he observes a peculiar incident. When they have completed the song, the four creatures begin to look at each other threateningly, and Abraham's angelic guide must turn their faces away from each other and teach them the song of peace (18:8–10). That this rowdy behavior is habitual is clear from Iaoel's words as he introduces himself to Abraham before the ascent: "I am he who is appointed by [God's] command to appease the strife the cherubic creatures have with one another . . ." (10:10).

The meaning of the creatures' behavior is not at all clear. It is quite different from the chaotic fiery worship that frightened Abraham during the ascent.[64] The emphasis on the rejection of idolatry in the first section of the Apocalypse of Abraham might suggest that the incident is intended to guard against idolatrous worship of the creatures that stand closest to God. What is important for my present purpose, however, is that Abraham watches the strife of the heavenly creatures without fear.

Further, remember that Abraham fainted the first time he heard the voice of the invisible God (ch. 9). Now he stands before the divine throne and again hears the voice of God, who remains unseen, as Iaoel had warned Abraham he would (16:3), although he manifests himself through fire (17:1).[65] Following his angelic guide, who bows his head in worship, Abraham wishes to prostrate himself, but he cannot since the ground rocks beneath him (17:2–3). Still, it appears that Abraham's desire to prostrate himself is a matter of etiquette rather than of fear.

Abraham does not undergo a transformation as explicit as that of Enoch, Isaiah, or Zephaniah, but he has now moved from fear to participation in the heavenly liturgy. Although Abraham is never actually provided with a garment, he has been promised one. Immediately before

Abraham's ascent, Azazel appears in the form of an unclean bird to attack the carcasses of the sacrifice, and Iaoel drives him away. He concludes his long rebuke: "The garment that of old was set apart in the heavens for you, is *now set apart* for him [Abraham]; and the corruption that was his has been transferred to you" (13:15).[66]

From the fire of the divine throne God speaks to Abraham, revealing to him the future of his descendants. In this vision of history the temple plays a central role. God begins by parting the heavens to demonstrate that though they are full of angels, they are empty of other gods (ch. 19). Then, echoing Genesis 15, he promises Abraham descendants as numerous and as mighty as the stars of the fifth heaven, "a people set apart for me in my heritage with Azazil [the spelling reflects the Slavonic]" (ch. 20). Whatever this phrase means, it introduces Azazel into the discussion, and he turns out to play a more prominent role in human history than his rather brief appearance in the Apocalypse of Abraham to this point might have led us to expect.

To explain this role, God shows Abraham the works of creation including paradise and hell, and humanity divided into two groups, Abraham's descendants on the right side of the picture, and all other people, some righteous and some wicked, on the left (ch. 21). Now the picture before Abraham's eyes changes as God shows him scenes from human history. First Abraham sees Adam and Eve in the Garden with the snake, whom God identifies as Azazel (ch. 23), followed by Cain with the murdered Abel and a variety of other sinners (ch. 24).

Next Abraham sees a beautiful temple, but in it a glittering idol worshiped with human sacrifices. God explains that although at first kings and prophets will assure that Abraham's descendants make proper use of God's temple, later the people will anger God with idolatrous worship. Those people whom Abraham sees sacrificed are apparently martyrs, whose death is associated with the coming of the end (ch. 25).

Now Abraham sees the nations burning the temple, sacking it, and slaughtering many of his descendants in punishment for their idolatry. God tells Abraham the duration of Israel's punishment in terms drawn from the prophecy of oppression in Egypt in Genesis 15, here understood as an eschatological prediction (ch. 27).

The last scene of the vision (ch. 29) is the most difficult and, as already noted, is often taken as Christian. A man emerges from the nations, and is worshiped by them and some of Abraham's descendants. Azazel too worships him. Some of Abraham's descendants, however, reject him. At the very end, God tells Abraham, Abraham's descendants too will come to worship him. Although the man in question seems to be Jesus, the picture of worship by Azazel does not fit well with any form of Christianity.[67] Even without regard to its Christian character, the passage is hard to square with God's promise to send his chosen one for the last judgment in his concluding address to Abraham after his return to earth (ch. 31). Further study is necessary to clarify the provenance of this scene, but it is unlikely that it belonged in this form to the original version of the apocalypse.

The vision concludes with a prophecy of the last judgment and the promise of restoration for the righteous among Abraham's descendants, including the restoration of the temple and its cult (29:14–22). Finally, Abraham returns to earth and, in response to his plea, God offers one more clarification of the eschatological plan involving ten plagues on the nations and the coming of the Elect One (chs. 30–31).

The vision shows us that for the Apocalypse of Abraham, as for 4 Ezra, the destruction of the temple is intimately connected to larger questions of God's expectations of humanity and human failure from the beginning of history. It is no accident that the sin of Adam figures prominently in both works, as it does also in 3 Baruch, another response to the destruction of the temple. Abraham is not as unrelenting in his questioning of God as Ezra, but the patriarch who charged God with injustice toward the people of Sodom and Gomorrah (Gen. 18:23–32) here too questions God's justice. Why has God given Azazel power over humanity? (23:10). Why has he willed people to desire evil? (23:12). Why cannot God change his mind about the punishment he intends for Abraham's descendants? (26:1). God's response, as I understand it, is that all have free will, including God himself, whose will is the punishment to which Abraham objects (ch. 26). The relationship between the two causes of evil—the figure of Azazel and the sin of idolatry— is not fully worked out: Azazel is entirely absent from the story of Abraham's rejection of idolatry.

The heaven of the Apocalypse of Abraham is clearly a temple. Abraham sacrifices in order to ascend to heaven, then ascends by means of the sacrifice, and joins in the heavenly liturgy to protect himself during the ascent. According to the Apocalypse of Abraham, the destruction of the earthly temple was caused by idolatry, that is, by corrupting the cult. There is no criticism of the cult properly performed. Indeed God promises that after the last judgment the righteous of Abraham's descendants will again offer sacrifices in the temple (29:17–18).

The depiction of heaven as a temple confirms the importance of the earthly temple. The prominence of the heavenly liturgy lends importance to the liturgy of words on earth, which at the time of the apocalypse provided a substitute for sacrifice, a substitute that in the apocalypse's view was to be temporary.

Ascent as Invasion?

In his recent book *The Faces of the Chariot: Early Jewish Responses to Ezekiel's Vision*, David Halperin offers a powerful reading of ascent in the hekhalot literature and in midrashim about Moses' journey to heaven to bring down the Torah as an invasion of heaven.[68] The hostility of the angels to Moses in the midrashim, like the dangers that the angels of the hekhalot literature put in the path of the ascending visionary, is a rational response by heaven's rightful inhabitants, who realize that their privileged status is being threatened by human beings.

The Śar Torah passages of the hekhalot texts, in which the initiate summons the angelic Prince of the Torah to reveal to him the secrets of the Torah that others must acquire through laborious study, play a central role in Halperin's thinking about the meaning of the hekhalot texts. Like the stories of Moses' ascent to take the Torah from the realm of the angels to human beings below, these incantations attempt to make the Torah accessible to ordinary people.[69]

The truly radical nature of these legends of ascent becomes apparent, Halperin claims, when we recognize them as the opposite side of the tales of unsuccessful invasion of heaven by figures like the boastful Morning Star son of Dawn in Isaiah 14. Although Isaiah intended his mythic antihero as a stand-in for the king of Babylonia, in later interpretation he became Lucifer, the model of overbearing pride, self-assertion, and rebellion against the will of God. The name Lucifer points to the relationship with the morning star.

The hekhalot texts and the midrashim about Moses are of course told from the point of view of the upstarts; the visionaries of the hekhalot succeed in standing before God's throne, just as Moses manages to wrest the Torah from the angels and bring it down to earth. The same pattern appears in some of the ascent apocalypses, where human ascent is correlated with angelic descent as in the fall of the Watchers (the Enoch apocalypses) or of Azazel (the Apocalypse of Abraham). The appeal of such stories through so many centuries derives from the universal human experience of growing up. The usurping heroes of the ascents speak to adolescents as they struggle to reach adulthood and eventually supplant the older generation.[70]

The traditions of the transformation of Enoch into Metatron in 3 Enoch (Sepher Hekhalot) play a particularly important role in Halperin's argument. Halperin claims that Moses can be viewed as a lesser Metatron, or Metatron as a greater Moses, and points to some striking parallels of detail in the ascents of the two heroes. Further, Halperin sees the title *na'ar*, youth, which is often bestowed on Metatron, as confirming his understanding of the psychological origins of the ascent legends. Some scholars have taken the epithet to mean nothing more than servant,[71] but Halperin insists that we must take Metatron's own explanation of the title in 3 Enoch (ch. 4, esp. v. 10) more seriously. He is called youth, Metatron tells R. Ishmael, because he is the youngest of the angels. The youngest of the angels—a fitting hero for adolescents as they attempt to become adults.[72]

To complement this psychological reading of the ascents, Halperin searches for a social setting in which the ongoing drama of generational conflict might take the particular form we find in the hekhalot texts. He suggests the *'am ha'areṣ*, the peasants excluded from the priveleged world of the rabbis by their lack of education, as the audience to whom the Śar Torah passages would appeal as a way to achieve mastery of the Torah, and thus equality with the rabbis, without rabbinic learning, which was virtually inaccessible to men of their social standing.[73]

It is a brilliant achievement to have made sense of the complex of quite different phenomena that can be placed under the heading of merkavah mysticism, as Halperin does in *The Faces of the Chariot*. But the emphasis on ascent as invasion, on the subversive aspect of the process, seems to me exaggerated, not only for the apocalypses, where it is perhaps unfair to take Halperin to task since they are not a central focus of the book, but also for the hekhalot literature. I will not pause here to criticize the reconstruction of the social setting of the hekhalot texts,[74] but will turn rather to the reading of the hekhalot literature on which it rests. While Halperin has certainly uncovered an important vein in this literature, which takes on added importance in light of its relationship to the traditions about Moses in the midrashim, he has more or less ignored a more irenic understanding of the process of ascent, in which the goal of the visionary is not to displace the angels but to join them.

Often in the hekhalot texts, as in the apocalypses we have examined, the manifestation of the visionary's equality with the angels at the culmination of the ascent takes the form of joining the angels in the heavenly liturgy. For example, after a series of hymns to be used to descend to the chariot in Hekhalot Rabbati, R. Ishmael says, "All these songs R. 'Aqiba heard when he descended to the chariot, and he took hold of them and learned them [as he stood] before the throne of glory, [the songs] that his ministers were singing before him" (Schäfer, *Synopse*, #106). Most of the songs contain the trishagion, and they show no signs of theurgic or magical efficacy. Rather, they are effective because, by singing them, the visionary takes his place among the angels. The hekhalot texts appear to have taken this idea from the apocalyptic tradition.[75] In other words, Halperin's reading, compelling though it is, is only a partial explanation of the texts in question.

In the apocalypses, as we have seen, ascent often means displacement of angels, for with surprising frequency human beings come to stand closer than the angels to God. This fact and the correlation already noted between human ascent and angelic descent in the traditions of the Book of the Watchers and the Apocalypse of Abraham would appear to make the apocalypses fertile ground for a reading of ascent as invasion. But such a reading is very difficult to sustain. Angelic hostility toward the ascending visionary is almost absent from the apocalypses.[76] Azazel in the Apocalypse of Abraham and the accuser in the Apocalypse of Zephaniah are exceptions, but Azazel is a wicked angel, and the accuser's hostility is a professional requirement. In the stream of traditions Halperin emphasizes it is the ordinary angels of heaven who oppose the hero. The fallen Watchers of the Book of the Watchers actually instigate Enoch's ascent, and in none of the Enoch apocalypses before 3 Enoch does Enoch encounter angelic opposition. The line from the prophetic traditions about participation in the divine council to the apocalypses is too direct to allow invasion to become an aspect of the understanding of ascent. In some of the apocalypses the human visionary goes to the head of the line in front of the angels, but the angels continue to perform their functions and to enjoy an exalted status.

The Meaning of Transformation

I propose a quite different reading of the ascents of the apocalypses based on the historical conditions that seem to have contributed to the concern for the heavenly temple. One result of the traumatic break with the traditions of the past caused by the destruction of the temple and the exile, it is often argued, is a new feeling of distance between God and humanity, a feeling unknown in the religion of Israel before the exile. Ezekiel's vision of God on a chariot-throne is a response to the fact that the temple, once the center of religious experience, is no longer available. The appeal to creation in the work of the other great prophet of the exile, Second Isaiah, a new departure in prophetic literature, also reflects a sense of distance between Israel and the God of history.

Such distance makes prophecy problematic. In the postexilic period there is a gradual movement away from prophecy toward interpretation as a primary mode of religious authority. In Zechariah, a postexilic prophet, prophecy has become interpretation, visions to be deciphered. Later the symbolic vision with angelic interpreter becomes one of the central forms of revelation in the apocalypses. Where the heroes of the Bible talked with God, the heroes of the apocalypses usually talk with angels. The Hellenistic period sees the emergence of angels with names and to a certain extent distinctive identities.[77] God is understood to dwell in the midst of myriads of angels, to whom he delegates the performance of various tasks.

Most scholars who attempt to describe the emergence of the angelologies[78] of early Judaism are unable to shake off the feeling that the new developments represent a falling away from the heights of classical biblical religion:

> Fundamentally the whole of angelology was an indication that the figure of God had receded into the distance and that the angels were needed as intermediaries between him, creation and man. . . . This strictly-ordered, pyramid-like hierarchical system probably corresponded to a general religious need of the time, as it exercised a profound influence, not only on the Greek-speaking Judaism of the Diaspora and early Christianity, but through them on gnosticism and indeed on the whole of popular religion in late antiquity, as is shown by its significance for magic. Even neo-Platonism could not escape its influence.[79]

The language used by this important historian of ancient Judaism—God "has receded into the distance," Neoplatonism "could not escape"—strongly suggests that the new development is undesirable. Other scholars make this judgment quite openly:

> There was . . . increasing stress on the role of angels and intermediaries as God was elevated above personal contact with human affairs. . . . An elaborate angelology was developed. . . . Under the archangels were a whole hierarchy of angels . . . through whom . . . God conducts his dealings with men. Though this developing angelology represented no perversion of Israel's faith, but rather an exaggerated development of one of its primitive features, it did pose the danger, as such beliefs always do, that in popular religion lesser beings would intrude between a man and his God.[80]

These reactions to the emergence of an elaborate hierarchy of angels are not unrelated to some of the old prejudices about "late Judaism."[81]

In *By Light, Light* E. R. Goodenough speaks of Philo's system as intended to solve "the problem of the relation of the Unrelated," of how God could "be brought into relation with the world, in spite of the fact that He was essentially beyond relation."[82] As both Goodenough and Hengel suggest, the perception of God's inaccessiblity was by no means restricted to Jews. Philo's solution to the problem is a variation on the standard ancient answer, to understand God through the image of the sun sending forth its rays, its brightness in no way diminished by the rays. This image gives rise to the more elaborate Neoplatonic system of emanations; the gnostic systems with their dizzying profusion of archons and syzygies can be seen as mythologically concrete versions of those more austerely philosophical systems. It is possible that the systems reflect the influence of Jewish angelology, as Hengel suggests. What is clear, however, is their structural similarity to Jewish angelology as a bridge between God and humanity.

Indeed once we have recognized how widely the problem of God's distance was perceived in the Greco-Roman world, we realize that angels, like emanations, are not its cause but an attempt at its solution. The idea that the heavens are full of angels assures human beings of contact with the sphere of the divine, even if only its periphery.

But the apocalypses do not restrict themselves to the periphery. Indeed it turns out that the boundaries between human beings and angels are not very clear. One group of apocalypses offers great heroes of the past as examples of how close human beings can come to God. Among the extant apocalypses this stream is represented primarily by Enoch works. By the end of this tradition, Enoch has become second only to God in the heavenly hierarchy. This understanding of ascent was not restricted to Enoch apocalypses, as the passages in the Mani Codex describing the transformations of Adam and Seth into exalted angels make clear. And the transformations of the apocalypses are clearly related to speculation about the exaltation of Moses in places as diverse as Ezekiel the Tragedian and Philo, on the one hand, and rabbinic sermons, on the other.[83]

The other stream of the apocalypses insists that if ordinary human beings are righteous, after death they can take their place in the heavenly hierarchy. In its milder form in the Apocalypse of Zephaniah, most of the righteous dead remain at a rank somewhat below that of the angels. In the more radical version in the Ascension of Isaiah, the righteous can expect to spend eternity contemplating God himself, having achieved a status even higher than the angels'. While for most this experience is reserved until after death, certain exceptional men can have a foretaste of angelic status while still alive, thus serving as examples of the future intimacy with God that all the righteous may hope for. The two streams of thought about equality with the angels—one stressing the future glory of all the righteous, the other the exaltation of one hero—are not in theory mutually exclusive, but the limits on the role of Isaiah in the Ascension of Isaiah show how the emphasis on the future glory of the righteous serves in practice to diminish the glory of the hero.

That the claims of these ascent apocalypses were sometimes shocking to their ancient readers is clear from the reactions of the authors of 3 Baruch and the Apocalypse of Paul. In 3 Baruch, Baruch pointedly continues to address his angelic guide as "lord" throughout the ascent—no equality here![84] In the Apocalypse of Paul even the mild form of angelic status of the Apocalypse of Zephaniah is too much. When the Apocalypse of Paul adapts the Apocalypse of Zephaniah's scene of crossing the heavenly lake, it omits all indications of fellowship with the angels.[85]

Alan Segal has suggested that in the literature of the Greco-Roman world the ascent of a human being to heaven is structurally equivalent to the descent of a divine figure to earth. Both accomplish mediation between the two opposed spheres.[86] But the journeys are certainly not equivalent in their anthropology. This is true even when the figure descending takes on a human identity, as does Christ in the Ascension of Isaiah or the angel Israel, who descends to earth and becomes Jacob according to the Prayer of Joseph. The descent of a divine figure expresses the certainty that God cares enough for the righteous to send them help. But the ascent apocalypses make greater claims for the nature of humanity: human beings, whether all the righteous or a single inspiring example, have the potential to become like the angels, or even greater than the angels. The standard assessment of the apocalypses as dualistic, pessimistic, and despairing of this world needs to be revised in light of the value the ascent apocalypses place on human beings. The examples of the heroes of the ascent apocalypses teach their readers to live the life of this world with the awareness of the possibility of transcendence.

4

The Secrets of Nature,
Primeval History, and
the Order of the Cosmos

One important aspect of the content of the ascent apocalypses remains to be discussed, their interest in nature. Nature is in fact one of the most ancient subjects of preserved apocalyptic speculation, for the Astronomical Book of Enoch is devoted almost entirely to the paths of the sun and moon and their implications for the calendar. The interest in nature takes a different form in the works with which we are concerned. In the Book of the Watchers, earthly geography is given more attention than heavenly, and nature serves as testimony to God's greatness and to the order of the universe. In the three later apocalypses to be discussed in this chapter (the Similitudes of Enoch, 2 Enoch, and 3 Baruch), earth has disappeared from the picture and heaven alone is the object of cosmological concern. Nature plays a central role in all three, in rather different ways. In the Similitudes of Enoch, God's ordering of nature is a model for his ordering of the fate of human beings. In 2 Enoch God's revelation about the creation of the world is the culmination of Enoch's ascent. In 3 Baruch certain natural phenomena are personified to dramatize their importance as testimony to the glory of God.

The Book of the Watchers and the
Tour to the Ends of the Earth

After Enoch ascends to the heavenly throne in the Book of the Watchers, he undertakes another journey (chs. 17–36). This time he travels to the ends of the earth in the company of the angels, and in the course of the

72

journey he sees wonderful sights. Two sources can be distinguished in the tour, the second (chs. 20–36) a later expansion of the first (chs. 17–19).[1]

The first tour offers only a very brief description of the geographical and cosmological phenomena it describes—mountains, luminaries, stars, thunder and lightning, rivers, winds, the foundations of the earth, the mountain of God—while devoting a great deal of attention to the place of the punishment of the Watchers. The second tour, on the other hand, places less emphasis on the fate of the Watchers and devotes considerable attention to the mythic geography of Jerusalem and the area around it, and to cosmology. It also describes the fate of souls after death.

On formal grounds, the best precedent to Enoch's tour is Ezekiel's tour of the eschatological temple and its environs, which concludes the Book of Ezekiel (chs. 40–48), the only such tour in biblical literature. As the angel guides Ezekiel, he offers comments of a form that I have elsewhere termed "demonstrative explanations," explanations of sights that begin with demonstrative pronouns or adjectives. In Enoch's tour these explanations serve as the angel's response to Enoch's questions or exclamations about the sights he is shown. This is not to deny the possibility, indeed the likelihood, that the tour in the Book of the Watchers is influenced by other, non-Jewish, literature, such as the *nekyia* of the Odyssey, but rather to insist that the primary model was Ezekiel.[2]

There are also connections between the content of Ezekiel's tour and Enoch's. At the beginning of Ezekiel's tour the angelic guide measures the dimensions of the temple that will someday replace the one so recently destroyed and gives instructions about the cult (chs. 40–44). The description of the temple leads to a more general sacred geography, including a description of the wonderful effects of the miraculous stream that issues forth from the temple (ch. 47) and the distribution of land to the tribes, restored in time to come to full number (ch. 48).

In his description of the stream from the temple, Ezekiel follows the lead of earlier biblical traditions by bringing the imagery of the Garden of Eden to the temple mount. The fertility caused by the stream is miraculous. As it flows from the temple, rich forests grow on either bank, and it sweetens the waters into which it flows so that the Dead Sea comes alive with fish. When Ezekiel's angelic guide describes the trees on the banks of the river, we cannot help being reminded of the tree of life from the Garden: "Their leaves will not wither nor their fruit fail, but they will bear fresh fruit every month, because the water for them flows from the sanctuary. Their fruit will be for food, and their leaves for healing" (47:12).[3] For Ezekiel the temple mount is as much a source of blessing and fertility as the primordial garden planted by God. This association appears elsewhere in Ezekiel as well and is clearly an important aspect of his understanding of the temple.[4]

Yet another sign of the debt of the Book of the Watchers to Ezekiel is the close association of Jerusalem, the city of the temple mount, with the Garden of Eden in Enoch's tour to the ends of the earth.[5] As he approaches Jerusalem from the west Enoch sees the tree of life, transplanted to a mountain that will serve as God's throne at the eschaton (chs. 24–25).[6] In Enoch's description, Jerusalem itself is full of trees. Significantly, a stream flows from Mount Zion (ch. 26). The wilderness to the east of Jerusalem is also full of trees, watered by a gushing torrent (ch. 28), a picture reminiscent of the luxuriant river banks of Ezekiel 47.

The Book of the Watchers goes farther than Ezekiel by making Eden itself—the Garden of Righteousness—a stop on its hero's itinerary. As Enoch travels east from Jerusalem, he sees spice trees (chs. 29–31), the Garden of Righteousness with the tree of knowledge (ch. 32), and beasts and birds (ch. 33). The inclusion of the Garden in the tour is particularly striking in view of the problems it raises for the Book of the Watchers. At the center of the Book of the Watchers is a story in which divine beings through their transgression introduce evil to humanity. By compressing any allusion to the traditions developed in the Book of the Watchers into four verses (Gen. 6:1–4), the editors of Genesis effectively subordinate it to the story for which the Garden provides the occasion, the rebellion of Adam and Eve. Any allusion to the Garden is sure to remind readers of this story, the dominant account in the biblical tradition of how evil came into the world.

The author of the tour overcomes the difficulties raised by the mention of the Garden quite cleverly. First, the Garden is never called Eden, but rather the Garden of Righteousness.[7] Next, as we have already seen, the tree of life has been transplanted from the Garden to the mountain west of Jerusalem.[8] Thus the importance of the Garden itself has been significantly diminished. Finally, while Michael gives Enoch an enthusiastic exposition of the virtues of the tree of life on the mountain, Raphael responds to Enoch's exclamation about the beauty of the tree of knowledge not with praise of the tree but with a brief version of the expulsion from Eden that is notable for what it leaves out. "This is the tree of knowledge of which your father of old and your mother of old before you ate; and they learned knowledge, and their eyes were opened, and they knew that they were naked, and they were driven out of the garden" (32:6). The author has avoided any mention of the serpent, the fruit, and the fact that Adam and Eve had sinned.

Why did our author include the Garden of Eden on Enoch's tour if it created so many difficulties for him? The answer must be that the Garden was so important a sight for the mythic geography of the biblical tradition that omitting it would also provoke comment. Further, the allusions to it in Ezekiel's tour of the restored temple made it impossible for him to pass over. Thus he set about including it in a way that would diminish as much as possible the dissonance caused by its presence. The measure of his success is how little comment there has been on the implications of its inclusion.[9]

The Tour to the Ends of the Earth and Wisdom Literature

In the course of his tour Enoch responds again and again to the sights he sees with praise of God.[10] The tour concludes:

> And when I saw, I blessed continually, and I will always bless the Lord of glory, who has wrought great and glorious wonders that he might show the grandeur of his work to his angels, to spirits, and to mankind, that they might glorify his work, and that every one of his creatures might see the work of his might, and glorify the great work of his hands, and bless him for ever. (36:4)

The view that the wonders of nature lead to praise of God appears also in wisdom literature, the primary locus for discussion of the meaning of creation in the Bible. In the optimistic view of early wisdom works (the Book of Proverbs and some of the Psalms), the created world speaks of its creator loud and clear. "The heavens are telling the glory of God; and the firmament proclaims his handiwork . . ." (Ps. 19:1 [2]).

In the period of doubt and despair following the destruction of the First Temple, the insistence that nature testifies to its maker takes on a new meaning. The author of Second Isaiah becomes the first prophet to appeal to creation as proof of God's power:

> To whom then will you compare me, that I should be like him? says the Holy One. Lift up your eyes on high and see: who created these? He who brings out their host by number, calling them all by name; by the greatness of his might, and because he is strong in power not one is missing. Why do you say, O Jacob, and speak, O Israel, "My way is hid from the Lord, and my right is disregarded by my God"? Have you not known, Have you not heard? The Lord is the everlasting God, the Creator of the ends of the earth. He does not faint or grow weary, his understanding is unsearchable. (Isa. 40:25–28)

As this passage makes clear, the prophet turns to nature because many of his contemporaries think that history has failed. God has not fulfilled his promises; he has not shown himself to be all-powerful in the arena of history. "My right is disregarded by my God," the prophet hears his contemporaries saying. In the prophet's insistence that God "does not faint or grow weary," we can surely hear the voices of those who took the destruction of the temple and the exile as signs of faintness and weariness. But the prophet insists that the God who can shepherd the heavenly host without losing a single star can also renew his people.

Over and over the prophet of Second Isaiah refers to God as creator of heaven and earth. The references are particularly plentiful in the Jacob/Israel poems (chs. 40–48),[11] where creation, past and future, plays a central role. God is several times said to have created (*br'*), formed (*ysr*), or made (*'sh*) Israel.[12] The coming redemption takes the form of a second exodus, a new journey through the wilderness. But this new exodus involves a new creation, the appearance of water in the wilderness to create a wonderful fertility.[13]

The theme of creation appears even in the Zion poems (chs. 49–55), where the prophet introduces another set of powerful images. The creator here stands in the background; God is represented rather as the husband of Zion the mother, who is now bereaved, but soon to be blessed with offspring. But here too God is called creator of heaven and earth,[14] and in one striking image that recalls Ezekiel, the redeemed Zion is compared to Eden: "For the LORD will comfort Zion, he will comfort all her waste places, and will make her wilderness like Eden, her desert like the garden of the LORD; joy and gladness will be found in her, thanksgiving and the voice of song" (51:3).

Like 2 Isaiah, Job is deeply concerned with creation. The speech from the whirlwind at the end of the book uses the greatness of God's creative activity to silence Job:[15]

> Where were you when I laid the foundation of the earth? Tell me if you have understanding. Who determined its measurements—surely you know! Or who stretched the line upon it? On what were its bases sunk, or who laid its cornerstone, when the morning stars sang together, and all the sons of God shouted for joy? Or who shut in the sea with doors, when it burst forth from the womb. . . . (Job 38:4–8)

A passage strikingly similar in its rhetoric appears at the beginning of 2 Isaiah:

> Who has measured the waters in the hollow of his hand and marked off the heavens with a span, enclosed the dust of the earth in a measure and weighed the mountains in scales and the hills in a balance? Who has directed the Spirit of the LORD, or as his counselor has instructed him? Whom did he consult for his enlightenment. . . . (Isa. 40:12–14)

The answer to both sets of questions is that no human being was there, that God alone accomplished the work of creation. Agreement on this central point leads to very different conclusions, however. The questions in 2 Isaiah are rhetorical, in Job sarcastic. The author of Job is arguing against those who use the evidence for God's power in the created world to prop up the God of history. Yes, the creator of the world is powerful, the Book of Job says, but no, he is not a god of history. He does not care about mankind, he is beyond such concerns. In contrast to the understanding of nature in 2 Isaiah, the mysteries of the created world in the Book of Job are beyond human understanding; their very inaccessibility demonstrates God's greatness. The Book of Job is notoriously difficult to date, but the parallels to 2 Isaiah make a reading of Job as a response to the destruction of the temple and the exile extremely attractive. It is a response so radical that the book can circulate only with the prose frame that softens its message.[16]

Like 2 Isaiah and Job, the Book of the Watchers is a response to the destruction of the temple, although that destruction was already centuries in the past. The tour to the ends of the earth represents a middle view about the way in which nature speaks of God, less pessimistic than

Job, less optimistic than 2 Isaiah. Many of the phenomena that cause Enoch to praise God are everyday aspects of nature: the rain, dew, wind, and stars of chapter 36, for example. But Enoch goes to their sources, as no other man has done. As the prophet of Second Isaiah would have it, the created world does indeed declare its creator's glory, though the declaration may be heard clearly only by the most righteous of men, the equal of the angels. But the emphasis of the tour is on the way the wonders inspire Enoch to praise God rather than on their inaccessibility to the average human being. All humanity can find hope in the fact that these mysteries have been revealed to at least one of their number.

Nature Elsewhere in the Book of the Watchers

The opening chapters of the Book of the Watchers offer a somewhat different understanding of the message of natural phenomena, one less continuous with the biblical tradition. In 1 Enoch 1–5, Enoch appeals to the regularity of the luminaries in heaven and to the seasonal changes of the waters, trees, and heat on earth as examples of faithfulness to God in contrast to human unfaithfulness.

> Consider all [his works] and observe the works (of creation) in heaven, / How the heavenly luminaries do not change their paths *in the conjunction of their orbits,* / How each of them rises and sets in order, at its appointed time, / And at their fixed seasons they appear, and do not violate their proper order. . . . See how the seas and rivers together perform and do not change their tasks by abandoning his commands. But you have changed your works, and have not been steadfast nor done according to his commandments, but you have transgressed against him, and spoken proud and hard words with your impure mouths against his majesty. . . . (2:1–5:4)[17]

This theme, which is taken up in several later apocalypses, implies a certain degree of personification of natural phenomena, a development with little precedent in biblical tradition, as Stone points out.[18] The idea of nature as the embodiment of faithfulness to God is never brought into relation with the idea of nature as testimony to the greatness of God, although both views understand nature to carry a message for humanity.

These attitudes toward nature are quite different from a third attitude that can be discerned in the Book of the Watchers. While the dominant theme of the story of the fall of the Watchers (1 Enoch 6–11) is angelic lust and its consequences, one of the traditions included in the final form of the story treats the revelation of secret knowledge as the great sin of the Watchers.[19] Here skills that make civilization possible are treated as corrupting and dangerous. Among the things revealed by the Watchers to humanity, astrology figures prominently (8:3). Thus knowledge of the very phenomena that are signs of faithfulness in the introduction to the Book of the Watchers and cause for praise of God in the tour to the ends of the earth here contributes to the corruption of humanity. The negative attitude of this strand of the story of the fall of the Watchers is quite isolated in apocalyptic literature.

Nature in Later Apocalyptic Literature

While the Book of the Watchers is extremely influential in shaping the later ascent apocalypses, its interest in nature appears in only three of them, the Similitudes of Enoch and 2 Enoch, both particularly close to the Book of the Watchers in many other ways as well, and 3 Baruch. Why is this aspect of the Book of the Watchers left aside as the apocalyptic tradition develops, both in the ascents and in the other apocalypses?

The lack of interest in mythic geography in the later ascents, including 2 Enoch and 3 Baruch, can be explained quite straightforwardly. The Book of the Watchers is the only one of the apocalypses to involve a journey on earth. When heaven becomes the only location for revelatory sightseeing, Jerusalem and the Garden of Eden are removed from the itinerary, as are the trees and mountains, birds and beasts of Enoch's tour. It is an indication of the debt of the Similitudes of Enoch to the Book of the Watchers that its heavenly journeys provide an opportunity to view important features of earthly geography as well.

It is harder to account for the disappearance of cosmological phenomena that are appropriately placed in the heavens, such as rain, snow, dew, winds, sun, moon, and stars. In the Testament of Levi, the fire, snow, and ice of the angel's description of the second heaven are intended as instruments of vengeance (3:2), and their origins probably lie in the description of the heavenly temple in the Book of the Watchers rather than in its tour to the ends of the earth. In the Apocalypse of Abraham, the Ascension of Isaiah, and the Apocalypse of Zephaniah the contents of the heavens have to do with angelology and the fate of souls after death. The several interests that were treated in a single tour in the Book of the Watchers have become quite separate for these apocalypses, and the interest in nature has been lost.

Between the Book of the Watchers and the other ascent apocalypses, of which none is earlier than the first century B.C.E., came the crisis of Antiochus's persecution and the Maccabean revolt. Several apocalypses were written in response to this crisis: Daniel, the Book of Dreams, perhaps the Assumption (or Testament) of Moses, and, a little later, the Epistle of Enoch. They are concerned primarily with collective eschatology; none includes revelations about nature or about the contents of the heavens. The crisis of contemporary events seems to have intensified interest in the end, which seemed imminent.

It seems plausible that the expectation of the imminent end of the world would create an atmosphere in which nature and the phenomena of this world were less likely than earlier to be viewed as a source of knowledge about God. But it is too simple to claim that expectation of an imminent end leads to lack of interest in nature. On the one hand, the Apocalypse of Zephaniah, as far as we can tell from what survives, lacks an interest in nature and collective eschatology. On the other hand, the Similitudes of Enoch has both intense eschatological expectations and also a deep interest in nature, although, as we shall see shortly, it views nature's message as hidden.

One last piece of evidence for the place of nature in the apocalypses remains to be considered, the "lists of revealed things." Michael Stone, who first called attention to these lists, points out that in a number of apocalypses, including some interested not in heavenly ascent but in collective eschatology, the content of a revelation to a hero of the past, to the visionary of the apocalypse in the text's present, or to the righteous in the future, is summarized in a list that includes cosmological phenomena. Such lists appear in 2 Baruch, the Epistle of Enoch, the Similitudes, 2 Enoch, and one work that is not an apocalypse, the Biblical Antiquities of pseudo-Philo. Related forms appear in ben Sira and the Wisdom of Solomon. Stone argues that the puzzles the angel poses for Ezra in 4 Ezra 5 are drawn from the contents of these lists to indicate the author's rejection of the claim that such knowledge has been revealed to humanity.[20]

The contents of the lists vary. The list in 2 Baruch includes natural phenomena in its wide range of revealed knowledge, from the eschatology of the individual and the world to angelology. The lists in the Similitudes of Enoch and 2 Enoch emphasize natural phenomena. Sometimes the lists are expanded into declarations or rhetorical questions. The antecedents of such lists can be found in Job 28 and 38, although the emphases of the apocalyptic lists are somewhat different. Individual elements of the lists find parallels elsewhere in biblical tradition.[21]

The function of the lists is more difficult to discern. Stone suggests that the lists represent "the contents of real or supposed visionary experiences."[22] In the Similitudes of Enoch and 2 Enoch, the contents of the lists fit the strong cosmological interests of the two works, but the Epistle of Enoch and 2 Baruch have nothing to say about the secrets of nature outside of the lists themselves. Still, the lists have sufficient prestige to appear even in works where the revelations bear little relationship to their contents—perhaps a vestige of the interests of earlier apocalypses.[23]

Finally, we must remember that our assessment of the development of the apocalypses is limited by the vagaries of transmission. It seems likely, for example, that the apocalypses of Enosh and Shem quoted by Baraies in the Mani Codex included revelations about creation, for the raptures of their heroes occur as they are meditating on the process of creation. If more or different apocalypses had survived, we might have a rather different picture of the rise and fall of nature as an interest of the apocalypses.

The Similitudes of Enoch

The Ethiopic term for "similitude" or "parable" is cognate with the Hebrew *mašal*. Enoch's prophetic poem about the coming judgment and the contrast between faithful nature and faithless humanity at the beginning of the Book of the Watchers is designated a parable. When Enoch calls himself a man "whose eyes were opened by God" (1 Enoch 1:2), the poem alludes to Balaam, who twice calls himself "the man whose eye is opened" (24:3, 15), and whose oracles are repeatedly called *mašal* in Numbers (23:7, 18; 24:3, 15, 20, 21, 23).[24]

In the New Testament and rabbinic literature, parables clearly involve a comparison. The situation in the Hebrew Bible is more complicated. There the term *mašal* is applied to a range of literary types, including proverbs, riddles, and Balaam's oracles. Usually these forms involve comparison, although the comparison can take many different forms.[25]

In its use of the term "parable," the Similitudes appears to be alluding to the opening of the Book of the Watchers. In what sense can Enoch's three discourses be called parables? David Suter argues that the Similitudes is a member of the *mašal* family because of the comparison between God's roles as the orderer of the cosmos, on the one hand, and judge of humanity, on the other. Further, the Similitudes shares not only form but also an element of content with many of the *mešalim* of the Hebrew Bible, the use of nature for purposes of comparison. This suggestion does not account for every aspect of the Similitudes, but it does make sense of a large part of what at first glance appears to be an almost incoherent mass of diverse materials.[26]

Just as the opening discourse of the Book of the Watchers contrasts the faithfulness of nature and the faithlessness of men, the Similitudes also emphasizes nature's faithfulness:

> And I saw the storehouses of the sun and the moon, whence they . . . go forth and whither they return, . . . and how they do not leave their courses, and neither lengthen nor reduce their courses, but they keep faith with one another in the covenant by which they abide. And first the sun goes forth and traverses his path according to the commandment of the Lord of spirits, and his Name will endure forever. . . . (41:5–7)

The contrast of nature with humanity is often left implicit in the Similitudes, but the emphasis on the faithfulness of nature places in relief the sinfulness of humanity:

> And I saw lightnings besides and the stars of heaven, and I saw how he called them all by their names and they hearkened to him. And I saw how they are weighed in a righteous balance according to their amount of light, according to the width of their spaces and the day of their appearing, and their movement produces lightning, and their motions according to the number of the angels, and (how) they keep faith with each other. And I asked the angel who went with me who showed me secret things, 'What are these?' And he said to me: 'The Lord of spirits has shown you a parable pertaining to

them. . . : these are the names of the holy who dwell on the earth and believe on the Name of the Lord of spirits for ever and ever.' (ch. 43)[27]

Other apocalypses describe the eschatological transformation of the righteous into stars. Here stars represent the righteous on earth.

In the Similitudes one important aspect of the comparison between nature and humanity is that the truth about both is hidden. The universe of the Similitudes is profoundly out of joint. Truth is everywhere concealed. On earth the righteous are persecuted, and the wicked are mighty and victorious. Only at the last judgment will their fates be reversed. The wicked will then realize their mistakes:

> In those days the mighty kings who possess the earth shall implore his angels of punishment to whom they were delivered up to grant them a brief respite that they might fall down and worship before the Lord of spirits, and confess their sins before him. . . .
> 'Every secret thing will be brought to light;
> Thy power is from generation to generation,
> And thy glory for ever and ever.
> Unfathomable are all thy secrets and innumerable,
> And thy righteousness is beyond reckoning.
> We have now learned that we should glorify
> And bless the Lord of kings and him who rules over all kings.'
>
> (63:1–4)

Notice the emphasis on secrets: the secret sins of the wicked that are known to God, and God's secrets, presumably including the future punishment of the wicked. Taken together with the Similitudes' picture of a small group of the elect, this insistence on the hiddenness of truth and the topsy-turvy nature of the present world suggest that the Similitudes is a sectarian document, although we cannot identify the sect from which it comes.

The workings of the phenomena of nature, the very sights Enoch sees in the Book of the Watchers in his journey to the ends of the earth, are also secrets. "And there my eyes saw the secrets of the lightnings and of the thunder, and the secrets of the winds, how they are divided to blow over the earth, and the secrets of the clouds and dew . . ." (41:3; cf. ch. 59, 60:11–15).

In a passage that represents wisdom as a woman in the traditional image of wisdom literature, the Similitudes contrasts the loneliness of Wisdom with the popularity of Iniquity:

> Wisdom found no place where she might dwell,
> And her dwelling-place came to be in heaven.
> Wisdom went forth to make her dwelling among the children of men,
> And found no dwelling-place: Wisdom returned to her place,
> And became established among the angels.

> And Iniquity went forth from her chambers;
> Those she did not seek she found,
> And dwelt among them,
> (Welcome) as rain in a desert and dew on a thirsty land.
>
>   (42:1–3)

In the universe of the Similitudes, Wisdom is available only in heaven.

In the great poem about wisdom in the Wisdom of ben Sira (ch. 24), Wisdom tells first of her role in creation and then of her search for a dwelling place among humanity. God directs her to take her place in Israel, indeed in the temple itself, and by the end of the poem, the wisdom inherent in creation has been explicitly identified with Torah. Whether the author of the Similitudes had ben Sira in mind or not, his point is clear. He has more in common with the author of Job than with ben Sira.[28]

In contrast to its inaccessibility on earth, Wisdom is readily available in heaven: "And in that place I saw the fountain of righteousness which was inexhaustible: / And around it were many fountains of wisdom; / And all the thirsty drank of them and were filled with wisdom, / And their dwellings were with the righteous and holy and elect" (48:1). The Elect One will be able to judge "the secret things" (49:4) because he possesses "the spirit of wisdom, / And the spirit which gives insight, / And the spirit of understanding and of might . . ." (49:3). Indeed "Wisdom has been poured out like water, / And glory fails not before him for evermore" (49:1).[29] Wisdom is available to the righteous, but only in heaven after death or on earth after the last judgment.

The use of natural phenomena in the Similitudes, then, develops one of the themes of the Book of the Watchers, the contrast between nature's faithfulness and humanity's faithlessness. It develops the analogy by describing God's judgment of natural phenomena as well as of humanity; both are weighed in the righteous balance (ch. 43, nature; 61:8, people). But because the author views the world as entirely out of joint, the idea that the wonders of nature testify to the glory of their maker is eclipsed. Only in one possibly interpolated passage is there mention of praise inspired by the works of creation, and there it is the works of creation themselves, not human beings, who offer praise (69:22–24).[30]

I have suggested that the loss of interest in the created world is a result of the development of a view in which this world is no longer worthy of much attention. The author of the Similitudes has not lost interest in the world, but he no longer sees it as speaking loud and clear of God's greatness. His view of truth as everywhere hidden, and of all but the few as wicked, is often taken as the typical apocalyptic view of the world. It should be clear from other works discussed here that that is by no means the only or even the dominant point of view in the apocalypses.

2 Enoch

The contents of the seven heavens in 2 Enoch represent an interpretation of the Book of the Watchers' account of the fall of the Watchers and its revelations to Enoch. The story of the Watchers provides inhabitants for the second and fifth heavens (chs. 4, 7), while the heavenly temple of the ascent in the Book of the Watchers is the inspiration for the contents of the sixth and seventh heavens (chs. 8–9). The place of souls after death is one of the sights of the tour to the ends of the earth in the Book of the Watchers; it finds its counterpart in paradise and hell, located in the third heaven of 2 Enoch (ch. 5).

Natural phenomena appear in the first and fourth heavens of 2 Enoch (chs. 3, 6). Stars and constellations, the heavenly sea, and the treasuries of snow, ice, clouds, and dew, are in the first heaven, together with their angelic supervisors. In addition to the account of the courses of the sun and moon and related calculations in the fourth heaven, which reflect the contents of the Astronomical Book, 2 Enoch introduces new elements: the chariots of the luminaries, the host of heavenly beings accompanying them in their travels, and the sun's crown.[31]

While the natural phenomena in the Book of the Watchers served to inspire Enoch's praise of God, the hero of 2 Enoch offers no comment on the sights his guide shows him in the first heaven, nor is any angelic praise heard. In the fourth heaven, however, there are some hints of an attitude similar to that of the Book of the Watchers. In the long version, as the sun dons its crown at sunrise, the phoenixes and khalkedras sing a song in praise of the sun, an action echoed by birds on earth when they flap their wings at the sight of the sun.[32] At the end of Enoch's sojourn in the fourth heaven he hears a host of angels with musical instruments praising God, a wonderful sound that delights Enoch (6:25).[33] This praise is not explicitly related to the sights that precede it, nor—since praise is a prominent aspect of angelic activity in the heavens of 2 Enoch—does it prove that the author understands the sun and moon as inspiring praise of God. Still, taken together with the song in praise of the sun, it points in this direction.

Another significant aspect of the depiction of the phenomena in the fourth heaven is the incipient personification of sun and moon. Both are shown riding in chariots (6:3–5, 23), and the sun is said to wear a crown (6:14–15). (A far more elaborate picture of the kingly sun and queenly moon appears in 3 Baruch.) The sixth heaven of 2 Enoch contains no natural phenomena, but among its supervising angels are those in charge of the movements of the stars, sun, and moon, and those in charge of seasons and years, rivers and seas, and vegetation (8:3–4). In these supervising angels we find a type of personification closer to that of the Similitudes of Enoch, which saw the regularity of natural phenomena as a kind of intentional faithfulness to God.

The Account of Creation: The First Day

Although natural phenomena do not play a central role in the course of the ascent in 2 Enoch, the ascent culminates in a revelation about creation. After Enoch has ascended through the seven heavens and has undergone the transformation that makes him "like one of the glorious ones," God reveals to him how he created the world, a secret never before made known, even to the angels (11:1–21). I shall argue that the revelation is an attempt to recast Genesis's account of creation in order to bring it into conformity with the popular philosophy of the author's contemporaries.[34]

Among the most striking deviations from Genesis 1 in the revelation of 2 Enoch is its account of the creation of light and darkness, a kind of prehistory of creation. Before God created the world, he tells Enoch, he moved about among the invisible things, unable to rest because the world was not yet created. So he decided to undertake creation (11:4–5).[35] This picture must reflect an interpretation of Genesis 1:2: "And the spirit [or wind] of God was moving over the face of the waters."

The first act of creation is God's command to the depths that "one of the invisible things should rise up *and become* visible." At this an enormous creature called Adoil emerges (11:7). The ending of the name suggests a Hebrew original in -*el*, but the inability of scholars to find a plausible etymology suggests that the original was pseudo-Hebrew.[36]

At God's command Adoil opens himself and something emerges from his belly. Here the manuscripts vary considerably, but it appears that first a great light emerges and then a great age (11:7–8).[37] God sees that what has emerged from Adoil is good. He places a throne for himself and sits upon it (11:9). Now he commands the light to establish itself on high as the foundation for the things above (11:9). The process of creation from Adoil is then complete.

God summons another creature from the depths, saying, "Let what is hard and visible come out from the invisible" (11:11). In response to this command there appears Aruchaz, "hard, heavy, and very black" (11:12). The name may be derived from Greek *arkhē*, beginning.[38]

God sees that Aruchaz is good and commands him to go down below to form the foundation of the things below (11:13). According to the long version, Aruchaz is commanded to disintegrate, and a dark age containing all the lower things emerges from him.[39] Even in the account of the long version, the process of emergence from Aruchaz is more compressed than the process of emergence from Adoil. Light and the great age emerged separately from Adoil, while a single entity, the dark age, emerges from Aruchaz.

Despite the lack of correspondence in certain details, the account of the creation of light and darkness offers a more or less symmetrical picture, in which two sets of opposing principles are born from the bellies of named creatures.[40] The account emphasizes the foundational quality of the principles when it insists, after the light is established above and the darkness below, that there is nothing higher than the light or lower than darkness (11:10, 14).

One of the few things that is perfectly clear from this account is that the author of 2 Enoch was not content with the account of the creation of light in Genesis 1, in which God speaks and brings light into being. The biblical creation story describes a God who creates quite directly. The problem so important to Hellenistic thought—how the immaterial, invisible God could come into relationship with the material, visible world—was not a problem for the biblical authors, who knew no radical divide between spirit and matter. But Hellenistic thinkers regularly interposed intermediaries between the highest god and the world he created. For philosophers this involved a development of Plato's position, but the structure of this solution, as we have seen, appeared also in more popular systems.

The story of the creation of light and darkness in 2 Enoch quite clearly has the biblical account in view. God moves about before creation, he sees that light and darkness are good. But 2 Enoch is uncomfortable with the simple act of speech by which God brings light into being quite directly. Instead it attempts to span the chasm it sees between God and creation with a pair of quite peculiar intermediary figures.

Adoil and Aruchaz are aspects of a process, hypostases of stages of creation. A more philosophical thinker would have described the stages without personifying them. But Adoil and Aruchaz are hardly independent creatures. They have neither personalities nor histories; they do not act on their own. Thus, although the influence of mythological cosmogonies can be felt in the way that Adoil and Aruchaz give rise to light and darkness—not by proper emanation but from their bellies—the account in 2 Enoch is not truly mythological.

The standard opinion about 2 Enoch is that it was written in Egypt before the destruction of the Second Temple. If this view is correct, our author would have been more or less contemporary with Philo. Comparison with Philo's treatment of the creation of the world is illuminating. Philo was a philosopher of considerable subtlety, and similarities of detail are certainly not to be expected. Yet there are some very interesting broad similarities. Like the author of 2 Enoch, Philo in *On the Creation of the World* (15–36) sees the first day of creation as qualitatively different from the others. It is the only day into which the author of 2 Enoch introduces anything like his story of the emanation of light and darkness. For Philo, the work of the first day was not the creation of physical entities but of the intelligible world, the world of forms that would serve as the model for the creation of the physical world. The great age that contains within it all the creation that God intends to create can perhaps be understood as a more concrete version of the forms.[41]

Philo's reading of Genesis in the light of philosophy is certainly more sophisticated than 2 Enoch's. The account in 2 Enoch is the effort of someone without technical philosophical education to make sense of the biblical account in light of the assumptions of the culture he lived in.

Where and when should we locate the author of 2 Enoch? The standard answer, Egypt in the first century, has never been provided with a convincing rationale. The first-century date is plausible enough, since the work seems to assume the existence of the temple; it could of course be earlier. But I suspect that one of the most important reasons for looking to Egypt is that Egypt is the only place in the diaspora from which literary works survive. My reading of 2 Enoch's account of the first day of creation would offer some real basis for the standard picture: first-century Alexandria is just the place where a literate but by no means philosophically learned Jew might arrive at the blend of biblical creation and popular Platonism reflected in the account.

The Rest of Creation

After the emergence of light and darkness, the short version of 2 Enoch offers a very brief retelling of the account of creation in Genesis 1, considerably shorter than the biblical story (11:15–21). The most striking addition is the mention of the creation of angels on the second day (11:18).

The much longer account of the long version includes the material of the short version and a great deal more. Andersen calls the long version "full and coherent," in contrast to the short version, where the manuscripts disagree among themselves and are often so brief that they hardly make sense.[42] Yet some of the features peculiar to the long version serve to bring its account of creation into closer alignment with Genesis 1, for example, the division of the account into days. This enterprise appears to represent revision of the shorter account, so problematic from the point of view of the biblical text. Other features of the long version are easily separable from the narrative: lists of planets (30:3); the substances from which man was created (30:8); the properties of man (30:9); the poem about man (30:10); and the acrostic explanation for the name Adam (30:13). Such material is also plausibly explained as later additions.

The long version also contains a story of the fall of Satan in its account of the creation of angels on the second day (29:4–6) and refers to a story of his role in the fall of Adam and Eve in the account of the creation of man on the sixth day (31:2–8). Further it includes an eighth day of creation, apparently to designate the first day of the week as worthy of special notice (ch. 33). The interest in the eighth day suggests Christian authorship. As for the material about Satan, Andersen points out in his careful notes that any dualism implicit in assigning such a role to a rebellious angel is subordinated to the strongly monotheistic outlook of the work as a whole. The Satan material thus seems unlikely to be of Bogomil origin. On the other hand, the passages include word play in Slavonic, so that the origin of at least this form of the material about

Satan's role in the fall of Adam and Eve must lie in the period during which 2 Enoch was transmitted in Slavonic.[43]

Finally, it is worth considering the relationship between the account of creation and the natural phenomena Enoch sees during his ascent. The natural phenomena are inherited from the Book of the Watchers, though with some significant developments. The account of creation in its original form is the author's own contribution, and he has not paused to rework inherited material in light of it. The continuity between the two aspects of the treatment of nature lies only in the belief that the created world is an appropriate subject for revelation.

3 Baruch

I have already noted that 3 Baruch stands apart from the other apocalypses considered here in its rejection of the possibility of the visionary's achievement of angelic status. Like other apocalypses attributed to Baruch, 3 Baruch uses the destruction of the First Temple as a way of considering the great event of the author's own time, the destruction of the Second Temple. Thus 3 Baruch can be dated with considerable certainty to some time shortly after 70 C.E. It is usually placed in Egypt. The points of contact with the Apocalypse of Paul discussed later in this chapter support this location.[44] It is preserved not only in Greek, but also in a Slavonic version that lacks some clearly Christian elements. Both versions are considered here.[45] Most scholars treat 3 Baruch as a Jewish work with Christian interpolations; I am inclined to see it as a Christian work, but the question requires careful reconsideration, with due attention to the Slavonic. For my purposes the question is not of great importance.

Since the revelation of 3 Baruch is a response to Baruch's lament about the fate of Israel (ch. 1), it is not surprising that its primary emphasis is reward and punishment. The first sights Baruch sees are the builders of the Tower of Babel, who occupy the first heaven, and the planners of the Tower, who occupy the second (chs. 2–3).[46] In the third heaven[47] Hades appears as the belly of a dragon that devours the wicked (ch. 4).[48] In the fourth heaven choirs of birds, identified in the Greek version as the souls of the righteous, praise God (ch. 10). The fifth heaven marks the entrance to the heavenly temple, and Baruch and his guide are unable to go any farther. As they stand there they see three groups of angels approaching the entrance. One group bears baskets full of flowers, which are the deeds of the righteous, another group carries partially filled baskets, containing the deeds of people of middle character, and a third group, bearing no baskets at all, laments its assignment to the wicked (chs. 12–13).

In 3 Baruch an interest in the phenomena of nature appears even in the descriptions of reward and punishment. In the description of Hades the monster is said to drink so much from the sea that only the 360 rivers that God has created can replenish it.[49] The pool around which the souls of the righteous gather in the fourth heaven is said to be the source for the rain that causes plants to grow on earth.

The Sun and the Phoenix

The most elaborate treatment of cosmological phenomena in 3 Baruch is the description of the sun and moon and their attendants (chs. 6–9), which is linked to questions of reward and punishment.[50] Here the personification of the sun and moon has been carried far beyond anything in the other apocalypses. The description of the two luminaries shows some relation to the description in 2 Enoch.[51] Like the sun and moon of 2 Enoch, the sun and moon of 3 Baruch travel in chariots (6:1–2, 9:3–4). Like the sun in 2 Enoch, the sun in 3 Baruch wears a crown (6:2, 8:3–5). In both works the sun is male, the moon female. But the personification that remains implicit in 2 Enoch becomes explicit in 3 Baruch. The sun in 3 Baruch is actually said to be a man wearing a crown of fire, while the moon is a woman.

The Similitudes of Enoch uses natural phenomena as examples of faithfulness, thus engaging in a mild type of personification. Third Baruch does not use the faithfulness of nature to criticize humanity, but does suggest a relationship between human unfaithfulness and nature: human sin tarnishes the perfection of nature. At the end of each day the sun's crown must be renewed because it has been defiled by the many sins it sees taking place on earth (8:3–5).

In the long version of 2 Enoch phoenixes form part of the sun's entourage. In 3 Baruch the description of the sun is overshadowed by the description of a single enormous phoenix, which flies in front of the sun to protect the earth from the sun's rays (chs. 6–8). The appearance and habits of the phoenix are described in striking detail. On its wings in huge letters appear the words, "Neither earth nor heaven brought me forth, but wings of fire" (6:8; my translation from the Greek).

In response to Baruch's question, his guide tells him that the bird eats the manna of heaven (Greek and Slavonic) and the dew of earth (Greek only) (6:11). In addition, the Greek describes the bird's excrement as a worm that in turn excretes cinnamon, which kings and princes use (6:12). Most of the Slavonic texts affirm only that the bird excretes.[52] (Perhaps the idea of cinammon excrement seemed too peculiar.) Baruch also learns that it is the bird's task to give the cry that wakes the cocks on earth, so that they in turn may awaken the inhabitants of the earth as the sun starts on its course (6:15–16).

Aspects of the description of the phoenix in 3 Baruch are found also in classical accounts, but with quite different functions. The worm appears in some classical sources as the first manifestation of the reborn phoenix after the death of the old, while in versions of the legend in which the phoenix immolates itself cinnamon figures as part of the bird's nest or as an important element of the funeral pyre.[53]

But I am less interested in the origins of the motif than in its function. The phoenix is surely the strangest of the many strange sights in 3 Baruch. What could the author have intended with his description of the bird's wonderful excrement? It is tempting to see it as humor, a satire on the wonderful sights of other texts, but there is nothing beyond the description itself, which sounds so bizarre to a modern reader, to warrant such a reading. Indeed, there are few internal indications of how we are to understand the sights Baruch sees. While the author of the Book of the Watchers conveys his message of the greatness of God's creation through Enoch's response to the sights on his tour to the ends of the earth, Baruch remains impassive through most of the ascent, asking questions about the sights he sees but hardly reacting to them.

Perhaps the single instance of a strong response from Baruch offers a clue to the author's intention. After the guide answers his question about the phoenix's excrement, he tells Baruch to wait and see the glory of God (6:12). A moment later Baruch *hears* God command the sun to shine, but does not see him.[54] At the end of his answer to the next question, about the sun, the guide again tells Baruch to wait and see the glory of God (7:2). While Baruch looks on, the phoenix appears and grows to full size, and angels place the crown on the sun's head. As the sun shines, the phoenix spreads its wings (7:3–4): "And when I saw such glory, I was overcome with great fear, and I fled and hid in the wings of the angel" (7:5; my translation from the Greek).[55]

The phoenix and the sun elicit Baruch's only strong response to a sight. The sun is a glorious figure, with his shining crown and fiery chariot, and the phoenix is a creature of amazing size and exotic, indeed miraculous, habits. Together the two show God's special care for the earth and its inhabitants, for without the accompanying phoenix the very glory of the sun would destroy the earth. From the point of view of a logician God might better have manifested his greatness by creating a well-regulated sun with no need for a phoenix. But for all of us who are not logicians, the multiplication of God's wonderous creations and their ingenious workings is more compelling proof of God's greatness.

The phoenix and the sun, then, are evidence of God's glory, but they evoke fear rather than praise. And the fear is expressed not in the ritual prostration required by heavenly etiquette, but in flight, the response of Daniel's companions to the appearance of the angel Gabriel, but not of Daniel himself (Dan. 10:7). In 3 Baruch, as in the Similitudes, the very works of creation that were once held up as accessible to all have come to be viewed as secrets or "mysteries";[56] thus fear is an appropriate response to them.

The Glory of God

The phoenix and the sun are not the only manifestation of God's glory made available to Baruch. Again, at the entrance to the fifth heaven, the angelic guide tells Baruch to wait and see the glory of God (11:2). The fifth heaven constitutes the entrance to the heavenly temple, and the angel promises Baruch that they will be able to enter after Michael arrives with the keys to the kingdom of heaven. Yet although Michael appears immediately, Baruch and his guide remain outside the gates for the duration of the ascent. Nor is there any indication in the Greek text that Baruch ever sees the promised vision of the glory of God. In the Slavonic text the group of angels assigned to the wicked address Michael as the "Glorious One" (13:4). Thus the angel's promise is at least partially fulfilled in the vision of Michael, the commander-in-chief and high priest of the angels.

After Michael has presented the deeds of humanity to God, addressed the angels who bore them, and given the angels their orders, the Slavonic text contains the guide's last promise of a vision of the glory of God and one further promise, of a vision of the resting place of the righteous—"glory and joy and rejoicing and celebration"—and of the punishment of the wicked (16:4). In a work so concerned with reward and punishment, this would be a fitting conclusion. Yet only the promise of a vision of punishments is actually fulfilled (16:4–8).

While 3 Baruch describes only five heavens, it implies others. Baruch's own ascent ends at the entrance to the heavenly temple in the fifth heaven, but Michael ascends further to confer with God. It is probably too fanciful to suggest that the fifth, sixth, and seventh heavens constitute the three chambers of the heavenly temple, but there is no reason to think that our author does not share the standard view of seven heavens. Origen refers to a book of Baruch that contained seven heavens (*De Principiis*, 2.3.6). Some scholars have argued, although not very persuasively, that the text of 3 Baruch that has come down to us is an abridgment of a work that originally contained seven heavens.[57] Recently, however, Richard Bauckham has made a case for this position on the basis of the obviously abbreviated ending of the Slavonic, an aspect of the work not previously considered in relation to this question.[58] Bauckham argues that 3 Baruch once contained an ascent through all seven heavens followed by a vision of the punishment of the wicked and the reward of the righteous, a schema that appears elsewhere.[59]

Bauckham has persuaded me that Baruch once entered the gates of the fifth heaven and ascended to the seventh heaven. At the gate to the fifth heaven, the angel tells Baruch that they must await the arrival of Michael, who bears the keys, to enter (11:2); in other words, the text suggests that entrance is possible. This reinforces the impression made by the conclusion of the Slavonic that some kind of abridgment has taken place. But I am not convinced by Bauckham's claim that Baruch would have seen God enthroned in the seventh heaven, like Isaiah in the Ascension of Isaiah or Enoch in 2 Enoch. I think Bauckham is mistaken to suggest that the angel's admonishments to Baruch to wait to see the glory of God are parallel to the Ascension of Isaiah's insistence that the glory of the lower heavens cannot be compared to the glory manifest in the seventh heaven.[60] Rather, I believe that 3 Baruch is engaged in a polemic against the understanding of the visionary's ascent in apocalypses like the Ascension of Isaiah.

Consider the relationship between Baruch and his guide. There is here no superiority of the visionary to angels, as in the Enochic tradition or the Ascension of Isaiah; there is not even equality. Baruch calls his guide "lord" throughout the work.[61] We learn in the Greek version of 3 Baruch that after Adam's sin in Eden, he was stripped of the glory of God (4:16). The glory of God was an attribute of humanity before the fall, but no longer. In the Ascension of Isaiah the ability to endure the vision of God, to look upon his glory without blinking, demonstrates the superiority of the righteous dead to the angels. In 3 Baruch the sight of the sun and the phoenix, natural phenomena that manifest the glory of God, is enough to induce terror in the visionary. If Baruch did once arrive in the seventh heaven, I doubt very much that he beheld the glory of God like Isaiah or that God addressed him "with his own mouth" as he addresses Enoch in the Book of the Watchers and 2 Enoch. Rather, in light of 3 Baruch's concern with reward and punishment I would guess that Baruch was able to see God engaged in judgment, an activity that from the point of view of the author of 3 Baruch surely constituted the glory of God.

Of course it is dangerous to argue about the message of a work that is missing so crucial an element as its conclusion. It is not impossible that the missing ascent through the sixth and seventh heavens contained a scene in which Baruch's angelic guide finally rejected the title of "lord" and Baruch underwent a transformation to angelic status. But such a passage would reverse the direction evident in the first five heavens.

Let me adduce a last piece of evidence in favor of my reading of 3 Baruch as standing apart from the other ascent apocalypses. The advantage of this evidence is that it comes from outside the text of 3 Baruch and is thus unaffected by the supposed contents of the lost portion of the ascent. M. R. James early noted a number of points of contact between 3 Baruch and the Apocalypse of Paul, an Egyptian Christian work of the third century that describes the apostle's tour of hell and paradise. These include accounts of the sun's defilement by humanity's sins and of angels bearing humanity's deeds to God.[62] I have already noted the Apocalypse of Paul's reluctance to attribute angelic status to human beings. Although it reworks the Apocalypse of Zephaniah's account of the visionary's passage on a boat across the Acherusian lake, it omits the account of the visionary joining the angelic choir of praise.[63] Since 3 Baruch appears to have influenced the Apocalypse of Paul at other points, the Apocalypse of Paul's subordination of human beings to angels may also reflect 3 Baruch's attitude.

Primeval History

The culmination of the ascent in 2 Enoch is a revelation about the creation of the world. The dominant concern of 3 Baruch, reward and punishment, is brought into relation with a story about the beginning of the world. At least that is how I believe we can make sense of the passage about the vine (ch. 4) that appears to interrupt Baruch's progress through the third heaven.

After Baruch first sees the dragon and Hades, he asks to be shown the tree that caused Adam to sin. The tree turns out to be a vine (4:8–17). This passage has long been suspect as an interpolation because it appears to interrupt the discussion of the dragon, to which Baruch and the angel return after the explanation of the vine. The claim of interpolation has been supported by reference to the clearly Christian elements in the passage.[64]

But even if the passage is an interpolation, why did the interpolator choose to put it where he did? The usual readings of the surrounding material provide no clue. The Greek of the description of the dragon and Hades is confused even without reference to the vine passage, but here the Slavonic can be of great help (4:3). Instead of the two creatures of the Greek, the Slavonic offers a single serpent. According to Baruch's guide, this enormous serpent[65] drinks a cubit of water from the sea each day, like the creatures of the Greek version. As in the Greek, this fact leads the angel to discuss the many rivers that God has created to keep the serpent's thirst from shrinking the sea.

It is at this point in both versions that Baruch inquires about the tree that led Adam astray. The connection between the tree in the Garden of Eden and the monster with Hades as its belly is far from obvious. But if the sight immediately preceding Baruch's question about the tree is a serpent, however oversized, the connection becomes much clearer. It should be remembered that the Garden of Eden plays a part in the tour to the ends of the earth in the Book of the Watchers, not as the future paradise of the righteous but as the primal garden.

The passage about the vine[66] goes on to tell us that after the flood Noah could not decide whether to plant the vine, since it had been the cause of Adam's sin. In response to Noah's prayer, God tells him that he should plant it and assures him that it will be changed in the future (4:9–15).[67] In the Bible, Noah did not undo the curse of the vine. Rather he became its victim when his son Ham uncovered Noah's nakedness as he lay drunk.

Why did the author of 3 Baruch not feel compelled to show us how this incident fits into the salvation history of the vine? Although in his lament at the opening of the work Baruch calls Israel God's vineyard, in this passage no connection is drawn between Israel and the vine. Collins argues that the original intention of the work was absolute condemnation of the vine, in keeping with the several passages where wine is identified as the source of many sins, and that it is only the Christian interpolator who introduces the prospect of the vine's future transformation.[68] Without any specifically Christian language the Slavonic version, too, says that the vine will be transformed. Nickelsburg suggests an original Jewish version of the fate of the vine in which the vine is transformed into the tree of life.[69]

But neither the details of the passage nor the question of Jewish or Christian authorship for this passage or for 3 Baruch as a whole are important for my immediate purposes. What I would like to emphasize is that the contents of the first three heavens of 3 Baruch represent a reuse of the materials of three stories of the primeval cycle from the book of Genesis: the story of the Tower of Babel in the first two heavens, and in the third heaven the fall of Adam and Eve and Noah and the flood.

The primeval cycle is an appropriate biblical text to contemplate for an author deeply concerned with the problem of evil, for all of the stories in the cycle, except the account of creation in Genesis 1, specifically address the question of the origins of evil. The author of 3 Baruch ignores the one story in the primeval history that squarely locates blame in the realm of the divine, the story of the descent of the sons of God in Gen. 6:1–4. This story, of course, forms the basis for the Enochic corpus and achieved wide influence through the Book of the Watchers. About this situation Bauckham writes, "The author [of 3 Baruch] is perhaps engaged in a polemical rejection of the Enoch traditions. . . ."[70] I agree that there is a polemic against the Enochic corpus here, and I would add that the polemic can be detected in other aspects of the work as well.[71]

Recently scholars have suggested that 3 Baruch is to be understood as a fundamentally unapocalyptic apocalypse. It insists that the destruction of the temple does not much matter for Israel or the world generally, for the heavenly temple continues to function, and God will punish the wicked and reward the righteous.[72] Like the biblical stories it uses, 3 Baruch blames humanity for the state of the world. Also like those stories, however, it is by no means pessimistic about the possibility of human righteousness. There is no indication that the righteous whose merits are brought in baskets to heaven are fewer than the wicked who cause such pain to the angels assigned to them.[73] Thus while 3 Baruch shares the Similitudes' view of the wonders of the created world as secrets or mysteries, it does not share the Similitudes' sectarian evaluation of the dominance of evil among human beings.

Conclusions

Early wisdom literature insisted that the created world spoke clearly of its creator, but the centuries after the destruction of the First Temple saw some thinkers retreating from this optimism. While the prophet of 2 Isaiah uses nature to affirm a God whose hand is no longer evident in history, the author of Job describes the wonders of nature but insists that their creator remains hidden. Centuries later the Book of the Watchers charts a middle course. Nature does indeed testify to the greatness of God, but only Enoch of all human beings sees its wonders. Still, Enoch's report allows the rest of humanity to see vicariously.

The understanding of the meaning of natural phenomena develops in different directions in later apocalypses that rework material from the Book of the Watchers. In keeping with its pessimism about life in this world, the Similitudes of Enoch treats natural phenomena as secrets available to the righteous at the eschaton rather than as evidence of the creator available to all. Despite its happier view of life in this world, 3 Baruch is even more cautious about the revelation of secrets of the cosmos. The heavenly mysteries are so awesome that even the righteous Baruch is terrified when they are revealed to him.

Second Enoch displays an entirely different attitude. Although the schema of the Book of the Watchers has here been rearranged to place nature in the heavens, nature is no more secret than it was in the tour to the ends of the earth. The major innovation of 2 Enoch is the revelation about creation that stands as the culmination of Enoch's ascent. This revelation offers a prologue to the biblical account of creation apparently intended to make it more convincing to readers whose ideas were formed by popular Hellenistic philosophy.

Despite the importance of nature for the Book of the Watchers and the three other apocalypses considered here, nature falls out of favor as a subject of revelation in the apocalypses and the texts descended from them. Rather, it is the other sights that 3 Baruch designates as revealing the glory of God—the archangel Michael, the rewards of the righteous and wicked—that contain the themes developed in later works, the former in the hekhalot texts, the latter in the tours of hell so popular among medieval Christians.

5

The Apocalypses as Writing

And I, Enoch, alone saw the visions, all things that exist: and no one of men shall see as I saw.

(1 Enoch 19:3)

I have by now explored the central themes of the ascent apocalypses: the understanding of heaven as temple, the visionary's achievement of angelic status in a process that echoes priestly investiture, and the phenomena of nature as a source of knowledge of God. This final chapter considers some basic but difficult questions: What kind of literature are these apocalypses? What kind of people wrote them, and for what purposes?

Any attempt to answer these questions inevitably runs up against the pseudepigraphy of the apocalypses. Pseudepigraphy was a widespread phenomenon in the ancient world, by no means restricted to Jews and Christians. With different functions depending on genre, it assumes a distinctive shape in the apocalypses because of their claim to represent divine revelation.[1] The epigraph, from Enoch's journey to the ends of the earth in the Book of the Watchers, poses the problem clearly and sharply. The author claims Enoch's authority for his account of sights that none of his readers has ever seen.

How are we to understand that claim? Some significant recent scholarship has claimed that, despite their pseudepigraphy, many apocalypses reflect the visionary experience of their authors.[2] This point of view stands in dramatic contrast to the older style of study of the apocalypses, represented by the grandfather of contemporary study, R. H. Charles.

Charles understood the pseudepigraphic attributions of the apocalypses as conscious deception, intended to confer authority on the views of the works to which they were attached in an age when the possibility of new revelation had been rejected by a Judaism dominated by the Law. Thus those who might once have offered visions in their own names as prophets could no longer do so. The only way to give authority to visions in the period after the return from Babylonia was for the visionary to hide his identity under the mantle of an ancient hero. For Charles, there-fore, the dominance of the Torah is stultifying, and the true heir of apocalyptic literature is not Judaism, but Christianity. Indeed, while Charles does not confront directly the morality of the deception of pseudepigraphy as he understands it, he seems to find it forgivable in light of the impossibility of other expressions of revelation for Jews of the Second Temple period.[3]

Charles's picture of the demise of prophecy during this period is of course contradicted by Josephus, who makes it clear that if the Second Temple sees the end of classical prophecy, it also sees the emergence of new kinds of prophecy. Josephus reserves the term *prophētēs* for the bib-lical prophets.[4] Many of the prophets he describes as active toward the end of the Second Temple were primarily wonder workers who patterned themselves on Moses and Elijah, sometimes acquiring large popular fol-lowings. In contrast to most of the classical prophets, they appear to come from among the poor and uneducated. Certainly their followers were drawn from the lower classes. Their claim to be prophets resides in their miracles, not in words of prophecy.[5]

Josephus also notes prophets who do not work wonders but preach impending doom, although, at least as Josephus reports them, their oracles are much shorter and less elaborate than those of the classical prophets.[6] He mentions brief predictions made by several Essenes and one Pharisee.[7] For Josephus prophecy as prediction is closely associated with the office of the priest, and with his pride in his priestly heredity, he seems to have believed that he had been entrusted with such a role.[8]

Josephus, then, demonstrates that prophecy had by no means dis-appeared during the later Second Temple period, but that the prophecy that persisted was very different from that of even the latest of the clas-sical prophets. Prophecy was no longer a mode of expression of the educated.

But perhaps more important in provoking the reaction of contem-porary scholarship than the theologically charged historiography that gave rise to Charles's understanding of pseudepigraphy is the propensity of Charles and his contemporaries for dividing works up into sources and for detecting interpolations at every turn. This approach effectively turns the apocalypses into storehouses of motifs, traditions, and ideas, while denying them a basis in religious experience. Charles was extremely sym-pathetic to the ideas he found in apocalyptic literature, but he and his contemporaries are rightly accused of insensitivity to their larger struc-ture and meaning.[9]

In an attempt to do justice to the apocalypses as literary wholes, recent scholarship has moved away from this atomizing approach. In taking authorial, or at least editorial, intent more seriously, it has attempted to arrive at an understanding of pseudepigraphy that sees it as an organic part of the author's activity rather than as a convention or, worse, deception. The following survey of recent scholarly discussion is meant to be exemplary rather than exhaustive.

In D. S. Russell's introduction to apocalyptic literature published in 1964, he argues that the visionary actually identified himself with the figure to whom he attributed his work because of the ancient Jewish sense of "corporate personality." Thus the visions can be genuine despite the pseudepigraphy. But this explanation could no longer be convincing after the notion of a peculiar "Hebrew psychology" had been discredited.[10]

More recently Christopher Rowland has suggested that many passages in the apocalypses are based on the author's ecstatic experiences as he contemplates particular scriptural passages, as, for example, in Daniel 9.[11] This approach emphasizes the importance of traditional material in apocalyptic visions while rejecting the view that their presence means that the visions are not genuine. The apocalypses are thus saved as documents of religious experience.[12] Rowland relates the practice of pseudepigraphy to the ecstatic experience of seeing oneself as if from outside, although he admits that he cannot explain why viewing the self as other should lead to attribution to a great hero of the past.[13]

David G. Meade puts the sense of continuity with the message of the ancient hero, although not with his personality, at the center of his understanding of the pseudepigraphy of the Jewish apocalypses, which he views as "*a claim to authoritative tradition, not a statement of literary origins.*"[14] Like Rowland, Meade emphasizes the role of interpretation in the apocalypses; their authors could write in the name of the pseudepigraphic hero because they understood their own work as inspired interpretation, an "actualization" of the message of the ancient hero. But despite the theological importance to Meade of his claim that the apocalyptic authors understood their interpretation as inspired, he does not address the question whether inspired interpretation necessarily involves visionary experience.[15]

Michael Stone has for some time argued for taking seriously the possibility of actual visionary experience behind the apocalypses. He suggests that the ascetic practices described in some of the apocalypses reflect the practices of actual visionaries, while the physical reactions of the heroes of the apocalypses to the awesome sights revealed to them reflect the reactions of the authors of the apocalypses to the visions they experienced.[16] Stone also sees the pseudepigraphy of the apocalypses as organically related to their content; in composing their works the authors drew on a body of lore associated with a particular ancient hero.[17] The frequency of the revelation of cosmic secrets to Enoch, for example, reflects the prominence of such secrets in the traditions about Enoch. With due caution, he suggests that in the course of their own visions the authors of the apocalypses may have felt a sense of relationship to the figure to whom they attributed the work.[18] Thus Stone shares Meade's understanding of pseudepigraphy as reflecting the sense of a continuing tradition, but Stone's psychological explanation for an author's identification with a pseudepigraphic hero puts greater emphasis on visionary experience.

Stone's new commentary to 4 Ezra is the most thorough and compelling attempt so far to read an individual apocalypse as reflecting the experience of its author. Ezra's movement from insistent questioning of God to acceptance of the comfort of eschatology that he had at first rejected is to be understood as reflecting the author's own journey from troubled doubts to peaceful trust and certainty. Stone even suggests that the author actually functioned in the role of prophet that the narrative attributes to Ezra, and that this was a public role, ratified by the author's community.[19]

These attempts to make sense of pseudepigraphy are extremely attractive. But despite their appeal, I shall argue that the apocalypses are literary documents in which the depiction of the hero's experience needs to be understood as an act of imagination, with its specifics determined by the author's manipulation of conventions, rather than as a literary representation of the author's own experiences.

Pseudepigraphy and Its Audiences

As my brief survey suggests, attempts to understand pseudepigraphy from the author's side almost inevitably become psychology. But it is an extremely problematic type of psychology. As is often true when psychology is applied to figures from the past, we have no access to the author's mind apart from the work that causes our puzzlement. More problematic still is that the flourishing of pseudepigraphy in a particular genre of literature at a particular time in history strongly suggests that it is less a psychological than a social phenomenon, dependent on the audience's understanding of how to interpret pseudepigraphy's claims.

Ancient readers who cite pseudepigraphic works with approval appear to accept their attributions. When the author of the New Testament letter of Jude quotes from the Book of the Watchers, he writes, "Enoch, the seventh from Adam, prophesied about these thus . . ." (14). Baraies, who valued the apocalypses he quotes, seems to understand them as autobiography.

As the canon of the Old Testament came to be defined by the Greek Church through the first four centuries, works like the apocalypses, which were part neither of the Hebrew Bible of the Jews nor even of the Greek translation that Christians had inherited from them, were gradually set aside as unsuitable, though without any general attack on their content or attributions. This situation stands in contrast to the debate about pseudepigrapha attributed to early Christian figures, in which questions about the authenticity of the attributions figured prominently. In some eastern churches some of the pseudepigrapha attributed to heroes of the Hebrew Bible achieved canonical status; in the Latin Church 4 Ezra became part of the canon. Meanwhile, in monasteries west and east, Old Testament pseudepigrapha continued to be copied into the Middle Ages and beyond. Just how these texts were understood and how their transmission could be squared with the existence of a well-defined canon, is a subject worthy of attention.[20]

But as Collins has suggested for Daniel, it may be appropriate to distinguish between different circles of the audience. An inner audience, the author's fellow *maśkilim* in the case of Daniel, may have understood the pseudepigraphic attribution as conventional, while the larger audience accepted it literally.[21] Knowledge of authorship not recorded in the work itself must have been lost during transmission. Jude wrote centuries after the Book of the Watchers, and the apocalypses Baraies quotes were no doubt written long before his time.

Morton Smith has pointed out that the Book of Deuteronomy has some claim to be considered the first Jewish pseudepigraphon.[22] When its authors wished to introduce their new work, they presented it as a long-forgotten ancient text recently rediscovered in the temple (2 Kings 22:8–20). The Apocalypse of Paul, probably composed in the third century, contains a preface (chs. 1–2) describing its discovery in the late fourth century in a box in the foundation of a house in Tarsus that had once belonged to the apostle himself. Here the account of the finding was added at some point in the text's career. In the works considered here there are no such attempts to provide a plausible explanation for the work's sudden reappearance. This suggests that our authors were not concerned to provide circumstantial support for the identification with pseudepigraphic heroes.

Pseudepigraphy and Writing

In the end, however, the attempt to understand pseudepigraphy in social terms comes up against the lack of evidence for the reception of the claims of pseudepigraphic works. Most of what we can learn about pseudepigraphy will have to be extracted from the texts themselves. To this end it is useful to examine a more accessible aspect of the texts, which may tell us something about the authors' self-understanding. That is the way in which the texts were composed, or how the authors of the apocalypses operated as authors.

The authors of the apocalypses often drew on oral tradition, and they may have meant their works to be read aloud. But the adaptation of earlier traditions (often written), the pervasive allusions to the Bible and to other apocalyptic works, and the centrality of interpretation are possible only in writing. The prominence of scribes as heroes surely indicates authorial self-consciousness on this point.

By the time of Zechariah in the late sixth century, prophecy had begun to take on some of the qualities of interpretation, and the inter-penetration of prophecy and interpretation is plainly visible at Qumran, where the eschatological interpretation of the pesharim explicitly claims inspiration.[23] Daniel 9 is a visionary interpretation of Jeremiah's prophecy of the seventy years of exile,[24] while Ezra's visions of the eagle (4 Ezra 11–12) and the man from the sea (4 Ezra 13) are elaborations of Daniel 7. The throne visions of the apocalypses, which are not strictly exegetical, are nevertheless deeply informed by interpretation of a series of biblical passages in light of each other, as Christopher Rowland and David Halperin have argued in different ways.[25]

Beyond these examples of biblical interpretation, the apocalypses are permeated by allusions to the Bible. As Lars Hartmann's study of 1 Enoch 1–5 has shown, these allusions set the apocalypse's explicit statements in a larger context of biblical themes.[26] This style of writing requires con-siderable learning, and it was used in the composition of apocalypses well into the Middle Ages. The Book of Zerubbabel, an early medieval Hebrew apocalypse, is a striking example, with its eschatological schema constructed from a pastiche of elements drawn from the Bible, especially Ezekiel, Zechariah, and Daniel.[27] Unlike the earlier ones, medieval Hebrew apocalypses include many verbatim quotations in addition to biblical allusions and echoes.

Not all early Jewish and Christian apocalypses exhibit the allusive style, and in some portions of individual apocalypses it is far more promi-nent than in others. Speeches in prophetic style such as the opening of 1 Enoch discussed by Hartmann or the woes and exhortations of the Epistle of Enoch, are more amenable to this style than are narratives. These often take as their point of departure biblical events (e.g., the fall of the Watchers in 1 Enoch 6–11, which explicitly refers to Gen. 6:1–4), or use imagery drawn from biblical sources (e.g., Enoch's journey to the ends of the earth in 1 Enoch 17–36, with its deep debt to the Book of Ezekiel), but by its nature narrative is less capable of the appropriation of biblical language. In some of the apocalypses the allusions are less to canonical works than to other apocalypses. This is particularly true in the Similitudes of Enoch and the ascent of 2 Enoch, which rework aspects of the Book of the Watchers, the Similitudes of Enoch, and the ascent of 2 Enoch.

The learned character of the apocalypses[28] considered here becomes evident when they are contrasted to an early Christian apocalypse, the Shepherd of Hermas. Its visions share the main structural features of the visions of Daniel, 4 Ezra, and 2 Baruch, but it lacks both their pseudepigraphy and their web of allusion. The Shepherd of Hermas quotes once from a lost "Book of Eldad and Modat" (Vision 2.3.4), and there are some possible allusions to the Hebrew Bible and New Testa-ment, but on the whole it does not draw from or imitate the Bible.

Although it contains some traditional elements, such as the female figure who is the heavenly Church, the imagery is not taken from earlier prophetic and apocalyptic visions.

The "writtenness" of the apocalypses breaks with classical prophecy. The classical prophets spoke their oracles. Writing them down and editing them were usually the work of others. Yet just as Zechariah provides us with an early example of prophecy as interpretation, so other prophetic books show us the beginning of the move to writing.

Writing is already important in Jeremiah, not so much in the oracles as in the stories about the prophet, which appear to come not from him, but perhaps from a contemporary.[29] These stories tell us that Jeremiah left the work of writing to his companion Baruch, but it is a measure of the importance of writing to Jeremiah's enterprise that this is the only place in prophetic literature where we hear of the scribe who works with the prophet.

Baruch steps out of the prophet's shadow when Jeremiah, in hiding, dictates a scroll to him. Baruch takes the scroll and goes to the temple to rebuke the Judeans assembled there. Writing allows the scribe to play the role of the prophet. In response to Baruch's reading of Jeremiah's words, the people proclaim a fast (Jer. 36:1–10).

After Baruch reads the scroll to a group of pious officials, they are so moved by its message that they make the risky decision to bring the scroll before the king themselves, first urging Baruch to join Jeremiah in hiding (36:11–20). But with neither prophet nor scribe present, the scroll fails to impress the king. As it is read to him, Jehoiakim cuts it in bits and tosses it into the fire that warms his winter quarters. At the conclusion of the reading he orders the arrest of Jeremiah and Baruch (36:21–26). But God hides Jeremiah and Baruch from the angry king and orders Baruch to rewrite the scroll. The medium of writing appears to triumph in the second scroll, which repeats the message of rebuke of the first and adds to it (36:27–32).

Ellen Davis has argued that in Ezekiel we encounter the prophet as author. In the work of this younger contemporary of Jeremiah no scribe intervenes between the prophet and the written word. Although Ezekiel probably intended his work to be read aloud, as the book itself testifies that some of it was, its "architectonic" structure and elaborate allusions are best explained on the assumption that Ezekiel composed his prophecy in writing.[30]

It is surely the use of writing that accounts for the prominence of narratives about the prophets in Jeremiah and Ezekiel. More than in the books of any of their predecessors, with the possible exception of Hosea, incidents from the lives of Jeremiah and Ezekiel figure in the books that bear their names. But Ezekiel functions as a character in a way distinctively different from Jeremiah. Most of the stories about Jeremiah are told in the third person, and, with the exception of the divine voice that makes him a prophet, nothing supernatural befalls him. Ezekiel, on the other hand, describes in the first person not only the wonderful visions he was shown, but also how he was transported by the hand of God from Babylonia to the land of Israel to see them. Visions play a far more prominent role in Ezekiel than in the other prophets, and this allows oracles to take on the form of first-person narrative. In the chariot vision (ch. 1) and the two temple visions, the vision of God's departure (chs. 8–11) and the vision of his return (chs. 40–48), Ezekiel serves as a character in the narrative. As we have seen, the form of Ezekiel's concluding vision was an important model for the Book of the Watchers and for the form of heavenly ascent in the apocalypses generally. Perhaps the role of Ezekiel as a character in his own work was a factor in the emergence of the apocalypses' depiction of revelation by means of narrative.

But there is a crucial difference between Jeremiah and Ezekiel as characters in the books that bear their names and Enoch, Baruch, and the others in the apocalypses. The narratives of the prophetic books are not pseudepigraphic. Even if the stories about Jeremiah were written by his followers, they surely bear a considerable relationship to the life of the prophet. In the case of Ezekiel, where the stories are more fantastic, even the most scissors-wielding of source critics assign some to Ezekiel himself, and the rest (e.g., chs. 40–48, in some views) can be seen as modeled on material going back to the prophet. But for an example of pseudepigraphic narrative and revelation, we have only to turn to Deuteronomy, which made its appearance at the beginning of the half-century that saw the activity of Jeremiah and Ezekiel as well. Deuteronomy presents its laws as God's revelation, reported by Moses in a first-person reminiscence of his career.[31] As in the apocalypses, the narrative draws on earlier traditions reshaped for the authors' purposes. Of course, the authors of the Book of the Watchers could not have modeled their pseudepigraphy on Deuteronomy, because they surely accepted the attribution to Moses. I do not know why writing emerged as a vehicle for prophecy and revelation in the decades preceding the destruction of the First Temple; the subject would surely reward further investigation. But the crucial point for my argument, I believe, is that the use of writing for these purposes provides the necessary conditions for the pseudepigraphy of the apocalypses.

Revelation and Narrative

Students of the apocalypses are often impatient to strip away the narrative "frame" to get to the revelatory core. In my view this practice is wrong, but it is at least feasible for the Ascension of Isaiah, the Apocalypse of Abraham, 2 Enoch, Daniel, 4 Ezra, or 2 Baruch. It is not feasible for the Book of the Watchers. Here I would like to consider the role of narrative in the Book of the Watchers and the ascent apocalypses generally.

The Book of the Watchers is clearly the result of a complex process of development, involving the use of oral traditions and written sources. The first author of the Book of the Watchers took the narrative of chapters 6–11, not his own composition, and added to it the story of Enoch's intercession for the Watchers, chapters 12–16, and Enoch's first journey on earth in the company of angels, chapters 17–19. A second author provided the prophecy of the eschaton that serves as an introduction to the book as a whole, chapters 1–5, and a second journey, chapters 20–36, which I understand as an expansion of chapters 17–19, intended to spell out some of the themes of the first journey and to establish its relationship to the sacred geography of the Bible.[32]

It is worth pausing for a moment to reflect on the manner in which our authors composed their work. The first author adapted a narrative of the fall of the Watchers and appended to it an account of Enoch's dealings with the Watchers. This account draws on earlier traditions, but our author shaped it to suggest that the sins of the Watchers were like the sins of the priests of his own time, thus offering a new perspective on the events of chapters 6–11. He drew extensively on biblical language and imagery, especially in his description of Enoch's heavenly ascent.

The second author tried to make more explicit some of the themes of the first stage of composition and to anchor them more firmly in the biblical tradition, so he added an introduction that depicts Enoch as a prophet. His expansion of the journey to the ends of the earth draws on themes found in Ezekiel to offer a version of the wonders of the earth more informed by biblical tradition. Enoch's frequent exclamations of praise make explicit the function of the journey.

The message of the Book of the Watchers is to be found not in snippets of divine revelation, but in the narrative itself. The heavenly ascent in chapter 14 is sometimes read as a record of the author's own visionary experience, but the culmination of Enoch's ascent is God's condemnation of the rebellious Watchers. This revelation is meaningless without the narrative context. The predictions of eschatological judgment in the course of the book are very brief and extremely general, hardly enough to justify such elaborate narrative scaffolding.

The authors of the Book of the Watchers saw the story of the Watchers and Enoch's career as deeply significant for their own times, and they told the story in such a way as to make the connections if not obvious then accessible to an appropriate audience. The parallels between Watchers and sinful priests emerge through the narrative, not through any divine revelation. So too the relation between human beings and the divine embodied in Enoch's fellowship with the angels emerges not through divine pronouncement but through the story of Enoch's ascent and travels.

I am inclined to think that to ask about the authors' identification with Enoch is to miss the point. In any case it is clear that if the authors did somehow identify with Enoch, this identification had no discernible

effect on how they wrote. There is no denying the conscious, artful use
of earlier material in the service of their understanding of the meaning
of Enoch's career.[33]

The Book of the Watchers is earlier than the other apocalypses considered here. In it narrative occupies a larger portion of the work than
in any of the later apocalypses; they contain a larger proportion of material
that has sometimes been interpreted as a more or less direct transcrip-
tion of what the authors saw in visions or experienced in ascents. But
even in the later apocalypses, extracting the visions from the narrative
cannot be justified. The narratives of the apocalypses and thus their
pseudepigraphy affect their message in a significant way. In the Ascension of Isaiah, for example, the attribution to Isaiah, perhaps the most
important prophet of Christ from the point of view of early Christians,
certifies the Christology of the vision as authentic, while the setting may
reflect the struggles of the prophetic school that held that Christology.
In the Apocalypse of Abraham the author's understanding of the causes
of the destruction of the temple is conveyed not only through the explicit,
although opaque, account in the vision of history, but also through the
story of Abraham's rejection of idolatry. On the other hand, the ascent
apocalypses in which narrative is least important, works like the Similitudes of Enoch and 2 Enoch, are reworkings of earlier Enoch materials,
in which the narrative played a determinative role. The narrative identification with the pseudepigraphic hero, then, is more than a device to
lend authority to the apocalypse; it is an integral part of its message.

Apocalyptic Communities

Since I have just emphasized that the narratives of the apocalypses are
crucial for understanding them, this is an appropriate moment to ask
whether these narratives can reveal anything about the authors and their
communities. In the narrative of Isaiah's martyrdom that precedes the
ascent in the Ascension of Isaiah, Isaiah is depicted as the head of a group
of prophets leading an ascetic life in the wilderness. Although this description appears in the Martyrdom of Isaiah—originally a separate source
from the Vision of Isaiah, in which the ascent appears—the final author
or redactor of the Ascension brings the followers into the ascent by
describing Isaiah seated among them as he undertakes his ascent (6:7).[34]
A number of scholars have seen the practices of Isaiah and his followers
described in the Martyrdom as reflecting the practices of an actual apocalyptic circle.[35] In their way of life they resemble John the Baptist and
his followers as described by Josephus and the Gospels, or, to a lesser
extent, the community at Qumran.

In the most influential modern theory the apocalypses are seen as
the product of "conventicles," small groups of the pious living in fear of
persecution as they awaited the imminent end. The Ascension of Isaiah
is the only ascent apocalypse to hint at such a conventicle, but several of

the apocalypses without ascents allude to companions or followers of the visionary in less detail than the Ascension of Isaiah. Daniel's companions figure in the court tales that make up the first, nonapocalyptic portion of that book. In the apocalyptic section companions are not mentioned until the last vision (chs. 10–12), where they appear only to tremble and flee although they have not actually seen the awesome angel who manifests himself to Daniel (10:7). In both 4 Ezra and 2 Baruch the heroes are provided with a group of followers (4 Ez. 5:16, 12:40–50, ch. 14; 2 Bar. 5:5–7, chs. 31–34, 44–47, 77).

Stone points out that in 4 Ezra, 2 Baruch, and the Ascension of Isaiah the followers appear to consist of inner and outer circles and a larger group of ordinary followers. He compares this picture to the accounts of Jesus' followers in the Gospels and to the circle of merkavah mystics in R. Neḥunyah's descent to the merkavah in Hekhalot Rabbati. The occurrence of this picture in unrelated sources must mean that it cannot have been invented independently by the various authors. Rather, Stone believes, it reflects the actuality of the situation of the apocalyptic visionary.[36]

In all the apocalypses with companions, the visionary engages in fasting and other ascetic practices. The Ascension of Isaiah, as we have seen, describes the prophet and his followers living in the wilderness, dressed in sackcloth, eating wild herbs, and lamenting Israel's sinfulness (2:9–11). Before Daniel's last two visions, he fasts and mourns (9:3, 10:2–3); the companions in the last vision are not described as participating in his ascetic practices. Both 4 Ezra and 2 Baruch describe their heroes fasting, weeping, and mourning before visions (4 Ez. 3:1–3, 5:20, 6:35, 9:26, 12:51; 2 Bar. 5:7, 9:2, 21:1, 35:1).

Yet plausible as may be the idea of apocalyptic literature emerging from small groups of ascetics, the presence or absence of such groups in the apocalypses is usually determined by literary considerations. We can learn little about the author's own situation from the way he depicted the life of his hero. For example, it is striking that in the Enoch apocalypses Enoch appears alone or accompanied only by family. In the Astronomical Book, the Book of the Watchers, and the Similitudes, Enoch's only companions are angels. In the first vision of the Book of Dreams, Enoch's grandfather Mehalalel wakes him from his terrifying dream and interprets it for him. There is no sign of a group of any kind. In the Epistle of Enoch, Enoch addresses his admonitions to his assembled relations (91:1–2). The concluding chapters of 1 Enoch, immediately following the Epistle, describe the birth of Enoch's great-grandson Noah. In 2 Enoch, after the ascent, Enoch exhorts first his children (13:1) and then the elders of the people (14:4–5). The concluding chapters of 2 Enoch tell the story of the birth of Melchizedek, again suggesting concern for the line of descent from Enoch. These Enoch apocalypses, with and without ascents, give a far less prominent place to ascetic practices than the "conventicle" apocalypses.

The absence of followers and ascetic practices, on the one hand, and the presence of family, on the other, may be different aspects of the understanding of Enoch as priest. The priest does not need a group of followers to validate his role or his work, and since contact with God is a priest's daily business, he does not need any special preparation in the form of ascetic practices. But the continuity of the priestly line in purity is of great importance.

The role of the figure of Enoch in determining the setting of the apocalypses attributed to him must raise some doubts whether the apocalypses that appear to hint at conventicles actually reflect such groups. It is clear that at least in literary terms the Enochic literature represents an ongoing tradition, and this may well imply a group with loyalty to the figure of Enoch.[37] If so, it is all the more striking that no such group appears in the apocalypses attributed to Enoch.

If for the Enoch apocalypses the narrative setting is determined by literary considerations, may not the small groups of some of the other apocalypses be equally conventional? Because of the important role of the *maskilim*, the enlightened ones who "lead the many to righteousness" (12:3) in Daniel, the author's allegiance to such a group seems especially likely. Nonetheless, the companions play a rather small role in the apocalyptic section of Daniel, and when they do appear they serve the clear literary purpose of emphasizing the awesomeness of the revelation to Daniel and his greatness in being able to receive it. Daniel was a powerful influence on 4 Ezra and 2 Baruch, which may be related to each other. In other words, the descriptions of the visionary's circle are not simply a reflection of the authors' own way of life. Conventions may grow out of reality—such groups are attested in the ancient Mediterranean—but they rapidly take on a life of their own.

Or consider the Apocalypse of Abraham, where ascetic practices play a role, although the visionary has no human companions. God commands Abraham to undertake a limited fast for forty days before sacrificing and receiving a revelation in clear immitation of Moses at Sinai (9:7–8), but Abraham goes beyond God's command. He spends forty days in the wilderness in the company of the angel Iaoel, neither eating nor drinking (12:1–2). The author's failure to provide Abraham with companions must be due to the requirements of his story, which emphasizes Abraham's uniqueness in rejecting idolatry and recognizing God.

Inducing Ascent in Ancient Judaism

The picture of the apocalypses as coming from small pious groups engaged in ascetic practices related to their visions is very appealing to those who wish to understand the apocalypses as reflecting the visionary experience of their authors. I have already suggested that the evidence for the existence of the groups is thin. The evidence for practices designed to produce ascent is even thinner.[38]

Ascetic practices such as fasting appear in only two of the ascent apocalypses, the Ascension of Isaiah and the Apocalypse of Abraham, and only in the Apocalypse of Abraham is the asceticism represented as preparation for the ascent. In several of the ascent apocalypses the hero is weeping or mourning as the angelic guide appears to summon him to ascend. Moshe Idel has shown that in medieval Jewish sources weeping was a technique for inducing mystical experience. In keeping with his view that much of medieval Jewish mysticism has roots in earlier Judaism, he claims 4 Ezra, 2 Baruch, and 2 Enoch as the earliest examples of the practice.[39] Idel might have added 3 Baruch and the Testament of Levi. In 2 Enoch the angels who lead Enoch to heaven find him weeping in bed (1:2) for reasons that are never specified. In 3 Baruch the angel appears to Baruch as he weeps and mourns the destruction of Jerusalem (1:1–3). In the Testament of Levi, Levi is grieving, though not weeping, about the sinfulness of humanity before his ascent (2:3–4). A similar scene appears in the fragment of an Enoch apocalypse preserved in the Mani Codex, where Enoch is weeping over the words of the impious when seven angels appear to him (58–59). The Ascension of Isaiah describes lamentation as part of the ascetic regimen of the prophets who retreat to the wilderness with Isaiah (2:10), but not in relation to the ascent. Daniel mourns before his final vision (10:2), while Enoch weeps *after* the second vision in the Book of Dreams (1 Enoch 90:41).

Thus the association of weeping or at least mourning with visionary experience and ascent is even more widespread in the apocalypses than Idel notes. But is weeping actually a technique in these texts? In some of Idel's medieval examples, weeping is recommended as a way to achieve revelation.[40] The closest the apocalypses come to this is the angel's command to Ezra to "pray again, and weep as you do now, and fast for seven days" (4 Ez. 5:13); elsewhere when Ezra weeps, it is not at the angel's command (6:31, 35; 9:24–25, 27). It is an unwarranted leap to assume that for the ancient apocalypses weeping is a technique as in the medieval texts. Rather, weeping and mourning in the apocalypses demonstrate the piety of the visionary, who feels deeply the sinfulness of humanity or the travails of his people. The cause of weeping and mourning is the crisis that vision or ascent is intended to resolve. The pyschological appropriateness of this association may account for the later development of a *technique* of weeping.[41]

It is often assumed that practices to achieve ascent were widely current among Jews and others in the Greco-Roman world, and that ascent was an important concern of magic. Morton Smith in particular has claimed that "one or more techniques for ascent into heaven were being used in Palestine in Jesus' day. . . ."[42] To support this claim Smith adduces the Dead Sea Scrolls, with their belief that angels are present with the sect, and the epistles of Paul, although he concedes that there are no references in either body of texts to techniques for ascent. But this should not surprise us, Smith argues. After all, such techniques were surely esoteric and thus unlikely to have been reported; the Mithras Liturgy and the hekhalot texts can help us to guess what those techniques were like.[43]

Now it is true that the Mithras Liturgy, a lengthy spell that forms part of the Paris Magical Papyrus, provides an elaborate ritual for ascent. The Chaldean Oracles also appear to have offered a technique for achieving immortality by means of ascent. But contrary to a claim made frequently in scholarly literature,[44] the magical papyri are not full of such techniques; the Mithras Liturgy, which differs from most of the texts of the magical papyri in so many ways, is the only spell for ascent to be found among them. The practitioners of magic must have thought there were better ways than ascent to attain their goals.

Nor are the hekhalot texts, as they have been read in recent scholarship, a clear source for techniques of ascent. The suggestion of continuity between the apocalyptists and the merkavah mystics goes back to Gershom Scholem, who pointed to the similarities between the visions of the merkavah in some of the apocalypses and those of rabbinic literature and the hekhalot texts.[45] This comparison is extremely appealing because the circles of merkavah mystics seem to provide a relatively well documented example of practices only hinted at in the ascent apocalypses. Although Scholem never developed his position on the apocalypses in any detail, he seems to have believed that the visions of the apocalypses drew on the visionary experiences of their authors.

For Scholem the central concern of the hekhalot texts is the practice of heavenly ascent. The famous account in Hekhalot Rabbati of the descent to the merkavah (as ascent is called in some of the hekhalot literature)[46] of R. Neḥunyah b. haQanah is understood as a description of how such ecstatic ascent was undertaken by ancient mystics. R. Neḥunyah b. haQanah, apparently in a trance, describes his ascent to colleagues assembled around him. As he speaks, scribes write down his words (*Synopse*, #228). This picture raises the immensely appealing possibility that the accounts of ascent in the hekhalot texts are just such records of the words of a mystic during ascent, the minutes of the meeting of a cell of merkavah mystics.

But this picture is problematic. First, the account of R. Neḥunyah's ascent is the only such account in the hekhalot literature. The other mentions of heavenly ascent leave the impression that the visionary undertakes the ascent without anyone present on earth to await his return, although they do not say so explicitly. Further, the part of the account that mentions the scribes, the recall of R. Neḥunyah from before the divine throne, turns out to be a later addition; it does not appear in a geniza fragment of Hekhalot Rabbati.[47] It becomes hard to maintain the view that the account is firsthand, even if pseudepigraphic.

Scholem read the hekhalot texts as reflecting visionary experience. Although Scholem distinguished between those earlier texts that represented ecstatic mysticism, marked by magical elements required to effect the ascent, and later texts that were merely literary,[48] it was essential for his view of the place of the hekhalot texts in the history of Jewish mysticism that at least some of them represent actual mystical practice, and thus he ignored such problematic features as their pseudepigraphy. Ithamar Gruenwald accepts the underpinnings of Scholem's position in his extensive and very useful study of the relations between the apocalypses and merkavah mysticism.[49]

Until recently this understanding was widely accepted.[50] But in the past fifteen years Halperin and Schäfer have argued that the heavenly ascents of the hekhalot literature should be understood not as rites to be enacted but as stories to be repeated. They point out that the mystic who studies the hekhalot literature is commanded to repeat particular passages. By doing so he will achieve the results that R. Ishmael, R. 'Aqiba, and R. Neḥunyah b. haQanah, achieved by actual ascent.[51] In Hekhalot Zuṭarti, after providing the seals that the mystic is to show to the keepers of the gates of the various palaces and the words that he is to use in the seventh heaven when requesting power over the angels for any purpose he desires, the instructions conclude, "Repeat this mishnah every day after prayer"[52] (*Synopse*, #419). A few paragraphs later, R. 'Aqiba reports that he heard a heavenly voice say, "I have instituted this blessing three times a day in the court above and the court below for my beloved, who troubles himself with descent and ascent to the chariot. I will love and redeem the household in which it is repeated" (*Synopse*, #423).

This does a great deal to explain some of the peculiarities of the instructions for ascent in the hekhalot literature, which contain information about the proper songs or passwords to use in the course of the ascent, but no directions for ascetic practices or other rituals to be performed in preparation for the ascent.[53] If the instructions are not intended for ascent but rather as a sort of itinerary to be repeated, the lack is easily understood.

Ascetic practices appear in the hekhalot texts as part of the procedure for adjuring angels, a central activity of the hekhalot texts, not for achieving ascent. They consist of fasts of various kinds, which are paralleled in a general way in the apocalypses, and of ritual baths, which do not appear in the apocalypses. Compared to the elaborate rituals of the magical papyri they are not very impressive.

Thus, Smith's claim that techniques for ascent are everywhere, and so can be assumed even when they are not mentioned, does not stand up. The authors of the apocalypses appear to have had in mind a model of ascent for which techniques are irrelevant. This model was clear to Baraies the Teacher. Rapture for him is a defining feature of revelation, and the noun *harpagē* as well as forms of the verb *harpazō* appear frequently in his comments.[54] The verb also appears in passages he quotes from apocalypses of Enosh and Shem and 2 Cor. 12:1–5.[55] Rapture—being snatched up—does not require rites because it takes place not at the visionary's initiative but at God's.[56] Fasting, mourning, and related practices are understood to make the visionary fit for the experience, but not to cause it. (This is probably the function of the ascetic practices that precede visions in the apocalypses without ascents too.) Rapture is not an experience that can be achieved at will on the basis of certain practices.

Visionary Experience and the Apocalypses

Despite their first-person accounts of the visions and ascents of ancient heroes, then, there is little to suggest that the authors of the apocalypses were themselves visionaries. They say rather little about the visionary's place in a community, and despite some mention of ascetic practices, they do not represent ascent as achieved by ritual, but rather as accomplished at God's initiative.

Further, the accounts of the experience of the visionary in the apocalypses are governed by convention. Visionaries regularly fall on their faces and wait for angels to raise them as they stand before the divine throne. This is the etiquette of being in God's presence as far back as Ezekiel. Even the most vivid descriptions of awe in the presence of the divine turn out to be conventional. In the Apocalypse of Enosh quoted in the Mani Codex, for example, Enosh reports that when he was taken up, "My heart became heavy, and all my limbs shook. My vertebrae were violently shaken, and my feet did not support my ankles" (53). The power of this description is undercut for the modern reader, though perhaps not for the ancient, when in his next quotation from an apocalypse Baraies records Shem's reaction to the appearance of an angel. "Then the appearance of my face was changed so that I fell to the ground. And my vertebrae shook, while my feet could not support my ankles" (57).

Conventions allow authors to make subtle points. Thus when Enoch falls on his face *twice* in the seventh heaven in 2 Enoch (9:8, 14), the intensification of the conventional response marks this as a particularly awesome revelation. In Enoch's transfiguration in the last chapter of the Similitudes, he does not wait to be raised by an angel, as in the standard description of prostration, but rather offers praise in a loud voice: "And I fell upon my face, / And my whole body became weak from fear, / And my spirit was transformed; / And I cried with a loud voice, / With the spirit of power, / And blessed and glorified and extolled" (1 Enoch 71:11). This variation on the standard response emphasizes Enoch's exalted status; he no longer requires angelic help.

Even in 4 Ezra, the most plausible example of an apocalypse of "personal experience," Ezra's reaction to the revelations he receives exploits such conventions. When the woman he has been comforting transforms herself into a city in the fourth and transitional vision, Ezra lies on the ground like a corpse until the angel raises him (10:29–30), and then expresses his distress at having been abandoned by the angel (10:31–37).

In his commentary to this passage, Michael Stone writes: "This aspect of the description is so much stronger than that which is found anywhere else in 4 Ezra that it must be regarded, at the very least, as a most sophisticated literary instrument. It is, however, much more probable that it is a faithful reflection of a particular experience of the author."[57] And yet, as Stone shows in his sensitive commentary, elements of the description of Ezra's reaction to the vision derive their power from his reaction to other visions earlier in the work and the behavior of other visionaries elsewhere in apocalyptic literature.

Stone takes the fear of death that Ezra expresses after the angel raises him (10:34) as particularly strong evidence for the view that this is a "real experience" because such fear is common in actual trance experiences but uncommon in the apocalypses. And yet as Stone himself notes, Ex. 33:20, "No one shall see me and live," provides a biblical basis for the fear of coming too close to God.[58] Further, as Abraham confronts the terrifying sight of the fiery people during the ascent in the Apocalypse of Abraham, he complains to his angelic guide, "Why have you brought me now to this place; for I cannot now see, my strength is gone, and I am at the point of death" (16:1). This parallel is particularly significant because of another parallel between the two works. Earlier Ezra experiences a sound like many waters and the ground rocking (6:13–17, 29); Abraham hears a sound like rushing waters and cannot prostrate himself because the firmament beneath him rises and falls (17:1–3). The authors of 4 Ezra and the Apocalypse of Abraham, then, have a shared repertoire of imagery to describe reactions to revelation.

The existence of literary parallels for an account of visionary experience does not necessarily mean that the account is entirely a literary creation rather than a reflection of experience. For moderns, individuality is a touchstone of authenticity. Not so in traditional cultures. The mystical testimonies of medieval Christians and Jews, for example, are written in the conventional language of their traditions. For them the truth of the vision is confirmed by its very resemblance to earlier visions, which have shaped their expectations.[59]

Here I would like to consider briefly a single passage from *Sepher haḤezyonot*, "the book of visions," of Ḥayyim Vital (1542–1620), the most important disciple of Isaac Luria.[60] A considerable part of the content of the visions and dreams (the two categories are not really separable) reflects neither Vital's kabbalistic interests nor his concern for the fate of Israel but his anxiety about his status in the community of mystics in Safed, of which he was a prominent member. Over and over, heavenly messengers confirm for him his exalted place relative to other disciples of Luria and Safed notables.

One such dream came to Vital after he had fallen asleep on a Sabbath eve weeping over his troubles, impotence after his marriage and neglect of the study of Torah; it offers a striking example of the use of traditional language and imagery in a vision dominated by personal concerns. In the course of the dream Vital receives reassurance from God himself, who is described seated on a throne, "with the appearance of the Ancient of Days, aged, and his beard white as snow." Vital reacts to the vision of God as the apocalypses have taught us to expect. He is afraid, he is seized with trembling, he falls on his face until God takes his right hand and raises him.[61]

Vital's picture of God refers to the Ancient of Days of Daniel (ch. 7). In Daniel it is the divine garment that is white as snow, not God's beard, which is not mentioned at all; rather the hair of God's head is "like pure wool." But despite the free use of biblical imagery, which is much like the practice of the apocalypses, Vital's description of God is deeply traditional. Similarly Vital's fear and trembling before the divine apparition can be traced back to Daniel, although not to the vision of the Ancient of Days, and Ezekiel; Vital would not have read the other apocalypses in which such reactions are standard features. But when God offers Vital a seat at his right hand, we return to the intensely personal anxieties underlying the dream. To Vital's protests that the seat had been prepared for the great R. Joseph Karo, his older contemporary, God responds that he has changed his mind and that the seat, which once belonged to the prophet Samuel, is now Vital's—an exalted seat indeed![62] Nor is the vision of God the only aspect of the dream with identifiable literary sources. Eshkoly notes that the opening setting of the dream, a mountain in the Galilee, and the old man who serves as a guide there, have their origins in earlier kabbalistic works.[63] In Vital's dream, then, a conventional vision of God, complete with standard visionary etiquette and scenery, offers a solution to the most individual and private problems.

Perhaps the best ancient parallel to Vital's dreams are the dreams of Perpetua recorded in the Martyrdom of Perpetua and Felicitas from the early third century.[64] Like Vital, Perpetua dreams of divine recognition of her spiritual greatness and of messages related to her immediate situation. The symbolism of the dreams includes some unusual features, such as the milking of the sheep, but also many traditional motifs, including the ladder, the dragon, the garden, the old man, and the white garments of the inhabitants of the garden.[65]

The only early Jewish or Christian apocalypse to hint at the presence of personal problems is the Shepherd of Hermas, where admonitions to Hermas about the conduct of his own family form an important part of the visions. The problem of sins committed after baptism that so concerns Hermas is a problem discussed elsewhere in early Christian literature, but the exhortations to Hermas include elements that apparently refer to his own family, as, for example, when he is told to instruct his wife to hold her tongue (Vision 2.2.3). Though there is nothing in the Shepherd of Hermas as unmistakably personal as the revelation to Vital or to Perpetua, the work suggests the author's family life in a way that none of the other apocalypses do. As we have seen, Hermas also stands apart from the other apocalypses in its lack of pseudepigraphy and its quite different relation to the traditional language and imagery that inform the other apocalypses.

The vision from *Sepher haHezyonot* is a clear example of a traditional description of visionary experience in the course of a vision with an unmistakably personal quality. Conventional language, then, does not preclude actual visionary experience. But in the apocalypses as a group the circumstances that give rise to the visions relate not to the authors' lives, but to the career of the pseudepigraphic hero. The messages of the visions are not personal but communal.

The meaning of pseudepigraphy for the authors of the apocalypses and for their audiences remains obscure. What can be known by studying the texts is how these authors worked as authors. Taking account of how they worked argues for reading the apocalypses not as fictionalized accounts of personal experiences[66] but as works of fiction from start to finish, although the authors themselves would never have accepted this anachronistic labeling of the genre in which they wrote.

Gershom Scholem concluded his great work *Major Trends in Jewish Mysticism* with the following story:

> When the Baal Shem [the founder of Hasidism] had a difficult task before him, he would go to a certain place in the woods, light a fire and meditate in prayer—and what he had set out to perform was done. When a generation later the "Maggid" of Meseritz was faced with the same task he would go to the same place in the woods and say: We can no longer light the fire, but we can still speak the prayers—and what he wanted done became reality. Again a generation later Rabbi Moshe Leib of Sassov had to perfom this task. And he too went into the woods and said: We can no longer light a fire, nor do we know the secret meditations belonging to the prayer, but we do know the place in the woods to which it all belongs—and that must be sufficient; and sufficient it was. But when another generation had passed and Rabbi Israel of Rishin was called upon to perfom the task, he sat down on his golden chair in his castle and said: We cannot light the fire, we cannot speak the prayers, we do not know the place, but we can tell the story of how it was done. And, the story-teller adds, the story which he told had the same effect as the actions of the other three.[67]

This wonderful tale might serve as a motto for the thought of the hekhalot literature as its recent interpreters have read it: no need for the mystic to ascend, for telling the story is enough. The actual performance of the acts is attributed to a mythic past, the era of the great rabbis of the Mishnah; recitation itself has become the ritual.[68]

No such claim can be made for the ascent apocalypses. Reading them was not a ritual act. Their stories performed no task, and they effected nothing outside the mind of the reader, which is where stories always perform their work. If I read them correctly, their most important accomplishment was to suggest an understanding of human possibility, of the status of the righteous in the universe, that goes beyond anything found in the Bible and was profoundly appealing to ancient Jews and Christians. In the midst of an often unsatisfactory daily life, they taught their readers to imagine themselves like Enoch, like the glorious ones, with no apparent difference.

Notes

Introduction

1. Tr. A. Pennington, "2 Enoch," in *The Apocryphal Old Testament*, ed. Sparks. Italics indicate words not actually found in the text; bold type indicates conjectural emendation.

2. This theme appears in 3 Baruch only negatively. I argue later that 3 Baruch is a polemic against the view that human beings can become equal to the angels.

3. Again 3 Baruch appears to be a polemic against the position of some of the other apocalypses, integrating the other stories of the primeval history into its ascent while neglecting Gen. 6:1-4 (see later discussion).

4. J. T. Milik, with the collaboration of Matthew Black, *The Books of Enoch: Aramaic Fragments of Qumrân Cave 4* (Oxford: Oxford University Press, 1976).

5. See, for example, reviews of Milik, *Books of Enoch*, by James Barr in *JTS*, n. s., 29 (1978): 517-30, primarily about Milik's treatment of the fragments; and George W. E. Nickelsburg, *CBQ* 40 (1978): 411-19, about the theories proposed in the introduction as well as the publication of the fragments.

6. John J. Collins, ed., *Apocalypse: The Morphology of a Genre, Semeia* 14 (1979).

7. Ibid., 19.

8. Schäfer's publication of the major manuscripts of the hekhalot texts marks the beginning of a new era in their study. See Peter Schäfer, in collaboration with Margarete Schlüter and Hans Georg von Mutius, *Synopse zur Hekhalot-Literatur*, Texte und Studien zum antiken Judentum 2 (Tübingen: Mohr [Siebeck], 1981). Schäfer has also published the geniza texts in *Geniza-Fragmente zur Hekhalot-Literatur*, Texte und Studien zum antiken Judentum 6 (Tübingen: Mohr [Siebeck], 1984). Schäfer's essays on the hekhalot literature have been collected in *Hekhalot-Studien*, Texte und Studien zum antiken Judentum 19

(Tübingen: Mohr [Siebeck], 1988). Halperin has published a number of articles on aspects of the traditions of merkavah mysticism, and his recent book, *The Faces of the Chariot: Early Jewish Responses to Ezekiel's Vision*, Texte und Studien zum antiken Judentum 16 (Tübingen: Mohr [Siebeck], 1988), discusses the theme of ascent in the apocalypses, rabbinic literature, and the hekhalot texts.

9. Segal, *ANRW* II.23.2, (1980): 1333–94.

10. Rowland (New York: Crossroad, 1982).

11. Collins (New York: Crossroad, 1984).

12. Dean-Otting, Judentum und Umwelt (Frankfurt: Peter Lang, 1984).

13. See my review, *JBL* 106 (1987): 126–28, for details.

14. These scholars and works are meant only to be representative: Fossum, *The Name of God and the Angel of the Lord: Samaritan and Jewish Concepts of Intermediation and the Origin of Gnosticism*, Wissenschaftliche Untersuchungen zum Neuen Testament (Tübingen: Mohr [Siebeck], 1985); Segal, most recently, *Paul the Convert: The Apostolate and Apostasy of Saul the Pharisee* (New Haven, Conn.: Yale University Press, 1990), 34–71; Morray-Jones, "Transformational Mysticism in the Apocalyptic-Merkabah Tradition," *JJS* 43 (1992): 1–31.

15. The understanding of the Testament of Abraham as an apocalypse is defended by Collins, *Apocalyptic Imagination*, despite his recognition of some of the difficulties: "Abraham's heavenly journey is only one episode in the story of his death and is narrated in the third person (so the work is not strictly pseudepigraphical). Yet the apocalypse proper is not merely a subordinate element but provides the crucial revelation on which the story turns" (201).

16. Nickelsburg, *Jewish Literature Between the Bible and the Mishnah* (Philadelphia: Fortress, 1981), 248.

Chapter 1

1. For references to previous discussions of Enoch's ascent, see George W. E. Nickelsburg, "Enoch, Levi, and Peter: Recipients of Revelation in Upper Galilee," *JBL* 100 (1981): 576–78. Nickelsburg, like others before him, thinks that Enoch's ascent stands in the tradition of the call vision.

2. Tr. Matthew Black, in consultation with James C. VanderKam, with an appendix on the "Astronomical" Chapters (72–82) by Otto Neugebauer, *The Book of Enoch or I Enoch: A New English Translation*, SVTP 7 (Leiden: Brill, 1985). Italics indicate "an emended or problematical text" (xii); parentheses apparently indicate words added to the text to improve the English. All quotations from 1 Enoch are taken from Black's translation unless otherwise indicated.

3. J. T. Milik, with the collaboration of Matthew Black, *Books of Enoch*. Paleographical evidence places the Book of the Watchers in the early second century B.C.E. Since the Book of the Watchers is a composite work with several stages of development, it must have its origins in the third century. The original language of the work was Aramaic. It was translated from Aramaic into Greek and from Greek into Ethiopic, although some think that the Ethiopic translation reflects independent knowledge of the Aramaic. The Aramaic fragments are generally quite close to the Ethiopic and to the Greek, as the Greek is to the Ethiopic. This is not true of the relationship between the Aramaic and Ethiopic in the Astronomical Book; 1 Enoch 72–82 represents a drastic condensation of the Aramaic form of the Astronomical Book.

4. There are textual problems associated with v. 18, the verse describing

the cherubim and the throne, as Black's italics indicate. The Ethiopic reads "the sound of Cherubim." See Black's discussion in his commentary to 14:18 (*Book of Enoch*, 149). Nickelsburg follows Milik's reconstruction (*Books of Enoch*, 199–200) and translates, "Its sides were cherubim" ("Enoch, Levi," 579). This reconstruction has the advantage of respecting the reading of the Greek as well as the influence of Ezekiel.

5. See Menahem Haran, *Temples and Temple Service in Ancient Israel* (Oxford: Oxford University Press, 1978), 276–88.

6. Johann Maier, *Vom Kultus zur Gnosis*, Kairos, Religionswissenschaftliche Studien 1 (Salzburg: Otto Mueller, 1964), 114–18; R. E. Clements, *God and Temple* (Oxford: Basil Blackwell, 1965), 28–39. The epithet "enthroned upon the cherubim" is sometimes associated with the ark (1 Sam. 4:4, 2 Sam. 6:2), but it also appears apart from it (Pss. 80:2, 99:1); see Frank Moore Cross, *Canaanite Myth and Hebrew Epic* (Cambridge, Mass.: Harvard University Press, 1973), 69. For the creatures on which God rides in heaven, see Ps. 18:11 (=2 Sam. 22:11) and discussion in Moshe Greenberg, *Ezekiel 1–20*, Anchor Bible 22 (Garden City, N.Y.: Doubleday, 1983), 54–55. On El enthroned on cherubim, see Cross, *Canaanite Myth*, 35–36.

7. Greenberg, *Ezekiel*, 43 (to 1:5), considers "living creatures" a neutral term. Maier, *Vom Kultus*, 116, sees the phrase as emphasizing that what Ezekiel saw was the real thing, of which the temple cherubim are only a representation.

8. The weight of scholarly opinion takes this identification in 10:20 as secondary harmonization. See, for example, Walther Eichrodt, *Ezekiel: A Commentary*, tr. Cosslett Quin (London: SCM, 1970); Walther Zimmerli, *Ezekiel 1*, Hermeneia, tr. Ronald E. Clements (Philadelphia: Fortress, 1979 [German original, 1969]), 256; C. B. Houk, "The Final Redaction of Ezekiel 10," *JBL* 90 (1971): 42–54. David J. Halperin, "The Exegetical Character of Ezek. X 9–17," *VT* 26 (1976): 129–41, sees the passage of his title as exegesis of Ezekiel 1. The identification of the "living creatures" with the cherubim is part of this process.

On the other hand, Greenberg and Maier take the identification as original. Greenberg, *Ezekiel*, argues against the common view that this verse is secondary (198–205, on conscious composition throughout chs. 8–11). He observes (183–84, to 10:20) that the cherubim of the temple would only have "approximated" the appearance of the heavenly cherubim of chapter 1. The same feeling that the heavenly counterparts of the earthly temple are far more wondrous than their earthly counterparts appears in the Songs of the Sabbath Sacrifice from Qumran discussed later. See also Maier, *Vom Kultus*, 116.

Haran (*Temples*, 276–84) argues that it was Manasseh who removed the furnishings of the holy of holies. Thus by Ezekiel's time the temple had already been emptied of ark and cherubim. If Haran is right, it may work against the view of Greenberg and Maier and in favor of the majority position. On the other hand, Ezekiel the priest surely would have known what furnishings should have been in the holy of holies. Finally, for my purposes it is not of crucial importance whether the identification of the living creatures with the cherubim goes back to Ezekiel himself, for it is certainly earlier than 1 Enoch 14.

All translations of passages from the Bible and the Apocrypha are taken from the RSV unless otherwise indicated.

9. For Mesopotamia, see, for example, B. Landsberger and J. V. Kinnier Wilson, "The Fifth Tablet of *Enuma Eliš*," *JNES* 20 (1961): 165–67, lines 119–

30: Babylon is modeled on Marduk's heavenly abode. For Canaan, see C. F. A. Schaeffer, *The Cuneiform Texts of Ras Shamra-Ugarit* (London: Oxford University Press, 1939), 66–68: Ba'al and the other gods actually participate in the building of Ba'al's temple. It is not clear whether the references to a "pattern," *tavnit*, for the tabernacle and its furnishings in the instructions for the tabernacle (Ex. 25:9, 40) imply that Moses is granted a vision of God's actual dwelling place or whether he is simply shown blueprints. Elsewhere, however, there are clear indications that God is understood to dwell in a heavenly temple. See, for example, David N. Freedman, "Temple Without Hands," in *Temples and High Places in Biblical Times*, ed. Avraham Biran, Proceedings of the Colloquium in Honor of the Centennial of Hebrew Union College–Jewish Institute of Religion, Jerusalem, 14–16 March 1977 (Jerusalem: Hebrew Union College–Jewish Institute of Religion, 1981), 21–30.

10. See Arvid S. Kapelrud, "Temple Building, a Task for Gods and Kings," *Orientalia*, n.s., 32 (1963): 56–62.

11. Richard D. Barnett, "Bringing God into the Temple," in *Temples*, ed. Biran, 10–20, for a discussion primarily of Mesopotamian and Hittite materials.

12. Richard J. Clifford, *The Cosmic Mountain in Canaan and the Old Testament*, Harvard Semitic Monographs 4 (Cambridge, Mass: Harvard University Press, 1972), 1–25. See also the remarks of Jonathan Z. Smith, *To Take Place: Toward Theory in Ritual* (Chicago: University of Chicago Press, 1987), 13–23.

13. Clifford, *Cosmic Mountain*, 34–97; summary p. 97.

14. See, for example, Clements, *God and Temple*, 63–67; Clifford, *Cosmic Mountain*, 98–181; Haran, *Temples*, 255–57; Maier, *Vom Kultus*, 34–54, 97–101; E. Theodore Mullen, Jr., *The Assembly of the Gods*, Harvard Semitic Monographs 24 (Chico, Calif.: Scholars, 1980), 128–75; Jon D. Levenson, *Sinai and Zion: An Entry into the Jewish Bible* (Minneapolis: Winston-Seabury, 1985), 111–37, 145–76.

15. Clements, *God and Temple*, 70–76; Clifford, *Cosmic Mountain*, 142–60; Levenson, *Sinai and Zion*, 151–76; John H. Hayes, "The Tradition of Zion's Inviolability," *JBL* 82 (1963): 419–26.

16. See Brevard Childs, *Isaiah and the Assyrian Crisis*, Studies in Biblical Theology, second series, 3 (London: SCM, 1967), for a discussion of these extremely complicated issues and a form-critical analysis of the relevant oracles and narrative. Childs considers it possible that Isaiah's advice to defy Sennacherib in 2 Kings 19:5–7 (=Isa. 37:5–7) reflects the historical Isaiah (76–83, 91–93). See also Clements, *God and Temple*, 80–84. For quite different views, see Hayes, "Inviolability," 424–26.

17. On Jeremiah and Micah and the attitude they combat, see Clements, *God and Temple*, 84–87.

18. Clements, *God and Temple*, 87–99; Yehezkel Kaufmann, *The Religion of Israel* (abridged), tr. Moshe Greenberg (Chicago: University of Chicago Press, 1960), 289–90; Moshe Weinfeld, *Deuteronomy and the Deuteronomic School* (Oxford: Oxford University Press, 1972), 191–209, in the context of a discussion of the differences between D and P. The understanding of Deuteronomic terminology is Kaufmann's.

19. See Greenberg, *Ezekiel*, 201–2, for a discussion of the idolatry depicted in chapters 8–11 and references to the literature. Greenberg writes, "Only a visionary and an audience at a remove from the reality of Jerusalem, and suffering the exile threatened for breach of covenant might have accepted and understood

at once the point of such a fantasy: to collect and display vividly the notorious instances of cultic pollution of the sanctuary, so as to bring home the awful realization that its sanctity had been hopelessly injured, and its doom irrevocably sealed" (202). See also Kaufmann, *Religion*, 430–32.

20. Ezekiel's visions of a mobile God have often been interpreted as representing a claim that God is not confined to the land of Israel, an issue of obvious importance to the exiles in whose midst Ezekiel lived. But Greenberg argues that there was no need to make such a claim because it had long been established that the God of Israel was accesible outside his land as well as within it. The function of the theophany of Ezekiel 1 is to confirm Ezekiel's prophecy of doom against the more numerous and certainly more popular prophecies of hope circulating among the exiles at the time. Indeed the existence of such prophecies, known to us from Jeremiah (29:8–9,15) and Ezekiel (13:8–10), is itself evidence that the exiles had no fear that their Babylonian location cut them off from the presence of their God. The strange and powerful images of Ezekiel's vision are perhaps an indication that nothing less spectacular stood a chance of convincing the exiles of Ezekiel's minority position (Greenberg, *Ezekiel*, 58–59, 80).

21. Nickelsburg, "Enoch, Levi," 580. See also Maier, "Das Gefährdungs-motiv bei der Himmelsreise in der jüdischen Apokalyptik und 'Gnosis,'" *Kairos* 5 (1963): 22–23. Maier understands Enoch's actions as parallel to cultic acts. For Maier the cult is the one place in the Bible where human beings initiate contact with God.

22. On the textual difficulties in the last clause, see Black, *Book of Enoch*, 150–51.

23. For example, Psalm 82, Isaiah 40. See Cross, *Canaanite Myth*, 186–90.

24. On the divine council in Israelite literature and its background, see Cross, *Canaanite Myth*, 186–90, and Mullen, *Assembly*, 175–209. Mullen argues that Yahweh's council is sometimes less passive than El's (206). On the accuser and other later developments, see Mullen, 274–75.

25. Cross, *Canaanite Myth*, 186–88; Mullen, *Assembly*, 209–26. This reading of Isa. 40:6 requires emendation of the pointing. See Cross, 188, and Mullen, 217.

26. For these references and discussion, see Mullen, *Assembly*, 226–33 and Cross, *Canaanite Myth*, 189–90. Note that I am not considering the heavenly host in its role as the army of the divine warrior here, although this function is certainly related to the function of council. See Mullen, 185–201.

27. Maier, "Gefährdungsmotiv," 22–23; Carol Newsom, *Songs of the Sabbath Sacrifice: A Critical Edition*, Harvard Semitic Studies (Atlanta, Ga.: Scholars, 1985), 60. In "Enoch, Levi," Nickelsburg refers to the *temenos* and the holy of holies, which suggests a less detailed correspondence between the layout of Enoch's heaven and the Jerusalem temple (580). Similarly in *Jewish Literature*, he speaks of Enoch's "progress through the courts of the heavenly temple right up to its holy of holies . . ."(53).

28. Ezekiel's vision of the temple includes such a vestibule (40:48), as well as other vestibules outside the temple proper (e.g., 40:8–9). So, too, does the temple of the Qumran Temple Scroll (col. 4).

29. The fact that the Greek uses *oikodomē*, building, for the first structure but *oikos*, house, for the other two, could point to the difference between the two inner chambers, where cultic activity takes place, and the vestibule, which

serves to separate the sanctuary proper from the area outside and which is not the scene of such activity. The very fact that two of the structures that Enoch sees are called "house" is for Nickelsburg further evidence that heaven is understood as a temple since the house of God "is by definition a temple" ("Enoch, Levi," 580 n. 19).

30. "Fire-balls" is Black's translation, *Book of Enoch*. Nickelsburg, "Enoch, Levi," 579, translates "shooting stars."

31. Nickelsburg emphasizes this point, "Enoch, Levi," 582. See Maier, "Gefährdungsmotiv," 30–38, on mythic associations of fire and water generally; Cross, *Canaanite Myth*, 147–69, on the storm theophany in the Bible and its Canaanite roots; Greenberg, *Ezekiel*, 54, on storm imagery in Ezekiel's first vision.

32. Maier, "Gefährdungsmotiv," 34–36.

33. *Jewish War* 5.222–23, tr. H. St. J. Thackeray, Loeb Classical Library (Cambridge, Mass.: Harvard University Press, 1928), 269. Maier refers to this passage, "Gefährdungsmotiv," 35.

34. See Maier, "Gefährdungsmotiv," 35, for parallels to Josephus in rabbinic and hekhalot literature, which suggest not dependence but use of similar traditions.

35. "Enoch, Levi," 579.

36. See Rowland, *Open Heaven*, 219; and Newsom, *Songs*, 301–2. 1 Kings 6:29 speaks of cherubim, palm trees, and open flowers on all the walls of the temple. Only cherubim are mentioned in 2 Chron. 3:7. Ezekiel's eschatological temple is to have cherubim and palm trees on the walls and doors of the sanctuary (41:15–26). Newsom points out that the eleventh Sabbath song from 4QShirShabb also seems to reflect this aspect of the temple (4Q405 14–15, line 5; tr. p. 281, discussion pp. 282–83; 4Q405 19, lines 5–6; tr. p. 295; discussion p. 296). Neither Rowland nor Newsom refers to the cherubim of the tabernacle hangings.

37. *Songs*, 51–52.

38. Ibid., 42–44.

39. Ibid., 49.

40. Ezek. 1:28, 3:23, 43:3, 44:4. In 9:8 and 11:13, Ezekiel falls on his face in distress.

41. See the discussion in chapters 2, 3, and 5.

42. Against Rowland, "The Visions of God in Apocalyptic Literature," *JSJ* 10 (1979): 141–42, who sees 1 Enoch 14 as significantly more anthropomorphic than Ezekiel 1.

43. Mullen, *Assembly*, 154–63. Mullen does not discuss 1 Enoch 14.

44. See also Isa. 33:20–21, Joel 4:18, and Zech. 14:8.

45. Most of the discussion has focused not on the Ancient of Days, but on the one like a son of man, because of the importance of this passage for understanding early Christian views of Jesus. The broad outlines of the reading of this passage suggested by J. A. Emerton, "The Origin of the Son of Man Imagery," *JTS*, n.s., 9 (1958): 225–42, have gained wide acceptance. The part of Emerton's argument that is important for my argument is his identification of the source of the imagery used to describe the two figures in this scene as Canaanite.

46. The Ugaritic word *šbt* is cognate with the Hebrew *śyb*. For references to El's beard and hair, see Mullen, *Assembly*, 160. I thank Edward Greenstein for help on this point.

47. Marvin H. Pope, *El in the Ugaritic Texts* (Leiden: Brill, 1955), 45–46.

48. I thank Edward Greenstein for pointing out the importance of this verse in Isaiah.

49. André Lacocque, *The Book of Daniel*, tr. David Pellauer, with a forward by Paul Ricoeur (Atlanta, Ga.: John Knox, 1979), 143. For biblical examples, see Isa. 1:18, Ps. 51:9.

50. Haran, *Temples*, 164–74; quotation, 164.

51. But in Ex. 39:28, we read that they made "the linen (*bad*) breeches of fine twisted linen (*šeš mašzar*)." Haran thinks that the phrase "fine twisted linen" is a mistake, taken from the verse following (*Temples*, 174 n. 54).

52. Haran, *Temples*, 165–74, esp. 173–74; quotation, 174.

53. The garment of God has a long career in Jewish literature. In Genesis Rabbah 3.4, God wraps himself in light in order to create the light of the first day of creation. According to some manuscripts of the midrash, it is in a white garment that God wraps himself (see the apparatus in the edition of J. Theodor-Ch. Albeck, *Midrash Bereshit Rabba*, 2d corrected printing [Jerusalem: Wahrmann, 1965], 1:19–20). The prooftext for the garment is Ps. 104:2, "He covers himself in light as a garment," rather than Daniel 7, so there is no clear literary link to the garments of the throne scenes in Enoch and Daniel.

In the hekhalot literature God is sometimes described wearing a wondrous garment referred to as *ḥaluq*, a long shirtlike robe. This garment is discussed by Gershom G. Scholem in *Jewish Gnosticism, Merkabah Mysticism, and Talmudic Tradition*, 2d rev. ed. (New York: Jewish Theological Seminary, 1965), 58.

54. Prayer shawl: The verb "wrap" used in Genesis Rabbah 3.4 and parallels (see the listing in Theodor-Albeck, *Bereshit Rabba*, at this passage) is the verb used for donning a tallit. The parallel in Midrash Tehillim 104:4 explicitly refers to the garment as a tallit. Phylacteries: b. Berakhot 6a–b.

55. Weinfeld, *Deuteronomy*, 205–6.

56. Philo: On Moses 2:109–35, Special Laws 1:84–97. Josephus: Antiquities 3.184–87.

57. Tr. Herbert T. Andrews, in *APOT*, ed. Charles, 2:104. Italics indicate words supplied in the translation for the sake of clarity.

58. Alexander A. Di Lella, in *The Wisdom of Ben Sira*, tr. Patrick W. Skehan, intro. and commentary Di Lella, Anchor Bible 39 (Garden City, N.Y.: Doubleday, 1987), 552.

Most commentators have assumed that ben Sira is describing Simeon's emergence from the holy of holies on the Day of Atonement, but it has recently been argued that the ceremony described is rather the daily whole offering (Fearghas Ó Fearghail, "Sir 50, 5–21: Yom Kippur or the Daily Whole Offering?," *Biblica* 59 [1978]: 301–16, followed by Di Lella, *Ben Sira*, 550–54). The argument hinges on parallels to the description of the ceremony for Yom Kippur in m. Yoma and of the daily offering in m. Tamid, as well as on the intended reference of the term I have translated literally as "house of the veil," usually taken to be the holy of holies. The high priest's rainbowlike appearance might seem to make Yom Kippur impossible, but, as Ó Fearghail notes (306–7), according to the Mishnah (Yoma 3:4, 6) the high priest officiated on Yom Kippur first in his elaborate daily garments and then in plain linen. It should also be noted that according to Josephus (*War* 5.236), the high priest wore what the Mishnah calls his "garments of gold" only on Yom Kippur.

59. *Songs*, 16, 72. On angelic high priests, usually "heads" or "princes," see 33–34. Although the angelic priests of our passage are not identified by

either of these names, their garments are called *'ephodim* (4Q405 23 ii 5); in the Torah the ephod is worn only by the high priest (Ex. 28:6–12, 39:2–7). See Newsom's note to line 5, p. 335.

60. On the types of workmanship in temple furnishings and vestments, see Haran, *Temples*, 160–61. "*'Oreg*," woven, work is a feature of the furnishings of the tabernacle and of both the vestments of ordinary priests and of Aaron. The term appears in the passage from the Sabbath Songs describing the garments of the angelic priests quoted below. Ranking above it in holiness, according to Haran, is "*roqem*" workmanship, involving a mixture of colors and materials. It is used for furnishings of the tabernacle and for Aaron's vestments, but not for those of the ordinary priests. The term appears in both the description of the garments of the angelic priests and the description of the glory of God from the Sabbath Songs quoted below. Newsom, *Songs*, translates with a phrase involving the word "color." Ranking highest of all in holiness is "*ḥošev*" workmanship, also involving variegated colors and materials, and, in Haran's view, figures as well. It appears in the furnishings of the tabernacle and in Aaron's garments. This term does not appear in the extant portions of the Sabbath Songs at all; I doubt that the community at Qumran would have realized along with Haran that *ḥošev* workmanship represented a higher level of holiness than *roqem* workmanship.

61. Text and translation, Newsom, *Songs*, 332–34; discussion, 335–39. Italics indicate "problematic translations," or, within brackets, "uncertain supplements" (ix).

62. Text and translation, *Songs*, 303–6; discussion, 316–17. The passage continues: "the spirits of living godlike beings which move continuously with the glory of the wondrous chariot(s)." Newsom takes the "spirits of living godlike beings" to be another description, or better, another understanding, of the glory on the chariot throne. "The appearance of the Glory of God is not directly described but is experienced as a multitude of angelic spirits . . ." (316). She also notes that the passage about the spirits could begin a new sentence (317), a construction that seems to me preferable to the very difficult picture presented by Newsom's translation.

63. For the controversial view that "P is the literary product of circles of the Jerusalemite priesthood of the First Temple . . . ," see Haran, *Temples*, esp. 1–12, 146–48; quotation, 5–6.

On Ezekiel's view of the priesthood, Haran, *Temples*, 58–61, 102–7, and "The Law-Code of Ezekiel XL–XLVIII and Its Relation to the Priestly School," *HUCA* 50 (1979): 61 n. 29, 64–65 n. 34; Greenberg, "The Design and Themes of Ezekiel's Program of Restoration," *Interpretation* 38 (1984): 194–99; Jon D. Levenson, *Theology of the Program of Restoration of Ezekiel 40–48*, Harvard Semitic Monographs 10 (Missoula, Mont.: Scholars, 1976), 129–51. Greenberg ("Design," 196 n. 31), is cautious about the absence of a high priest in Ezekiel's vision of the restored temple. In the light of all the other omissions it is difficult to draw conclusions (203). Haran (*Temples*, 59) holds a position similar to Greenberg's. In "Law-Code" (61, esp. n. 29), he suggests that the absence of a high priest from the code is the result of the fact that by Ezekiel's time the high priest no longer had a function since the furnishings of the holy of holies had been removed under Manasseh (*Temples*, 208–21). Levenson believes that Ezekiel has dispensed with the high priest because in the renewed Israel the roles of king and high priest are to be combined in a single figure, the *nasi'* (140–44).

64. For a convergence of the rainbow as garment for Moses and comparison

of Moses to the high priest in the Zohar, see Moshe Idel, *Kabbalah: New Perspectives* (New Haven, Conn.: Yale University Press, 1988), 225–28, esp. n. 114.

65. There are serious textual problems in v. 22; see Black's commentary, *Book of Enoch.*

66. Nickelsburg, "Enoch, Levi," 580–81 n. 19, 585 n. 37. There are a number of Hebrew verbs that are used to mean "approach" in the cultic sense, *qrb* and *ngš*, for example. *Engizō* is one of several terms used by the Septuagint to translate them.

67. Nickelsburg translates: "the high heaven, the eternal sanctuary," "Enoch, Levi," 584.

68. David Suter, "Fallen Angel, Fallen Priest: The Problem of Family Purity in 1 Enoch 6–16," *HUCA* 50 (1979): 119, thinks that 1 Enoch 10:11, in which God accuses the Watchers of defiling themselves with the women "in their uncleanness" suggests that menstrual blood may be intended here. I thank Milton Himmelfarb for persuading me of the position I hold here.

The following discussion is indebted to Nickelsburg, "Enoch, Levi," and Suter, "Fallen Angel," who independently offer compelling arguments for placing the accusations of sexual improprieties directed at the Watchers in the context of polemics against the Jerusalem priesthood in the Second Temple period.

69. Nickelsburg, "Enoch, Levi," 585; Suter, "Fallen Angel," 119–22.

70. Since the passage from the Damascus Covenant includes the sin of profanation of the temple and refers its charge to the words of Levi, Suter ("Fallen Angel," 128–29) takes the passage to refer to priests.

71. Tr. Marinus de Jonge, "The Testaments of the Twelve Patriarchs," in *Apocryphal Old Testament*, ed. Sparks. From the point of view of the rabbis, no woman born a gentile could ever be purified so as to be a fit wife for a priest.

72. Suter, "Fallen Angel," 129–31.

73. Martin Hengel, *Judaism and Hellenism: Studies in Their Encounter in Palestine During the Early Hellenistic Age*, tr. John Bowden (Philadelphia: Fortress, 1974), 1:133–34.

74. Enoch appears in the introductory poetic predictions of chapters 1–5 of the Book of the Watchers, which do not form part of the narrative proper, but he is not even mentioned in the account of the descent of the Watchers in chapters 6–11. This of course has important implications for the history of the various traditions and sources brought together in the Book of the Watchers.

75. The Greek translates "righteousness" as *dikaiosunē* in 12:4, *alētheia* in 15:1. The Aramaic is not preserved in either place, but the Greek probably reflects Aramaic *qušṭa'*, which can mean either truth or righteousness. In 10:16, where *qušṭa'* is preserved (4QEn^c1 v), both Greek and Ethiopic provide both terms (see Milik, *Books of Enoch*, 191, to line 4). In 32:3 Garden of Righteousness is *pardes qušṭa'* in Aramaic (4QEn^c1 xxvi), *ho paradeisos tēs dikaiosunēs* in Greek.

Charles suggested that Enoch deserved the title "scribe of righteousness" both because he is a righteous man (15:1) and because the judgment he is announcing is righteous (*Book of Enoch*, 28, note to 12:3). James C. VanderKam agrees (*Enoch and the Growth of an Apocalyptic Tradition*, Catholic Biblical Quarterly Monograph Series 16 [Washington: Catholic Biblical Association of America, 1984], 133).

76. Charles and others saw the description of Enoch's role as modeled on that of the Babylonian god Nabu, a heavenly scribe, who also served in their

view as the model for the man dressed in linen of Ezek. 9:16 (*Book of Enoch*, 28). VanderKam rejects this identification, arguing that Nabu is associated with the tablets of destiny, which appear only in later layers of 1 Enoch (the Epistle of Enoch [1 Enoch 92–105] and the addition to the Astronomical Book [1 Enoch 80–81]) (*Enoch*, 132–33).

77. These roles are much better documented outside Israel than within, but it seems reasonable to assume a certain similarity, although the difficulty of mastering cuneiform must have created special circumstances for the scribes of Mesopotamia. Jonathan Z. Smith, "Wisdom and Apocalyptic," in *Religious Syncretism in Antiquity*, ed. Birger A. Pearson (Missoula, Mont.: Scholars, 1975), 135–36 (rpt. in Smith, *Map Is Not Territory: Studies in the History of Religions* [Leiden: Brill, 1978]) offers an interesting description of the scribal mentality.

78. Weinfeld, *Deuteronomy*, esp. 158–78.

79. See, for example, Gerhard von Rad, *Wisdom in Israel*, tr. James D. Martin (Nashville, Tenn.: Abingdon, 1972), 15–23.

80. On scribes, see Elias Bickerman, *From Ezra to the Last of the Maccabees* (1947; reprint New York: Schocken, 1962), 67–71; Hengel, *Judaism*, 78–83; Victor Tcherikover, *Hellenistic Civilization and the Jews* (1959; reprint New York: Athenaeum, 1974), 124–26.

81. Nehemiah is never called "scribe" in the biblical text, but he is a layman and civil servant who engages in interpretation of the law.

82. I am indebted for my understanding of Nehemiah to Morton Smith, *Palestinian Parties and Politics That Shaped the Old Testament* (New York: Columbia University Press, 1971), 126–36.

83. Ibid., 133.

84. Rabbinic reports about the conflicts between Pharisees and Sadducees appear to be of little historical value (see Jack Lightstone, "Sadducees versus Pharisees: The Tannaitic Sources," in *Christianity, Judaism, and Other Greco-Roman Cults: Studies for Morton Smith at Sixty*, ed. Jacob Neusner [Leiden: Brill, 1975]), but they show that the issues were not forgotten even after the destruction, when the rabbis "remember" that the Pharisees were able to impose their interpretation of proper temple practice on the Sadducees.

85. *Biblical Interpretation in Ancient Israel* (Oxford: Oxford University Press, 1985), 78–79. Fishbane arrives at these conclusions on the basis of a detailed study of scribal usage in the Hebrew Bible, which leads him to conclude that the tradents of "cultic-legal" material were not the same as the tradents of prophetic literature, who in turn have a scribal vocabulary distinct from the tradents of wisdom literature. If some scribes were trained at the temple rather than at the royal court, differences in technique are to be expected.

This point has important implications for the contrast between priestly and scribal thought as manifested in P and D that Weinfeld develops, *Deuteronomy*, esp. 179–89. Weinfeld attributes learning and writing, the prerequisites for scribal activity, to the priests, but sees the spheres of interest of priest and scribe as completely separate.

86. "'They Shall Teach Your Statutes to Jacob': Priest, Scribe, and Sage in Second Temple Times," *JBL* (forthcoming).

87. Nickelsburg sees the figure of Enoch in the Book of the Watchers as reflecting aspects of Ezra's career, including his condemnation of marriage to foreign women ("Enoch, Levi," 585).

88. Ibid., 589. Suter, "Fallen Angel," takes God's words to the Watchers

via Enoch, "It is you who should be petitioning on behalf of men, and not men on your behalf" (15:2), as representing a protest against "scribal encroachment on priestly roles" (134). But the rebuke is directed not at the scribe who acts as priest, but at priests who fail to act as priests. If priests performed their roles properly (according to scribal demands), such scribal intervention would not be necessary.

89. Tr. R. H. Charles, rev. C. Rabin, "Jubilees," in *Apocryphal Old Testament*, ed. Sparks. See VanderKam, *Enoch*, 185–86, on Enoch as priest in Jubilees. VanderKam considers Jubilees to be the first place where Enoch is so depicted.

90. Nickelsburg, "Enoch, Levi," 588–90.

91. For Enoch as prophet in the Book of the Watchers generally, see Michael E. Stone, "Lists of Revealed Things in Apocalyptic Literature," in *Magnalia Dei: The Mighty Acts of God (Essays on the Bible and Archeology in Memory of G. Ernest Wright)*, ed. Frank M. Cross, Warner Lemke, and Patrick D. Miller (Garden City, N.Y.: Doubleday, 1976), n. 2. Stone points out that Enoch is depicted in the opening chapters of the Book of the Watchers as a prophet comparable to Moses, the greatest of the Israelite prophets; Balaam, the greatest prophet of the gentiles; and Ezekiel, the prophet who has the most vivid visions of God. VanderKam, *Enoch*, 115–19, develops the parallels to Balaam, whom he sees as a figure particularly close to Enoch because he is a diviner.

92. Michael Stone in particular has treated these questions. See his "Lists"; "The Book of Enoch and Judaism in the Third Century B.C.E., *CBQ* 40 (1978): 479–92; "Enoch, Aramaic Levi and Sectarian Origins," *JSJ* 19 (1988): 159–70.

93. See, for example, John J. Collins, *Apocalyptic Imagination*, 1–11; Stone, "Lists," 439–43.

94. The two leading exponents of this view are Otto Plöger in *Theocracy and Eschatology*, tr. S. Rudman (Richmond, Va.: John Knox, 1968); and Paul D. Hanson in *The Dawn of Apocalyptic: The Historical and Sociological Roots of Jewish Apocalyptic Eschatology*, rev. ed. (Philadelphia: Fortress, 1979). While Hanson himself does not seem to see his work as a development of Plöger's, others have also noted the similarity in their positions (see, e.g., Joseph Blenkinsopp, *A History of Prophecy in Israel* [Philadelphia: Westminster, 1983], 243). Here I will refer primarily to Hanson, because his work is more recent (although not recent enough to reflect the new dates for the Enochic material) and more detailed, and also because he considers at some length the model for the temple in Ezekiel 40–48, an issue of particular importance for my discussion.

95. The terminology is Hanson's.

96. *Dawn*, 228–40.

97. Ibid., 233.

98. Ibid., 238.

99. Ibid.

100. See Greenberg, "Design," 208; Haran, "Law-Code," 66–71; and the discussion of the lack of a high priest in Ezekiel's vision, n. 63.

101. "Rebellion in Heaven, Azazel, and Euhemeristic Heroes in 1 Enoch 6–11," *JBL* 96 (1977): 220–26; quotations, 226.

102. See Devorah Dimant, "1 Enoch 6–11: A Methodological Perspective," *SBL Seminar Papers 1978*, 1: 326–27, for a position that accepts a relationship between Leviticus 16 and the Asael traditions without any such view of the attitude to the temple. Dimant criticizes some of the specifics of Hanson's position, 336 n. 38.

103. For a different reading of 3 Isaiah's attitude toward the temple with an explicit rejection of Hanson's view, see Blenkinsopp, *History*, 247–48, esp. nn. 47–48.

104. See the references in Susan Niditch, "Ezekiel 40–48 in a Visionary Context," *CBQ* 48 (1986): 210 n. 5, for a sample.

105. See, for example, Greenberg, "Design," 181–89, for a radical insistence on unity and Ezekiel's authorship; and Niditch, "Ezekiel," 209–11, for a position less extreme than Greenberg's.

106. "Ezekiel," 212–20. Niditch notes the relationship of the themes and imagery of the chapters to myths of creation and compares the model of the temple to Buddhist mandalas.

107. See Niditch, "Ezekiel," 220–23, for a discussion of the significance of this placement.

108. Note Niditch's comment about the gospel/law distinction in many treatments of Ezekiel, "Ezekiel" 211.

109. *Dawn*, 20.

110. *Vom Kultus*, 131–35.

Chapter 2

1. This position is not uncontroversial. It has been advanced with great conviction and energy by Marinus de Jonge, starting with his doctoral dissertation, published as *The Testaments of the Twelve Patriarchs: A Study of Their Text, Composition, and Origin* (Assen, Netherlands: Van Gorcum, 1953). For a history of the discussion of the question through the mid 1970s, see H. Dixon Slingerland, *The Testaments of the Twelve Patriarchs: A Critical History of Research* (Missoula, Mont.: Scholars, 1977). For de Jonge's most recent contributions on the subject, see several of the essays collected in Part II of *Jewish Eschatology, Early Christian Christology and the Testaments of the Twelve Patriarchs: Collected Essays of Marinus de Jonge* (Leiden: Brill, 1991).

2. Among the most influential works that maintain that the Testaments was an originally Jewish composition are Jürgen Becker, *Untersuchungen zur Entstehungsgeschichte der Testamente der Zwölf Patriarchen*, Arbeiten zur Geschichte des antiken Judentums und des Urchristentums 8 (Leiden: Brill, 1970), and Anders Hultgård, *L'eschatologie des Testaments des Douze Patriarches*, 2 vols. (Uppsala: Almqvist & Wisksell, 1977 and 1982).

3. On the geniza document, see Jonas C. Greenfield and Michael E. Stone, "Remarks on the Aramaic Testament of Levi from the Geniza," *RB* 86 (1979): 214–15. On MS e, see Marinus de Jonge et al., *The Testaments of the Twelve Patriarchs: A Critical Edition of the Greek Text* (Leiden: Brill, 1978), xvii. The parallels between MS e and the geniza text are quite close, but the way in which the copyist of a Greek MS came to have access to Aramaic material has yet to be explained.

4. Stone, "Enoch, Aramaic Levi," 168–70.

5. Nickelsburg, "Enoch, Levi," 588–90. The Testament of Levi even refers to a "writing of Enoch" (14:1), which seems likely to be the Book of the Watchers.

6. On the setting in early Christianity, see H. W. Hollander and M. de Jonge, *The Testaments of the Twelve Patriarchs: A Commentary* (Leiden: Brill, 1985), 76–79.

7. Against Adela Yarbro Collins, "The Seven Heavens in Jewish and

Christian Apocalypses," in *Essays in Memory of Ioan P. Culianu*, ed. John J. Collins and Michael Fishbane (Albany: SUNY Press, forthcoming), who reads the very fragmentary text of 4QTestLevi[a] col. 2, lines 11–18, as indicating more than one heaven. Milik, who published the text, reconstructs it as containing only a single heaven, "Le Testament de Lévi en Araméen," *RB* 62 (1955): 404. See also the comment of Marinus de Jonge, "The Aramaic text does not necessarily presuppose more than one heaven" ("Notes on Testament of Levi II–VII," in *Studies on the Testaments of the Twelve Patriarchs: Text and Interpretation*, SVTP 3 [Leiden: Brill, 1975], 253).

R. H. Charles (e.g., "The Testaments of the Twelve Patriarchs," *APOT* 2:304 [notes]), followed by Yarbro Collins, claims that three was the original number of heavens in the Testament of Levi. I follow de Jonge ("Notes," 248–51, esp. n. 13), who argues that no form of the text with three heavens ever existed.

8. This rare phrase, *hē doxa hē megalē*, appears also in 1 Enoch 14:20, but there Black translates, "the glory of the Great One," in accordance with what he takes to be the original phrase, following 1 Enoch 104:1 (*Book of Enoch*, 149–50).

9. Angels "bear answers" to the angels of the presence. See Hollander and de Jonge, *Commentary*, 138–39, for this understanding.

10. All translations from the Testaments of the Twelve Patriarchs are taken from Hollander and de Jonge, *Commentary*.

11. "Notes," 253.

12. See Marinus de Jonge, "Levi, the Sons of Levi and the Law in *Testament Levi* X, XIV–XV and XVI," and "The Testament of Levi and 'Aramaic Levi,'" in *Jewish Eschatology*.

13. As Maier notes, "Gefährdungsmotiv," 20–22.

14. These apocalypses are by no means easy to date, but the works that contain seven heavens (the Testament of Levi, 2 Enoch, the Apocalypse of Abraham, the Ascension of Isaiah, and, as I argue in chapter 4, 3 Baruch, although it mentions only five) all seem to date from the first century C.E. or later. Those ascent apocalypses that hold on to a single heaven (the Similitudes of Enoch, the Apocalypse of Zephaniah) may well be earlier, perhaps from the first century B.C.E.

15. Some long MSS of 2 Enoch contain ten heavens. The last three are clearly a later addition, since they are inserted between Enoch's prostration and his approach to God's throne (2 Enoch 21:6, MS J in Frances I. Andersen, "2 (Slavonic Apocalypse of) Enoch," in *The Old Testament Pseudepigrapha*, ed. Charlesworth, 1:136).

16. "The Seven Heavens." She argues that the seven planetary spheres come to play a role in thinking about the heavens only later, with the rise of Mithraism.

17. In the course of her discussion of the importance of the number seven for the groupings of angels (31–35) and the heavenly temple and its furnishings (48–51), Newsom writes, "The entire composition seems at times to be a rhapsody on the sacred number seven . . ." (*Songs*, 49).

18. As de Jonge notes in passing, "Notes," 259, "The final redactor superimposed a system of seven heavens and obviously looked for traditional material to 'fill' this."

19. Nickelsburg, "Enoch, Levi," 588.

20. References to actual sacrifice in heaven are quite rare in the apocalypses and elsewhere. See Hans Bietenhard, *Die Himmlische Welt im Urchristentum*

und Spätjudentum (Tübingen: Mohr [Siebeck], 1951), 123–37; only Hebrews and Revelation are discussed in detail.

21. Collins, *Apocalyptic Imagination,* 198–201.

22. The Slavonic version speaks consistently of prayers, while the Greek has prayers, virtues, and good deeds (11:4, 9; 12:5; 15:2).

23. De Jonge, *Testaments of the Twelve Patriarchs: A Study,* 48–49. In the passages from early Christian literature cited here, "bloodless" is always *anaimaktos,* but a number of different Greek terms are used for "offering."

More recently de Jonge has reaffirmed his view that "in its present redaction the passage is undoubtedly Christian," but he has accepted the criticism of Becker and others that this view of the true sacrifice as spiritual rather than physical has its background in Hellenistic Judaism ("Notes," 259 n. 42).

Becker discusses the question in *Untersuchungen,* 267–68 n. 6. De Jonge himself notes Plutarch's use of the phrase (*Testaments of the Twelve Patriarchs: A Study,* 49 n. 51). Becker even points to Palestinian works that share the idea if not the language. But when Azariah prays that "a contrite heart and a humble spirit" may substitute for sacrifice in Babylonia (Prayer of Azariah 16), the text does not reject sacrifice. Rather, it seeks a substitute suitable for people unable to sacrifice (v. 15). (Becker's reference to "37ff." is mistaken.)

24. *Recherches sur le vocabulaire du culte dans la Septante,* Études et commentaires 61 (Paris: Klincksieck, 1966), 188–91. I thank Gideon Bohak for calling this discussion to my attention.

25. *Songs,* 372–73.

26. 2 Chron. 29:27–28, Sir. 50:14–16. See Newsom's discussion of rabbinic evidence, *Songs,* 18.

27. The hymns of the Similitudes are brief hymns based on Isaiah's trishagion (39:10–14) sung before the divine throne, while the hymn of the Apocalypse of Abraham (17:7–17) is sung by Abraham to protect him in the course of ascent and is far lengthier and more elaborate.

28. Martha Himmelfarb, "Heavenly Ascent and the Relationship of the Apocalypses and the *Hekhalot* Literature," *HUCA* 59 (1988): 91–96.

29. "The Aim and Purpose of Early Jewish Mysticism," in *Hekhalot-Studien,* 287–88.

30. Indeed, Hollander and de Jonge comment on this passage: "T. L. is clearly not interested in cultic affairs; hence the variations and lack of coordination between vv. 2f. and 4–11 and the lack of logic in the sequence of the actions of the angels" (*Commentary* to 8:2, p. 151).

31. For details of the parallels, see Hollander and de Jonge, *Commentary,* 151–52.

32. See Hollander and de Jonge, *Commentary,* 152–53, for a discussion of the individual elements and their background.

33. Tr. Greenfield and Stone, in Hollander and de Jonge, *Commentary,* 461. Greenfield and Stone translate *rbwt* "anointing" rather than "greatness" or some synonym, not on the basis of the parallel passage in the Testament of Levi, but on the basis of Ex. 40:15, where the targumim use the root *rby.*

34. There is of course no way to be sure what exactly was included in the vision of the Aramaic. I am inclined to think that something like the list of priestly accessories in 8:2 appeared in the Aramaic because of the priestly interests of the document. There is nothing in the list as it stands that is implausible in a work in a Semitic language or out of keeping with the outlook of the surviving portions of the Aramaic document.

35. Jubilees does not offer the details of the ceremony in its vision, but the account of Levi's consecration in both the Testament of Levi and the Aramaic deviates from the account of Aaron's consecration in Exodus 29 in one particularly striking fashion. According to the instructions in Exodus, the high priest is first dressed in his garments and then anointed. In both documents considered here, anointing precedes dressing in priestly clothes. Since it appears in Aramaic as well as in the Testament, the change in order cannot be attributed to the influence of Christian baptismal practice. In any case it is contrary to the order of baptismal practice too (de Jonge, *Testaments of the Twelve Patriarchs: A Study*, 44–45). It is perhaps worth noting that some think that anointing of priests was not actually practiced in the Second Temple period (Haran, "Law Code," 64).

36. The fragments of the Aramaic document do not contain such a clear expression of the sentiment, which in some sense underlies the whole document. Jubilees makes the point very clearly: "And the descendants of Levi were chosen for the priesthood, and to be Levites, that they might minister before the Lord (as we *do*) continually" (30:18; the angel of the presence who reveals the entire book of Jubilees is the speaker) and in Isaac's blessing of Levi, "And may the Lord . . . set you and your descendants apart from all mankind to minister to him and to serve him in his sanctuary like the angels of the presence and the holy ones" (31:14, tr. R. H. Charles, rev. C. Rabin, in *Apocryphal Old Testament*, ed. Sparks; italics indicate words added to improve the sense of the translation).

37. Andersen, "2 Enoch," 93–94.

38. Ibid., 92–93.

39. A. Vaillant, *Le livre des secrets d'Hénoch*, Textes publis par l'Institut d'études slaves 4 (Paris: Institut d'études slaves, 1952), argues that 2 Enoch is an early Christian work. His arguments (ix–xiii) are not convincing.

40. "The Date and Place of Writing of the Slavonic Book of Enoch," *The Observatory* 41 (1918): 309–16. The comments of R. H. Charles, "The Date and Place of Writing of the Slavonic Book of Enoch," *JTS* 22 (1921): 161–63, especially #5 pointing out the absence of the Bogomils' style of dualism in 2 Enoch, have been widely accepted as refuting Maunders's claims about authorship, although some of her objections to the view of Charles, which has become the scholarly consensus, deserve further consideration even after the lapse of so many years. See also Émile Turdeanu, "Apocryphes bogomiles et apocryphes pseudo-bogomiles," in *Apocryphes slaves et roumains de l'Ancien Testament*, SVTP 5 (Leiden: Brill, 1981), 37–43, for a more recent rejection of a Bogomil origin for 2 Enoch in the context of a wider study of the role of the Bogomils in the transmission of pseudepigrapha in Slavonic.

41. See Nickelsburg, *Jewish Literature*, 185–88. Vaillant, *Livre des secrets*, calls 2 Enoch a Christian revision of 1 Enoch (ix).

42. There are no standard divisions of chapter and verse for 2 Enoch. I follow the divisions of A. Pennington, "2 Enoch," in *Apocryphal Old Testament*, ed. Sparks, which represents the short version, unless I have reason to refer to the longer version published by Andersen, "2 Enoch." Translations are also taken from Pennington unless otherwise indicated.

43. In the long version only (MS J, ch. 15, in Andersen, "2 Enoch"), the sun is attended by birds that sing in its honor.

44. The short version suggests that the angels of the fifth heaven neglect their liturgical duties because they are mourning their fallen brethren in the second heaven, not because of any sin of their own. "These are the Watchers, who did not join their brothers. . . . And these are bewailing their brothers and

the punishment which was laid upon them" (7:4–5). Thus it is not the inhabitants of the fifth heaven who sinned, but rather some of their former leaders. When the angels resume the liturgy at Enoch's urging, God seems to accept their praise (7:8–10).

The picture of the long recension is different and less clear: "These are the Grigori, who turned aside from the LORD, 200 myriads, together with their prince Satanail. And similar to them are those who went down as prisoners in their train, who are in the second heaven imprisoned in great darkness" (Andersen, "2 Enoch," MS J, 18:3–6). But even in the long recension, the renewal of praise in the fifth heaven is apparently accepted (18:9). The long recension fails to explain why the sinful angels of the fifth heaven are expected to praise God while those in the second heaven are not.

45. These are the chapter and verse divisions in K. H. Kuhn, "The Apocalypse of Zephaniah and an Anonymous Apocalypse," in *Apocryphal Old Testament*, ed. Sparks.

46. See Himmelfarb, *Tours of Hell: An Apocalyptic Form in Jewish and Christian Literature* (Philadelphia: University of Philadelphia Press, 1983), 149–51.

47. Ibid., 147–53. It is possible that the angel's admonition to Daniel, *ḥazaq vehazaq* (11:19), "Be strong, be strong" (not "Be strong and of good courage," as RSV translates), also echoes these words of encouragement to Joshua, but Daniel is an unlikely source of influence for the other apocalypses discussed here because of their very different interests.

48. It must be noted that the short recension never actually describes Enoch putting on the clothes of glory. After God orders Michael to remove Enoch's earthly clothing and to put on the clothes of glory, Michael takes off Enoch's old clothes and anoints him with oil. The long version says explicitly that Michael first anoints and then clothes Enoch (Andersen, "2 Enoch," MS J, 22:9), but it never reports stripping Enoch of his old clothes. Thus both versions leave a certain amount implicit.

49. For references to some instances, see R. H. Charles, "The Book of the Secrets of Enoch," *APOT* 2:443, to 22:8.

50. Andersen raises the possibility that the oil with which Enoch is anointed represents baptismal oil ("2 Enoch," ch. 22 n. o, 138–39), although he points out that there is no mention of washing. I referred earlier to de Jonge's argument for the influence of Christian baptismal ritual on the investiture scene of the Testament of Levi. In the absence of any other indications of Christian influence in 2 Enoch, however, priestly consecration is surely a better place to look for the rituals underlying Enoch's transformation.

51. Nickelsburg, *Jewish Literature*, 187–88.

52. On this circumstance, see Andersen, "2 Enoch," ch. 71 n. c, 204–5. Andersen downplays the likelihood of Christian influence here.

53. For example, Arie Rubinstein, "Observations on the Slavonic Book of Enoch," *JJS* 13 (1962): 14–15; perhaps Charles in W. R. Morfill, tr., and R. H. Charles, ed., *The Book of the Secrets of Enoch* (Oxford: Oxford University Press, 1896), 85, who does not make this connection explicit, but does see the Melchizedek section as a Christian addition in distinction to the Jewish body of 2 Enoch.

54. On Melchizedek at Qumran, see Paul J. Kobelski, *Melchizedek and Melchireša*ʿ, Catholic Biblical Quarterly Monograph Series 10 (Washington:

Catholic Biblical Association, 1981). On early Jewish Melchizedek traditions generally, see David Flusser, "Melchizedek and the Son of Man," *Christian News from Israel* (April 1966): 23–29.

55. Andersen, "2 Enoch," ch. 69 n. a, 196. Andersen takes ch. 73, the last chapter, as the work of a learned Christian scribe (ch. 73 n. a, 212); here he follows Vaillant (*Livre des secrets*, xxi–xxii, 117–18; for Vaillant this is ch. 24). Vaillant also treats the Melchizedek section as original to 2 Enoch, which he views as Christian, but sees the last chapter as a scribal addition.

56. Nickelsburg, *Jewish Literature*, 188.

57. There is no ch. 12 in the form of the text Pennington translates ("2 Enoch").

58. Rubinstein, "Observations," 15, points out that the animals sacrificed by Methuselah and Nir are said to be bound before they are sacrificed (21:9, 22:23) in accord with Enoch's exhortation in 15:7–9. Rubinstein suggests that this means either that both sections are the work of the same author or that the author of the concluding chapters wished to bring his work into line with the rest of 2 Enoch. He does not consider the possibility that the final editor introduced this detail to bring the sources on which he drew closer together. In light of the striking difference just noted and others noted later, it seems unlikely that the original form of these chapters was the work of the author of the ascent.

59. The three possible references to sacrifice appear in 13:46–48, 15:7–9, and 15:17–20. The first of these might well be read as a rejection of sacrifice, especially in the long recension (Andersen, "2 Enoch," MS J, ch. 45), echoing as it does the prophetic preference for a pure heart over sacrifice. On 15:7–9, see later discussion. The last passage speaks of paying a vow to God in language that suggests sacrifice, but is not unequivocal.

60. De Jonge, "Levi, the Sons of Levi," in *Jewish Eschatology*, 183–85.

61. *Eschatologie und Jenseitserwartung im hellenistischen Diasporajudentum* (Berlin: de Gruyter, 1978), 40–41.

62. "Eschatology and the Concept of Time in the Slavonic Book of Enoch," in *Types of Redemption*, ed. R. J. Zwi Werblowsky and C. Jouco Bleeker, Supplements to *Numen* 18 (Leiden: Brill, 1970), 74–75. The passage in 2 Enoch is not as clear as Pines took it to be: "All you have for food, bind it by the four legs. . . ." Andersen, "2 Enoch," ch. 59 n. c, 185, writes that the slaughter in question could be "dietary, cultic, or magical." On the other hand, the mention of binding the sacrificial animals in the Melchizedek section (21:9) suggests that the slaughter in question was understood as cultic by the author of the section or by the redactor who joined it to the rest of 2 Enoch.

63. Tr. Saul Lieberman, *Hellenism in Jewish Palestine* (New York: Jewish Theological Seminary, 1950), 158. The brackets are Lieberman's; I have added the parenthetical Hebrew roots.

64. Pines, "Eschatology," 75 n. 8; Rashi to b. Tamid 30b.

65. *Hellenism*, 158. Lieberman does not address the reading of the Venice first edition, but he surely was aware of it. He may have preferred the standard reading because while no sect is known to have endorsed a practice that can be identified with that forbidden in the Mishnah, the Egyptians show that the practice did exist among non-Jews.

66. Pines suggests on the basis of irregularities of sacrificial practice that 2 Enoch may be an Essene text, but he points out that other aspects of 2 Enoch,

like its account of creation and its eschatology, do not match accounts of the Essenes or the Dead Sea Scrolls themselves ("Eschatology," 75).

67. For example, Collins, *Apocalyptic Imagination*, 198; Nickelsburg, *Jewish Literature*, 188.

68. On evidence for knowledge of the Enochic corpus in Christian Egypt, Nickelsburg, "Two Enochic Manuscripts: Unstudied Evidence for Egyptian Christianity," in *Of Scribes and Scrolls: Studies on the Hebrew Bible, Intertestamental Judaism, and Christian Origins Presented to John Strugnell on the Occasion of His Sixtieth Birthday,* ed. Harold W. Attridge, John J. Collins, and Thomas H. Tobin (Lanham, Md.: The College Theology Society and University Press of America, 1990).

69. More precisely, it is the only comparable transformation in extant apocalyptic literature. The summary of an Apocalypse of Adam in the Cologne Mani Codex claims that Adam "became more exalted than all the powers and angels of creation" (Ludwig Koenen and Claudia Römer, eds. and trs., *Der Kölner Mani-Kodex: Über das Werden seines Leibes*, Abhandlungen der rheinisch-westfälischen Akademie der Wissenschaften, Papyrologica Coloniensia 14 [Opladen: Westdeutscher, 1988], Codex p. 50).

70. 3 Enoch stands out among the hekhalot texts for a number of reasons. Although it may appear to a reader unfamiliar with the hekhalot literature as a rather loosely related set of traditions about the heavenly palaces (or temples: *hekhal* means palace or temple, as well as the middle chamber, or sanctuary, of the temple), relative to the other hekhalot works 3 Enoch is a more or less coherent whole. On the problem of the hekhalot texts as *works* with a defined beginning and end, Schäfer, "Tradition and Redaction in Hekhalot Literature," in *Hekhalot-Studien*, 8–16 (first published in *JSJ* 14 [1983]: 172–81). 3 Enoch also stands apart from the other hekhalot texts in its avoidance of theurgy (Philip Alexander, "3 (Hebrew Apocalypse of) Enoch," in *Pseudepigrapha*, ed. Charlesworth 1:235). The hekhalot work that stands closest to it in this regard is Hekhalot Rabbati, but unlike Hekhalot Rabbati, 3 Enoch contains no angelic songs at all.

71. Chapter and verse references are taken from Alexander, "3 Enoch"; Alexander follows Hugo Odeberg, *3 Enoch, or The Hebrew Book of Enoch* (Cambridge: Cambridge University Press, 1928).

72. Alexander, "3 Enoch," 225–29.

73. Metatron is called high priest of the heavenly temple in Numbers Rabbah 12:12. On the attestation of the chapter in question, ch. 15B in Alexander, "3 Enoch," see Alexander, ch. 15 n. a, 303. The reference to the "heavenly tabernacle of light" (15B:1) may suggest Metatron is here understood to serve as high priest.

74. The relationship between Metatron's robe and priestly dress is clear in a work entitled Alphabet of Metatron, quoted by Odeberg, *3 Enoch*, note to 12:1, p. 32, from a British Museum MS, where Metatron is said to be dressed in eight garments. As Alexander, "3 Enoch," notes (ch. 12 n. a), eight is the number of garments of the high priest.

Chapter 3

1. The scholarly discussion about Jesus as *theios anēr*, a divine man who manifests his divinity through the miracles he performs, has shown the difficulty

of isolating a single such type in Greco-Roman literature. See, for example, David Lenz Tiede, *The Charismatic Figure as Miracle Worker*, SBL Dissertation Series 1 (Missoula, Mont.: Society of Biblical Literature, 1972), and Carl R. Holladay, *Theios Aner in Hellenistic Judaism: A Critique of the Use of This Category in New Testament Christology*, SBL Dissertation Series 40 (Missoula, Mont.: Scholars, 1977), and literature discussed in these two works.

2. Tr. M.W. Meyer in *The Greek Magical Papyri in Translation Including the Demotic Spells*, ed. Hans Dieter Betz (Chicago: University of Chicago Press, 1986): 50–51.

3. Hans Lewy, *Chaldean Oracles and Theurgy: Mysticism, Magic, and Platonism in the Later Roman Empire* (Cairo: L'Institut Français d'Archéologie Orientale, 1956), 177–226.

4. Tr. E. N. O'Neil in *Magical Papyri*, ed. Betz, 41–42. Morton Smith's translation in *Jesus the Magician* (San Francisco: Harper & Row, 1978) is even more striking: "'I have been united with thy sacred form. I have been empowered by thy sacred name. I have received the effluence of thy goodness, Lord, God of gods, King, Demon.'. . . When you have done this, descend, having attained that nature equal to the God's which is effected by this ritual union" (103). It is interesting to consider the presuppositions reflected in the differences between the translations.

5. Koenen and Römer, eds. and trs., *Mani-Kodex*. Parenthetical references to the Mani Codex refer to pages of the Codex itself. All translations from the Greek of the Mani Codex are mine.

6. Baraies is summarizing the content of the Apocalypse of Adam in the passage I quote, but he indicates that he is quoting the passage from the Apocalypse of Sethel.

7. These categories are suggested by Larry W. Hurtado, *One God, One Lord: Early Christian Devotion and Ancient Jewish Monotheism* (Philadelphia: Fortress, 1988), 17–18; on Enoch traditions, see 51–56. In addition to Hurtado, recent literature on intermediary figures includes Fossum, *The Name of God*, which has rather little to say about the ascent apocalypses; and Segal, *Paul the Convert*, 34–71, esp. 40–52, where the ascent apocalypses receive considerable attention.

8. See, for example, Tiede, *Charismatic Figure*, 101–240; Hurtado, *One God*, 51–69.

9. Tr. F. H. Colson, *Philo*, Loeb Classical Library, vol. 6 (Cambridge, Mass.: Harvard University Press, 1935), 357–59.

10. Smith, "Ascent to the Heavens and Deification in 4QM^a," in *Archeology and History: The New York University Conference in Memory of Yigael Yadin*, ed. Lawrence H. Schiffman, Journal for the Study of the Pseudepigrapha Series 8, JSOT/ASOR Monographs 2 (Sheffield: JSOT, 1990). The portions of the translation cited come from 183–84, line 12 and line 19; the discussion of the identity of the speaker and the relation to early Christianity appear on 185–88. See also Collins, "A Throne in the Heavens: Apotheosis in pre-Christian Judaism," *Essays in Memory of Ioan P. Culianu*, ed. Collins and Fishbane.

The view of Jesus as a human being who had achieved divine status is by no means the only early Christian view. Alan Segal (*Paul the Convert*, 56–71) offers a powerful argument that Paul understands Jesus as the Glory of God. See also Carey Newman, *Paul's Glory-Christology: Tradition and Rhetoric* (Leiden: Brill, 1992).

11. Tr. Geza Vermes, *The Dead Sea Scrolls in English*, 3d ed. (London: Penguin, 1987), 173.

12. See the discussion and references in Michael Newton, *The Concept of Purity at Qumran and in the Letters of Paul*, SNTS Monograph Series 53 (Cambridge: Cambridge University Press, 1985), esp. 49–51.

13. Newsom, *Songs*, 17–21.

14. I am indebted to Collins, "Apocalyptic Eschatology as the Transcendence of Death," *CBQ* 36 (1974): 21–43, which concentrates on Daniel and literature contemporary with it. All of the texts I cite are cited by Collins, with the exception of the passage from 2 Baruch, which is too late for the time span that Collins defines.

15. Nickelsburg, *Resurrection, Immortality, and Eternal Life in Intertestamental Judaism* (Cambridge, Mass.: Harvard University Press, 1972).

16. Tr. R. H. Charles, rev. L. H. Brockington, "The Syriac Apocalypse of Baruch," in *Apocryphal Old Testament*, ed. Sparks.

17. The essay was originally published in *Archiv für Religionswissenschaft* 4 (1901): 136–69, 229–73; it was later reprinted as a separate booklet (Darmstadt: Wissenschaftliche Buchgesellschaft, 1960). The claim just stated appears in the very first paragraph of the essay (p. 5 in the reprint). For discussion of this classic essay, see Segal, "Heavenly Ascent," 1341–42; Ioan Petru Culianu, *Psychanodia I: A Survey of the Evidence Concerning the Ascension of the Soul and Its Relevance* (Leiden: Brill, 1983), 18–22.

18. On the complicated issues associated with the preservation of this work, see Kuhn, "Apocalypse of Zephaniah," 915–19. I cite the Apocalypse of Zephaniah according to chapter and verse divisions and translation of Kuhn. These chapter and verse divisions are entirely different from those of O. S. Wintermute, "Apocalypse of Zephaniah," in *Pseudepigrapha* 1, ed. Charlesworth. Italics in Kuhn's translation indicate words not actually present in the Coptic.

19. Since both the Sahidic and the Akhmimic MSS contain versions of the Apocalypse of Elijah, the assumption is that the fragment of the second work in the Sahidic is a version of the anonymous apocalypse in the Akhmimic. While the content of the Sahidic fragment is very close to the Akhmimic, it does not correspond exactly to anything in the preserved Akhmimic. The passage from an Apocalypse of Zephaniah quoted by Clement is not much help here since it corresponds neither to the Sahidic fragment nor to the extant Akhmimic, nor does it seem possible to locate its description of the angels of the fifth heaven in one of the lacunae of the Akhmimic with its single heaven.

Kuhn, "Apocalypse of Zephaniah," refers to the apocalypse from the Akhmimic MS that is the subject of discussion here as anonymous.

20. Tr. Charles Cutler Torrey, *The Lives of the Prophets: Greek Text and Translation*, Journal of Biblical Literature Monograph Series 1 (Philadephia: Society of Biblical Literature and Exegesis, 1946), 44.

21. I accept the view of David Satran, "The Lives of the Prophets," in *Jewish Writings of the Second Temple Period*, ed. Michael E. Stone, Compendia Rerum Iudaicarum ad Novum Testamentum, 2.2 (Assen: Van Gorcum, 1984), 56–60, that the Lives is a Christian composition of the fourth or fifth century. See also Satran's forthcoming monograph, *Biblical Prophets in Byzantine Palestine: Reassessing the Lives of the Prophets*, SVTP (Leiden: Brill, forthcoming).

22. Himmelfarb, *Tours*, 147–51.

23. In the terms Maier suggests in "Gefährdungsmotiv," this is danger, not merely awe. On parallels to hekhalot literature, see n. 26.

24. The name does not appear at all in the indices to Victor A. Tcherikover, Alexander Fuks, and Menahem Stern, eds., *Corpus Papyrorum Judaicarum*, 3 vols. (Cambridge, Mass.: Harvard University Press, 1957–64).

25. Italics indicate words added to improve the English.

26. See my discussion in *Tours*, 153–55. My claim that the iron bars of the Apocalypse of Zephaniah find a parallel in the hekhalot literature is misleading; see my "Heavenly Ascent," 89 n. 73. I would also revise the more general comments on the relationship of the apocalypses to merkavah mysticism in *Tours*, 155–58; see "Heavenly Ascent," 98–100.

27. "Apocalypse of Zephaniah," 513–14 (in the body of the text).

28. See, for example, the introduction of J. M. T. Barton, "The Ascension of Isaiah," in *Apocryphal Old Testament*, ed. Sparks, 775–81. All quotations from the Ascension of Isaiah are taken from this version, which is Barton's revision of the translation of R. H. Charles.

29. Himmelfarb, *Tours*, 136–37, 156 n. 56.

30. Robert G. Hall, "*The Ascension of Isaiah*: Community Situation, Date, and Place in Early Christianity," *JBL* 109 (1990): 300–306, reviews earlier opinions and argues convincingly for the early second century.

31. In the first heaven, no mention is made of one seated on the throne. This may be intended to suggest a distinction between the first heaven and the next four, but this is by no means obvious, and the omission may be accidental.

32. For this verse, I follow the literal translation in Charles-Barton, "Ascension of Isaiah," 799 n. 30.

33. Charles-Barton here follow the Latin and Slavonic against the Ethiopic ("Ascension of Isaiah," 805 nn. 35–36). According to the Ethiopic, it is Christ who is transformed into an angel at this point. But there is no reason for Christ to be transformed into a being of lesser status before Isaiah worships him.

34. Here all three versions read that it is the Holy Spirit that does not transform itself (Charles-Barton, "Ascension of Isaiah, 805 n. 39). The reading of the translation of Charles-Barton is based on Charles's emendation. This emendation seems to me necessary to the sense of passage. But in any case the point I wish to make is clear in 9:37–38, where there are no textual problems. See immediately below.

35. See Himmelfarb, "Heavenly Ascent," 80–88.

36. Andrew K. Helmbold, "Gnostic Elements in the 'Ascension of Isaiah,'" *New Testament Studies* 18 (1972): 222–27, finds gnostic elements in both sections.

37. Himmelfarb, *Tours*, 136–37.

38. Paul himself does not see God, but rather hears him announcing judgment; the souls themselves apparently see God (chs. 14, 16).

39. Mullen, *Assembly of the Gods*, 182–85, and references there. Mullen takes the adjective "princely" to point to the originally military function of the gods of the council. Whatever the original connotations, it is easily understood as royal.

40. See, for example, Louis F. Hartman and Alexander A. DiLella, *The Book of Daniel*, Anchor Bible 23 (Garden City, N.Y.: Doubleday, 1978), 218.

41. Collins, *Apocalyptic Imagination*, 145–47, emphasizes sectarian provenance. On date see, for example, Nickelsburg, *Jewish Literature*, 221–23; Collins, *Apocalyptic Imagination*, 142–43.

42. For some brief remarks on the development from Daniel through the Similitudes to the Gospels, Nickelsburg, *Jewish Literature*, 222–23.

43. In Black's translation (*Book of Enoch*), the name of God is "Chief of Days." Black discusses the complexities of the title and its relationship to Daniel, 192–93.

44. David Suter, *Tradition and Composition in the Parables of Enoch*, SBL Dissertation Series 47 (Missoula, Mont.: Scholars, 1979), 11–33, argues that the author of the Similitudes used traditions that also appear in the Book of the Watchers without dependence on the Book of the Watchers, since the Similitudes knows other traditions about the fallen angels as well. I think Suter is mistaken. Because of his concentration on the relationship between the Similitudes and chapters 6–11 of the Book of the Watchers, he fails to take account of the many links between the Similitudes and the ascent to heaven and tour to the ends of the earth in the Book of the Watchers. See Nickelsburg, *Jewish Literature*, 214–21, who notes many of the points of contact, and my discussion in this chapter on the Similitudes' use of the ascent of the Book of the Watchers and in the next chapter on its use of the tour to the ends of the earth.

45. On this reading, rather than Son of Man and Lord of spirits, see Black, *Book of Enoch*, note to 70:1, 250.

46. On the relationship of the last chapter to the rest of the work, see Collins, *Apocalyptic Imagination*, 151–53; Nickelsburg, *Jewish Literature*, 221.

47. Nickelsburg, *Jewish Literature*, 221.

48. *Apocalyptic Imagination*, 152–53.

49. *Jewish Gnosticism*, 23; for discussion of the song, Scholem, *Major Trends in Jewish Mysticism*, paperback ed. (New York: Schocken, 1961), 61. Other points of contact between the Apocalypse of Abraham and the hekhalot literature are the qualities of the angel Iaoel and the details of Abraham's vision of the chariot throne. Scholem discusses the experience of the visionary in the Apocalypse of Abraham in *Major Trends*, 52; he treats the angel Iaoel in *Major Trends*, 68–69.

On the relationship of the Apocalypse of Abraham to merkavah traditions, see also Ithamar Gruenwald, *Apocalyptic and Merkavah Mysticism*, Arbeiten zur Geschichte des antiken Judentums und des Urchristentums 14 (Leiden: Brill, 1980), 51–57, and now David Halperin's very interesting treatment of the text, *Faces of the Chariot*, 103–14.

50. On this passage and its difficulties, see, for example, Nickelsburg, *Jewish Literature*, 297. Michael E. Stone, "Apocalyptic Literature," in *Jewish Writings*, 415–16, points out that the passage presents difficulties even if it is presumed to be Christian. A. Pennington in the introduction to his translation, "The Apocalypse of Abraham," in *Apocryphal Old Testament*, ed. Sparks, considers the possibility that despite the use of Jewish traditions, the Apocalypse of Abraham is a Christian work (365–67).

51. See G. H. Box with J. I. Landsman, *The Apocalypse of Abraham* (London: SPCK, 1918), Appendix 1, 88–94. There are also some very broad similarities to the stories in Jubilees and Philo.

52. All translations of the Apocalypse of Abraham are taken from Pennington, "Apocalypse of Abraham."

53. MSS J and K; see Pennington, "Apocalypse of Abraham," 11:2 n. 1.

54. Fossum, *Name of God*, 318–20, uses the similarities between Iaoel's appearance and God's as part of his argument that Iaoel is the Glory of God; in addition he suggests that the divine throne Abraham sees has no occupant because

Iaoel has stepped off to guide Abraham. But Hurtado, *One God*, 87–89, shows that Fossum's reading of the Apocalypse of Abraham is problematic: God does appear on the throne, although he appears as fire rather than a human form (17:1, 19:1). While Hurtado connects Iaoel's appearance to the imagery of the imperial court, I would insist on the centrality of priestly imagery, although the two are by no means mutually exclusive.

55. I would like to thank Gideon Bohak for pointing this out to me.

56. For the use of royal elements for priests, see T. Levi 8:4, 8.

57. Halperin, *Faces of the Chariot*, 104, calls the ascent "apocalyptic midrash" and offers an admirable analysis of the debt of the Apocalypse of Abraham to the biblical text.

58. Gen. 15:17: *tannur 'ašan*, a smoking oven; *lappid 'eš*, a fiery torch. Ex. 19:18, *'ašan*, smoke; *'eš*, fire; *ke'ešen hakkivšan*, like the smoke of a furnace. Ex. 20:18: *lappidim*, lightning. On this appropriation and its relation to the larger complex of traditions associated with Moses' ascent to receive the Torah in rabbinic literature, Halperin, *Faces of the Chariot*, 109–12.

59. At 19:6 all the MSS refer to the angels of the *eighth* firmament, but the translations of Box (*Apocalypse of Abraham*), Pennington ("Apocalypse of Abraham"), and R. Rubinkiewicz ("Apocalypse of Abraham," in *Old Testament Pseudepigrapha* 1, ed. Charlesworth), all question this reading. On the probability of scribal error, Rubinkiewicz, "Apocalypse of Abraham," 698 n. f. Rubinkiewicz emends "eighth" to "sixth"; Pennington emends to "seventh."

60. Italics indicate words not found in the original. Here Rubinkiewicz's translation differs considerably at one point, which affects the meaning of the passage as a whole. In 15:6, for Pennington's "And behold, by that light *I saw* a burning fire of people," Rubinkiewicz translates, "And behold, in this light a fiery Gehenna was enkindled. . . ." The men of changing appearance are then inhabitants of Gehenna rather than the angelic host as in Pennington's translation. But Rubinkiewicz's translation involves an emendation (see his n. f to ch. 15, "Apocalypse of Abraham," 696), and there are no hints elsewhere in the Apocalypse of Abraham that Gehenna is to be found in the seventh heaven, a placement unparalleled in apocalyptic literature. Further, the point of taking Abraham through Gehenna is not clear. I prefer to understand Abraham's first impression of the scene in relation to other visionaries' fear in the face of the heavenly hosts.

61. The italicized words are added in MSS JK (Pennington, "Apocalypse of Abraham," ch. 16, n. 5, 380).

62. Tr. Meyer, in Betz, *Magical Papyri*, 49.

63. The text of the song varies somewhat in the MSS. On the types of hymns in hekhalot literature, see Alexander Altmann, "Kedushah Hymns in the Earliest Hechaloth Literature (From an Oxford MS)" (in Hebrew), *Melilah* 2 (1946): 1–24; Scholem, *Major Trends*, 57–63. Scholem calls the type of hymn involving the piling up of adjectives, "numinous," and mentions the hymn from the Apocalypse of Abraham as early evidence for this type of hymn, 61. Some of the numinous hymns that appear in the hekhalot texts became part of the synagogue liturgy.

64. It may also be a kind of comic relief, since the narrative of Abraham's discovery of God contains some comic incidents. For the suggestion that this incident implies "something fundamentally savage and chaotic" about the creatures, see Halperin, *Faces of the Chariot*, 112–13 (quotation, 113).

65. Halperin sees the absence of a vision of God as another aspect of the transfer of Sinai traditions: "For a man cannot see me and live" (Ex. 33:20) (*Faces of the Chariot*, 110).

66. On the relationship between Azazel's descent and Abraham's ascent, see Halperin, *Faces of the Chariot*, 111.

67. Stone, "Apocalyptic Literature," 416–17.

68. This section and the following one expand on my comments in "Revelation and Rapture: The Transformation of the Visionary in the Ascent Apocalypses," in *Mysteries and Revelations: Apocalyptic Studies since the Uppsala Colloquium*, ed. John J. Collins and James H. Charlesworth, Journal for the Study of the Pseudepigrapha Supplement Series 9 (Sheffield: JSOT Press, 1991), 88–90.

69. On Moses in the midrashim, see *Faces of the Chariot*, 289–322. On Śar Torah, see *Faces of the Chariot*, 376–87, 414–46.

70. Ibid., esp. 439–46.

71. For example, Scholem, *Jewish Gnosticism*, 49–50; Saul Lieberman, "Metatron, the Meaning of His Name and His Functions," Appendix to Gruenwald, *Apocalyptic*, 238–39.

72. Halperin, *Faces of the Chariot*, 420–27.

73. Ibid., 437–39.

74. See my review of Halperin's *Faces of the Chariot*, in *Critical Review of Books in Religion* 3 (1990): 342, and also Rachel Elior's comments in her review of *Faces of the Chariot* in *Numen* 37 (1990): 241–47. Elior insists on the importance of ecstatic ascent for understanding the hekhalot literature, a view I follow Halperin in rejecting, but I share her opinion that Halperin overemphasizes the antagonism they depict and presumably reflect.

75. Himmelfarb, "Heavenly Ascent," 91–93. The recent challenge to Scholem's view of the centrality of heavenly ascent to the hekhalot literature has also called into question his view of an unbroken tradition of merkavah mysticism reaching from the apocalypses through rabbinic literature to the hekhalot texts. Still, there are some important parallels between the transformation of the visionary in the ascent apocalypses and the hekhalot texts. For a succinct statement of Scholem's position, see *Major Trends*, 41–43. For the critique, see Halperin, *The Merkabah in Rabbinic Literature*, American Oriental Series 62 (New Haven, Conn.: American Oriental Society, 1980). Halperin argues that the tannaim did not practice merkavah mysticism but rather put Ezekiel's vision to homiletical use.

76. Schäfer, *Rivalität zwischen Engeln und Menschen*, Studia Judaica (Berlin: de Gruyter, 1975), 9–33, discusses the various ways in which angels function in the pseudepigrapha.

77. See the fine new study by Michael Mach, *Die Entstehung des jüdischen Engelglaubens. Entwicklungsphasen des jüdischen Engelglaubens in vorrabbinischer Zeit*, Texte und Studien zum antiken Judentum 34 (Tübingen: Mohr [Siebeck], 1992).

78. I use the plural to emphasize that there was no single dominant angelology.

79. Hengel, *Judaism and Hellenism*, 1:233.

80. John Bright, *A History of Israel*, 3d ed. (Philadelphia: Westminster, 1981), 447–49.

81. Bright makes a real effort to defend "late Judaism" against the charges

of legalism and spiritual dryness; he treats the elaboration of angelology as nonnormative, thus rescuing normative Judaism.

Hurtado, *One God*, traces the negative view back to Bousset and suggests an understanding of the significance of angelology quite similar to mine (22–35).

82. E. R. Goodenough, *By Light, Light: The Mystic Gospel of Hellenistic Judaism* (New Haven, Conn.: Yale University Press, 1935), 11.

83. On Philo and Ezekiel, see n. 8 in this chapter. On rabbinic sermons, see Halperin, *Faces of the Chariot*, 262–358.

84. I argue for this understanding of 3 Baruch in some detail in the next chapter.

85. Himmelfarb, "The Experience of the Visionary and Genre in the Ascension of Isaiah 6–11 and the Apocalypse of Paul," in *Early Christian Apocalypticism: Genre and Social Setting*, ed. Adela Yarbro Collins, *Semeia* 36 (1986): 104–5.

86. "Heavenly Ascent," 1338–40.

Chapter 4

1. See, for example, Nickelsburg, *Jewish Literature*, 54–55.

2. Himmelfarb, *Tours of Hell*, 50–60. Nine out of ten of the instances of the form appear in the second tour. The content of the second tour is also clearly influenced by Ezekiel. See later discussion.

3. It is even possible to translate the "very many trees" on either side of the banks of the river (Ezek. 47:7) as "a very great tree" (Levenson, *Program*, 30–31). We would thus have two very great trees, one on either side of the river, further emphasizing the correspondence to the Garden of Eden of Genesis, with the tree of knowledge and the tree of life in its midst. Compare Rev. 22:2, where the stream in the Jerusalem that descends from heaven has on either side "the tree of life."

4. See the taunt against the prince of Tyre (ch. 28) and oracle against Pharoah (ch. 31). In neither place is the holy mountain the temple mount. On the use of Eden traditions in the taunt against Tyre, see Carol A. Newsom, "A Maker of Metaphors—Ezekiel's Oracles Against Tyre," *Interpretation* 38 (1984): 161–64. On this subject generally, see Levenson, *Program*, 25–36; Himmelfarb, "The Temple and the Garden of Eden in Ezekiel, the Book of the Watchers, and the Wisdom of Ben Sira," in *Sacred Places and Profane Spaces: Essays in the Geographics of Judaism, Christianity and Islam*, ed. Jamie S. Scott and Paul Simpson-Horsley (Westport, Conn.: Greenwood, 1991), 64–66.

5. The discussion of the Garden of Eden in 1 Enoch 17–36 is adapted from Himmelfarb, "The Temple," 69–72.

6. As the mountain of the temple, Mount Zion is widely understood as God's throne. The mountain Enoch sees, however, is clearly not Mount Zion; it is part of a range of seven mountains, and only after visiting it does Enoch proceed to Jerusalem (26:1).

7. The Aramaic is *pardes qušṭa'*, the Greek, *paradeisos tēs dikaiosunēs*. *Paradeisos* is the Septuagint's translation of *gan* in Genesis 2.

Although Rabbinic literature knows the Garden of Eden as the place where the righteous are rewarded after death, no such view is expressed in the Book of the Watchers. The tree of wisdom in the Garden seems to be given an eschatological function: it is the tree "of the fruit of which those who partake understand great wisdom" (32:3), presumably at the eschaton.

8. Pierre Grelot, "La géographie mythique d'Hénoch et ses sources orientales," *RB* 65 (1958): 41–44, suggests that the author doubled Eden in an attempt to make sense of various biblical traditions about location. He also suggests that the author drew on a tradition of exegesis of Genesis 2–3 that understood God to have removed the tree of life from the Garden of Eden after the fall.

9. I know of no discussion of the subject.

10. The praise appears in the second source, but it only makes explicit what is implicit in the first.

11. For example, 40:12, 22; 42:5; 44:24, 45:7, 12, 18; 48:13.

12. For example, 43:1; 44:2, 21.

13. For example, 41:18–20, 43:16–21. The theme of fertility in the wilderness probably goes back to Baal mythology. See Cross, *Caananite Myth*, 116–20.

14. 51:13, 16.

15. On rhetorical questions like this, see Stone, "Lists," 421 n. 15.

16. Cross, *Caananite Myth*, 343–45.

17. In Black's translation (*The Book of Enoch*), brackets indicate omissions in the text or a "putative Greek variant"; italics indicate an emended or problematic text.

18. Stone, "The Parabolic Use of Natural Order in Judaism of the Second Temple Age," in *Gilgul: Werblowsky Festschrift*, ed. Shaul Shaked, David Shulman, and Gedaliahu G. Stroumsa, Numen Supplement 50 (Leiden: Brill, 1987), 298–303.

19. For a brief analysis of the sources combined in the story of the fall of the Watchers, see Nickelsburg, *Jewish Literature*, 49–52.

20. Stone, "Lists," 414–26.

21. Ibid., 426–37.

22. Ibid., 436.

23. "Formulaic, traditional lists were included in the apocalyptic books without having more than partial overlap with the actual concerns of the apocalyptic authors" ("Lists," 419).

24. The translation of the Hebrew phrase *šetum ha'ayin* is not certain. RSV translates as above, with a note "or closed or perfect." What is important for my purposes is not the original meaning of the phrase but how the author of the Book of the Watchers understood it. The Septuagint translates both instances of the pharse, "who sees truly."

25. David Suter, "Mašal in the Similitudes of Enoch," *JBL* 100 (1981): 195–202.

26. Ibid., 202–12.

27. Suter, "Mašal," 204, uses this passage as an example. Stone, also discusses it, "Lists," 428–29.

28. Nickelsburg reads the description of Wisdom's failure to find a place on earth as a parody of ben Sira (*Jewish Literature*, 216). Burton Mack points out that ben Sira's view of wisdom's presence in Israel is not easy optimism but a self-conscious program (*Wisdom and the Hebrew Epic: Ben Sira's Hymn in Praise of the Fathers* [Chicago: University of Chicago Press, 1986], 139–71).

The passage about Wisdom appears to be out of place in its present context in the Similitudes, but there is no question that the view of the passage matches the author's view, expressed throughout the work.

29. "Him" here seems to refer to the Elect One, especially in light of the end of the paragraph, but it is conceivable that the reference is to God himself.

30. This passage is part of a Noah apocalypse incorporated into the Similitudes. It was probably originally an independent composition.

31. Nickelsburg, *Jewish Literature*, 185–86.

32. Chapters 14–15 in MS J, Andersen, "2 Enoch." I follow Andersen's spelling for the birds.

33. MS J, chapter 17 (Andersen, "2 Enoch") provides a more elaborate description than the short version.

34. Most of the little that has been written about this very difficult passage treats the origins of individual motifs rather than the meaning of the passage as a whole. In relation to his discussion of the creation of a primordial aeon in *Sefer habahir*, the earliest kabbalistic text, Gershom Scholem sketches an understanding of the account of creation in 2 Enoch as related to the Jewish "gnosticism" of the *Bahir*, and points to parallels with individual elements of the account in rabbinic literature (*Origins of the Kabbalah*, tr. from the German by Allan Arkush [Philadelphia and Princeton: Jewish Publication Society and Princeton University Press, 1987], 73–74).

In a reading in many ways close to Scholem's, Fossum treats Adoil as the "celestial Man" and demiurge (*Name of God*, 287–92). I find this reading unpersuasive because it fails to relate this aspect of 2 Enoch's account of creation to the rest of 2 Enoch.

Individual elements of the account are discussed by Marc Philonenko, "La cosmologie du 'Livre des secrets d'Hénoch,'" in *Religions en Égypte hellénistique et romaine*, Colloque de Strasbourg, 16–18 mai 1967 (Paris: Presses universitaires de France, 1969), 109–16. Philonenko treats the account as an example of syncretism, discerning Jewish, Egyptian, and Persian elements in it. He does not offer a reading of the account as a whole, nor does he explain how Jews in Egypt had access to Persian traditions.

The view that 2 Enoch was influenced by Zoroastrianism goes back to Rudolf Otto, *Reich Gottes und Menschensohn* (Munich: Beck, 1934), 160–64. It is developed also by Pines, "Eschatology," 72–87. Pines does not consider the account of creation itself, nor does he discuss the channels through which such influence might have made itself felt.

35. This is the sense of Andersen's translation ("2 Enoch"): "I did not find rest, because everything was not yet created" (24:5). Pennington's translation ("2 Enoch") is somewhat different: "I found no rest, for I was creating everything."

36. For example, R. H. Charles in his edition of 2 Enoch (Morfill and Charles, *The Book of the Secrets of Enoch*, 32) suggests *yad'el*, hand of God (note to 25:1). L. Gry, "Quelques noms d'anges ou d'êtres mystérieux en II Hénoch," *RB* 49 (1940): 200–203, takes it as a corruption of Uriel. Vaillant, *Livre des secrets d'Hénoch*, xi, derives it from *'ado*, his eternity. Scholem, "Die Lehre vom 'Gerechten' in der jüdischen Mystik," *Eranos-Jahrbuch* 27 (1958): 252, takes it as a corruption of a name derived from *ṣaddiq*, righteous. Andersen's MS A ("2 Enoch," 145) reads Adail.

37. Pennington's text ("2 Enoch") reads rather differently. Like MS A (Andersen), it describes only the great age emerging from the disintegration of

Adoil and make no mention of the emergence of light. Since God shortly afterward issues commands to the light, an original reference to its emergence must have fallen out of the text of these short MSS. According to the long version of MS J (Andersen), there first emerges a great light, followed by a great age "reveal[ing] all the creation which I had thought up to create" (25:2–3).

38. The name Aruchaz also suggests Hebrew *'arokh*, long, but this meaning does not seem appropriate to the creature. The name differs slightly in some of the MSS.

39. Andersen, "2 Enoch," MS J, 26:2.

40. As Andersen notes, "2 Enoch," ch. 26 n. d., 145.

41. In his close analysis of the odd eschatology of 2 Enoch, Fischer (*Eschatologie und Jenseitserwartung*, 57–58) rejects Pines's claim for the importance of Persian background. Instead he suggests Philonic and Platonic beliefs about the visible and noetic worlds as an influence that gives 2 Enoch's apocalyptic eschatology its peculiar twist. Thus the careful study of a different aspect of 2 Enoch leads Fischer to a view similar to mine about the intellectual background of the work.

42. "2 Enoch," ch. 27 n. a, 145. But Andersen concludes that it is impossible to decide at this stage of research which form of the account of creation is closer to the original.

43. "2 Enoch," ch. 31 n. d, 154–55. It is important to emphasize that the material about Satan does not influence the rest of the work in any way. The ethical exhortations that form the largest part of the work show no traces of it, nor is any attempt made to bring it into relation to the story of the fall of the Watchers that lies in the background of the ascent.

44. Parallels to 2 Enoch are often invoked in the introductory literature. They are much less persuasive, both because 2 Enoch's Egyptian provenance has not been adequately demonstrated and because the parallels are not very compelling.

45. I use H. E. Gaylord, Jr., "3 (Greek Apocalypse of) Baruch," in *Pseudepigrapha* 1, ed. Chartesworth, which includes translations of both versions.

46. For a convincing explanation of the use of the story of the Tower of Babel, see Nickelsburg, *Jewish Literature*, 299–303. For another view, see Jean-Claude Picard, "Observations sur l'Apocalypse grecque de Baruch," *Semitica* 20 (1970): 77–103.

47. There is considerable confusion in both versions about the beginning and end of the third and fourth heavens. Although entrance into the third heaven is never noted in the text (Greek or Slavonic), the Greek later refers to the heaven in which the sun and moon appear as the third (7:2). The sun and moon seem to be in the same heaven as Hades. Later in the Greek version Baruch enters the third heaven (10:1), where he sees the lake with birds. The Slavonic does not indicate entrance into a new heaven at this point. Gaylord assumes that the fourth heaven is intended ("3 Baruch," ch. 10 n. a, 673).

48. The description in the Greek of a serpent, a dragon, and Hades, all somehow related, is extremely obscure. The perhaps harmonizing claim that Hades is the belly appears in 5:3. The Slavonic makes no mention of Hades; in the Slavonic it is the serpent of Genesis 3 that is punished for its role in the fall of Adam and Eve. This reading seems to me likely to be original; Gaylord thinks so too ("3 Baruch," 657), although he does not argue the case.

49. The same picture appears in the Slavonic, where it is the serpent who drinks. There the statement about the number of rivers is somewhat confused.

50. Dean-Otting treats this portion of 3 Baruch as "a polemic against the solar pantheism of the age" (*Heavenly Journeys*, 137–48; quotation, 141). While she provides a good sketch of the background against which the interest in the sun should be understood, her suggestion that 3 Baruch represents a polemic is misguided. Rather, 3 Baruch provides a way of integrating reverence for the sun into a monotheistic system.

51. I am by no means convinced that the relation is literary, especially since the most striking common element, the association of the phoenix with the sun, is found only in the long, presumably later, version of 2 Enoch. Further, as Gideon Bohak points out to me, this association is so common that it cannot be taken as evidence for dependence of one text on another.

52. According to Gaylord, the family of Slavonic MSS he designates B2 goes on to say that the excrement becomes black cumin, used in anointing kings ("3 Baruch," ch. 6 n. i, 670).

53. R. van den Broek, *The Myth of the Phoenix According to Classical and Early Christian Traditions* (Leiden: Brill, 1972), 212–17 on the worm, 164–72 on cinnamon. Van den Broek comments that 3 Baruch may be attempting to incorporate elements of other accounts into his quite different understanding of the phoenix (216), which van den Broek understands to derive from an enormous bird that appears associated with the sun in some rabbinic sources (e.g., Genesis Rabbah 19.4, Leviticus Rabbah 22.10) (264–65). The bird is called the *ziz*; it takes its name from a playful reading of Ps. 50:11.

54. Presumably the commanding voice is God's. See Dean-Otting, *Heavenly Journeys*, 110.

55. The description of the phoenix and the sun and Baruch's reaction to them (7:3–5) is lacking in Slavonic, which describes Baruch's fear and flight into the wings of the angel as a response to the sight of the sun's crown (ch. 8). The reaction better fits its context in the Greek, where it has been more adequately prepared for.

56. The term "mysteries" appears in the Greek only at the beginning of the tour (1:6, 8: 2:6). In the Slavonic the term appears also during the tour (1:4, 6; 2:6; 5:3; 17:1).

See Dean-Otting, *Heavenly Journeys*, for an elaborate discussion of the term and its background (102–9). Picard reads this language in line with his view of 3 Baruch as an initiation text for a mystery ("Observations," 84; mysteries: 90, 102). Dean-Otting's comments on cultic silence (108–9) relate to this, but unlike Picard she does not invent Jewish mysteries.

57. The argument is an old one. See, for example, H. M. Hughes, "The Greek Apocalypse of Baruch or III Baruch," in *APOT*, ed. Charles, who writes that the work is incomplete, that other heavens are implied, and also that both the extant Greek and Slavonic are condensations of a longer Greek original (2:527). This seems to me an excess of solutions.

58. Richard Bauckham, "Early Jewish Visions of Hell," *JTS*, n.s., 41 (1990): 373–74.

59. Bauckham's examples, "Early Jewish Visions," are the Syriac Transitus Mariae, from the fifth century in its present form (361), and the medieval Gedullat Mosheh (370–71).

60. Ibid., 373–74.

61. Compare also Revelation, where John's angelic interlocutor tells him not to worship him since they are fellow servants (Rev. 19:10).

62. *Apocrypha Anecdota II* (Texts and Studies 5:1; Cambridge: Cambridge University Press, 1897), lxvii, lxix. The passages are 3 Bar. 8:3–5 and Apocalypse of Paul 4, and 3 Baruch 11–16 and Apocalypse of Paul 7–10.

63. Apoc. Zeph. 3:3–8, Apocalypse of Paul 23. See the discussion in Himmelfarb, "The Experience of the Visionary," 104–5.

64. See A. W. Argyle, "The Greek Apocalypse of Baruch," in *Apocryphal Old Testament*, ed. Sparks, 899.

65. The Slavonic text is corrupt. Gaylord's translation reads, "a serpent on a stone mountain," but in his note he repeats the emendation of M. R. James and others, "two hundred plethra in length" ("3 Baruch," ch. 4 n. d, 666).

66. The Slavonic includes a large block of material about which angels planted which trees in paradise. This tradition does not appear independently elsewhere. Gaylord ("3 Baruch," ch. 4 n. m, 666–67) is unsure whether it is an original part of the work or an addition in the Slavonic.

67. In the Slavonic, God commands Noah to change it: "Alter its name, and change it for the better" (4:15). In the Greek, God predicts that the vine will be transformed from curse to blessing, and here appears an obviously Christian passage: "Its fruit will become the blood of God, and just as the race of men have been condemned through it, so through Jesus Christ Emmanuel in it (they) will receive a calling and entrance into Paradise."

68. "The Genre Apocalypse in Hellenistic Judaism," in *Apocalypticism in the Mediterranean World and the Near East: Proceedings of the International Colloquium in Apocalypticism, Uppsala, Aug. 12–17, 1979,* ed. David Hellholm (Tübingen: Mohr [Siebeck]: 1983), 539–40.

69. *Jewish Literature*, 300.

70. "Early Jewish Visions," 372. Bauckham even suggests that the two groups of builders of the Tower of Babel in the first and second heavens are intended as substitutes for the two groups of Watchers in the second and fifth heavens of 2 Enoch. I am less convinced about a relation between 3 Baruch and 2 Enoch.

71. Compare 4 Ezra's "pointed rejection of the very sort of apocalyptic speculation that greatly interests other apocalypses" (Stone, *Fourth Ezra*, 81).

I have modified my conclusions about the polemical aspects of 3 Baruch in light of Bauckham's arguments for an original form of the work that included the sixth and seventh heavens and paradise and hell.

72. Collins, *Apocalyptic Imagination*, 198–201; Nickelsburg, *Jewish Literature*, 299–303.

73. I leave aside the problem of 3 Baruch's attitude toward the people of Israel. It would require a thorough discussion of the relation of the Jewish and Christian elements of the work and its literary development.

Chapter 5

1. See, for example, Wolfgang Speyer, *Die literarische Fälschung im heidnischen und christlichen Altertum*, Handbuch des Altertumswissenschaft 1.2 (Munich: Beck, 1971), and Martin Hengel, "Anonymität, Pseudepigraphie und

'Literarische Fälschung' in der jüdisch-hellenistischen Literatur," in *Pseudepigrapha I*, ed. Kurt von Fritz.

2. The authors of the apocalypses are today generally granted good faith; see, for example, Anthony Grafton, *Forgers and Critics: Creativity and Duplicity in Western Scholarship* (Princeton: Princeton University Press, 1990), where the Letter of Aristeas is treated as a sophisticated example of ancient forgery (15–17), while the Jewish apocalypses are considered "pseudepigrapha rather than forgeries until the *mens rea* of the author is established" (6).

3. Introduction to *APOT* 2: vii–xi.

4. Joseph Blenkinsopp, "Prophecy and Priesthood in Josephus," *JJS* 25 (1974): 240.

5. On these prophets, see Richard A. Horsley, "'Like One of the Prophets of Old': Two Types of Popular Prophets at the Time of Jesus," *CBQ* 47 (1985): 443–47, 454–61, and Horsley and John S. Hanson, *Bandits, Prophets, and Messiahs: Popular Movements at the Time of Jesus* (Minneapolis: Winston, 1985), 135–72.

6. Horsley, "'Like One of the Prophets of Old,'" 45–54, and Horsley and Hanson, *Bandits, Prophets*, 172–87.

7. Horsley, "'Like One of the Prophets of Old,'" 446–49; Horsley and Hanson, *Bandits, Prophets*, 153–60.

8. Blenkinsopp, "Prophecy and Priesthood."

9. On R. H. Charles, for example, Collins, *Apocalyptic Imagination*, 11–13. For a critique of the approach, Stone, *Fourth Ezra*, 11–13, on Kabisch and Box.

10. *The Method and Message of Jewish Apocalyptic* (Philadelphia: Westminster, n.d.; first published London: SCM, 1964), 132–39. The concept of corporate personality is taken from H. Wheeler Robinson (see, e.g., "The Hebrew Conception of Corporate Personality," in *Werden und Wesen des Alten Testaments*, ed. Paul Volz, Friedrich Stummer, and Jonathan Hempel, Beihefte zur Zeitschrift für die altestamentliche Wissenschaft 66 [Berlin: Töpelmann, 1936]; repr. in Robinson, *Corporate Personality in Ancient Israel* [Philadelphia: Fortress, 1964].) For criticism of the idea of corporate personality, see, for example, J. W. Rogerson, "The Hebrew Conception of Corporate Personality: A Re-Examination," *JTS*, n.s., 21 (1970): 1–16.

11. *Open Heaven*, 214–28.

12. Ibid., 228–40, for a discussion of criteria of authenticity.

13. Ibid., 240–47. Rowland sees himself as following J. Lindblom, who discusses an "extraordinary *ego*" that allows the prophet to see his everyday self as if from outside in the course of his vision (*Prophecy in Ancient Israel* [Oxford: Basil Blackwell, 1962], 44).

14. David G. Meade, *Pseudonymity and Canon: An Investigation into the Relationship of Authorship and Authority in Jewish and Earliest Christian Tradition*, Wissenschaftliche Untersuchungen zum Neuen Testament 39 (Tübingen: Mohr [Siebeck], 1986), 102; italics in the original.

15. Ibid., 73–102; summary, 101–2. Meade restricts his discussion to Daniel and 1 Enoch, although in principle it could be extended to other apocalypses.

16. Michael E. Stone, "Apocalyptic—Vision or Hallucination?" *Milla wa-Milla* 14 (1974): 47–56, esp. 55–56, and "Apocalyptic Literature," 430–31, for the apocalypses generally.

Mention should also be made here of a more technical psychological discussion of the practices and experiences of the visionaries of the apocalypses, Daniel Merkur, "The Visionary Practices of Jewish Apocalyptists," in *The Psychoanalytic Study of Society* 14, ed. L. Bryce Boyer and Simon A. Grolnick (Hillsdale, N.J.: The Analytic Press, 1989).

17. "Apocalyptic Literature," 428.

18. "Indeed a relationship between the seer in his ecstatic state and the pseudepigraphic author is a possibility which might be entertained as a partial explanation of pseudepigraphy" (ibid., 431). This position goes somewhat beyond John Collins's understanding of pseudepigraphy in Daniel and elsewhere in the apocalypses as reflecting the author's "sense of affinity" with his hero (*The Apocalyptic Vision of the Book of Daniel*, Harvard Semitic Monographs 16 [Missoula, Mont.: Scholars, 1977], 72–74; the phrase in quotation marks appears on 74).

19. *Fourth Ezra*, esp. 121, 326–27, 429–31. See also Stone, "On Reading an Apocalypse," in *Mysteries and Revelations*, ed. Collins and Charlesworth, 73–78.

20. For a thoughtful discussion of the attitude of the Greek Fathers to the canon of the Old Testament, see Éric Junod, "La formation et la composition de l'Ancien Testament dans l'Église grecque des quatre premiers siècles," in *Le canon de l'Ancien Testament: sa formation et son histoire*, ed. Jean-Daniel Kaestli and Otto Wermelinger (Geneva: Labor et Fides, 1984), 105–51. He emphasizes the importance of the development of Jewish attitudes for the Church, which comes to feel that a book rejected by the Jews cannot form part of the Old Testament. Junod takes Judaism to be rabbinic Judaism, although he does not designate it as such. Indeed he does not consider the complexity of Judaism in the period. It seems unlikely that all Jews shared the rejection of noncanonical literature.

21. *Apocalyptic Vision*, 74.

22. "Pseudepigraphy in the Israelite Tradition," in *Pseudepigrapha I*, ed. von Fritz. Smith uses the term "forgery" rather than pseudepigraphon.

23. 1QpHab col. 7, lines 3–4.

24. See Michael Fishbane, "From Scribalism to Rabbinism: Perspectives on the Emergence of Classical Judaism," in *The Garments of Torah: Essays in Biblical Hermeneutics* (Bloomington: University of Indiana Press, 1989), 67–69, for an interesting discussion of exegetical aspects of Daniel 10–12.

25. Rowland, "Visions of God," 137–54, *Open Heaven*, 214–40; Halperin, *Faces of the Chariot*, 63–114.

26. Lars Hartmann, *Asking for a Meaning: A Study of 1 Enoch 1–5* (Lund: Gleerup, 1979).

27. See the introduction and translation of Himmelfarb, "Sefer Zerubbabel," in *Rabbinic Fantasies: Imaginative Narratives from Classical Hebrew Literature*, ed. David Stern and Mark Jay Mirsky (Philadelphia: Jewish Publication Society, 1990).

28. This learned or "scribal" character is more or less a consensus now. See, for example, Collins, *Apocalyptic Imagination*, 30.

29. The prose narratives about Jeremiah are sometimes attributed to Baruch (e.g., John Bright, *Jeremiah*, Anchor Bible 21 [Garden City, N.Y.: Doubleday, 1965], lxx). Others have argued that even if they go back to Baruch, they have reached us only after reworking by a Deuteronomic editor (e.g., Blenkinsopp, *History of Prophecy*, 157).

30. Ellen Davis, *Swallowing the Scroll: Textuality and the Dynamics of Discourse in Ezekiel's Prophecy*, JSOT Supplement Series 78, Bible and Literature Series 21 (Sheffield: Almond, 1989).

31. For a more detailed consideration of Deuteronomy as a pseudepigraphon and its use of sources, see Smith, "Pseudepigraphy."

32. I believe this view is compatible with the position of Nickelsburg, *Jewish Literature*, 48–55. I take seriously his suggestions about the relationship between the introductory chapters, 1–5, and the second tour, chapters 20–36 (49). For that reason I prefer this schema to an alternative in which the second author is responsible for chapters 20–36 only, while a third author adds chapters 1–5. Of course, there are other possible reconstructions of the earlier stages of composition, but for this discussion the specifics are not important. What is important is the fact of a process of composition that draws on earlier materials, oral or written, and reworks them.

33. The seams visible to the modern reader may reflect different conventions of composition rather than lack of art.

34. See Hall, "Ascension of Isaiah," 290–91, on chapter 6 as redactional.

35. Morton Smith, "Palestinian Judaism in the First Century," in *Israel: Its Role in Civilization*, ed. Moshe Davis (New York: Jewish Theological Seminary, 1956), 69; Stone, "Apocalyptic Literature," 430. Hall thinks that the picture of the prophetic school in chapter 6 is a reflection of the early Christian prophetic school to which the author/redactor of the Ascension of Isaiah belonged ("Ascension of Isaiah," 293–94). He suggests that the references to a prophetic group in the Martyrdom (chs. 1–5) may also reflect this author's situation (294–96): "Three passages (*Asc. Is.* 1:1–13; 2:7–11; 3:6–12) echo chap. 6 sufficiently to suggest that the author's perception of the school has colored the retelling of the martyrdom story" (294).

36. "On Reading an Apocalypse," 76–77; *Fourth Ezra*, 429. I have combined the references to other instances from Stone's two works.

37. See Nickelsburg, "The Apocalyptic Construction of Reality in *1 Enoch*," in *Mysteries and Revelations*, ed. Collins and Charlesworth, on continuities in the literature contained in 1 Enoch; Nickelsburg points out that the editors and compilers of 1 Enoch must have seen such continuities in order to undertake their work. For a discussion of the growth and use of Enoch literature by a socially distinct group in early Judaism, see Collins, *Apocalyptic Imagination*, 56–63.

38. I discuss the subject of the following section in greater detail in "The Practice of Ascent in the Ancient Mediterranean World?," in *Essays in Memory of Ioan P. Culianu,* ed. Collins and Fishbane.

39. Idel, *Kabbalah*, 76–77.

40. Ibid., 80–88.

41. Ibid., 88; Stone, *Fourth Ezra*, 121–22; Merkur, "Visionary Practices," 125–34.

42. Morton Smith, "Ascent to the Heavens and the Beginning of Christianity," *Eranos-Jahrbuch* 50 (1981): 415. The sentence quoted concludes, "and that Jesus himself may well have used one"; the article is part of Smith's larger agenda of demonstrating that Jesus is best understood as a magician.

43. Ibid., 411–15.

44. For example, Elior's review of Halperin, *Faces of the Chariot*, 242. This is an extremely interesting review, and I do not wish to single out Elior; I have said the same thing myself. Smith is in part responsible for establishing this view,

this view, although he surely knew better; unlike most of us, he had read the papyri from start to finish.

45. For a summary statement of Scholem's view, see *Major Trends*, 43.

46. On this puzzling locution, see Scholem, *Jewish Gnosticism*, 20 n. 1.

47. The geniza fragment is published by Schäfer, *Hekhalot-Studien*, 96–103; see his comments, 101. On the redaction history of the recall of R. Nehunyah, see Margarete Schlüter, "Die Erzählung von der Rückholung des R. Nehunya ben Haqana aus der *Merkava*-Schau in ihrem redaktionellen Rahmen," *FJB* 10 (1982): 65–109.

48. *Major Trends*, 50–51.

49. *Apocalyptic and Merkavah Mysticism.*

50. The most recent voice in favor of Scholem's position, against Schäfer and Halperin, is Morray-Jones, "Transformational Mysticism." Morray-Jones sees in Jewish apocalyptic, early Christian, gnostic, and rabbinic texts, evidence of an ongoing tradition in which "exceptionally worthy human beings or 'men of righteousness' were able to achieve a transformation into the likeness of the divine Glory" (20); his view is much like Alan Segal's in *Paul the Convert*, a similarity Morray-Jones notes (30 n. 153).

51. Halperin, review of Schäfer's *Synopse*, "A New Edition of the Hekhalot Literature," *JAOS* 104 (1984): 549–51; Schäfer, "The Aim and Purpose of Early Jewish Mysticism," in *Hekhalot-Studien*, 293–94.

52. In his *Übersetzung der Hekhalot-Literatur*, vol. 3 (with Klaus Herrmann, Lucie Renner, Claudia Rohrbacher-Sticker, and Stefan Siebers, Texte und Studien zum antiken Judentum 22 [Tübingen: Mohr (Siebeck), 1989]), Schäfer takes "prayer" to be the Eighteen Benedictions despite the absence of the definite article (174 n. 52).

53. See Schäfer, "Aim and Purpose," 284; I make the claim more categorically than Schäfer. This is against Scholem, *Major Trends*, 49, as Schäfer points out. Scholem has retrojected onto the hekhalot texts the claims of Hai Gaon in his famous responsum from around 1000, which says that the visionary prepared for ascent by fasting, assuming a position with his head between his knees, and reciting hymns. The absence in the hekhalot texts of ritual fasting or purification associated with ascent is implicitly admitted by Gruenwald, *Apocalyptic and Merkavah Mysticism*, 100–103, despite his adherence at most points to Scholem's view of the hekhalot literature.

54. Cologne Mani Codex, 46, 48, 52, 60, 62, 63, 70, 71.

55. Ibid., 53, 55, 61.

56. See Maier, "Gefährdungsmotiv," 22–23, on this distinction.

57. Stone, *Fourth Ezra*, 330.

58. Ibid., 330–31, and see n. 14.

59. Steven T. Katz, "The 'Conservative' Character of Mystical Experience," in *Mysticism and Religious Traditions,* ed. Katz (New York: Oxford University Press, 1983).

60. Ed. Aaron Ze'ev Eshkoly (Jerusalem: Mosad haRav Kook, 1954), 42–47. I thank Elliot Wolfson for calling the passage to my attention. Idel discusses it in the context of visions induced by weeping (*Kabbalah*, 81), but he prefers the version of the story quoted by R. Isaac Judah Yehiel Safrin of Komarno, *Netiv Miṣvotekha*, p. 87 (*Kabbalah*, 314 n. 45). On impotence in the passage, Idel, *Kabbalah*, 81 and 314 n. 43.

61. *Sepher haHezyonot*, ed. Eshkoly, 45–46.

62. Ibid., 46.

63. Ibid., 43 n. 67. On the history of these motifs, see Eshkoly, "Some notes to the history of the Messianic movements" (in Hebrew), *Sinai* 12 (1942): 84–89.

64. The status of Perpetua's testimony is less clear-cut than that of Vital's. Vital's visions come from a sort of diary. The larger account into which Perpetua's dreams have been incorporated claims that she herself wrote them down, but of course she died soon after dreaming them, leaving them in the hands of others.

65. For the Latin text of the Martyrdom with facing English translation, Herbert Musurillo, *Acts of the Christian Martyrs* (Oxford: Oxford University Press, 1972), 106–31.

66. Rowland has argued that it is possible to detect in the visions of the apocalypses the presence of material not necessary for the manifest message of the vision. This material, never interpreted or deciphered, may be a clue that genuine experience stands behind the literary crystallization of the vision; if it were invented from scratch, no such loose ends would appear (*Open Heaven*, 236–40). This view requires that the conscious imagination work without any recourse to the unconscious and dreamlike.

67. *Major Trends*, 349–50. Although he notes (424 n. 36) that the "core" of the story appears in a collection about Israel of Rishin, *Keneset Yisrael*, Scholem offers the story as told by S. Y. Agnon (349). Thus the strikingly modern tone of the story as Scholem reports it is perhaps less surprising than it at first appears.

68. Scholem did not make this connection because his understanding of the hekhalot literature was so different.

Bibliography

Alexander, Philip. "3 (Hebrew Apocalypse of) Enoch." In *The Old Testament Pseudepigrapha*, ed. Charlesworth.

Altmann, Alexander. "Kedushah Hymns in the Earliest Hechaloth Literature (From an Oxford MS)" (in Hebrew). *Melilah* 2 (1946): 1–24.

Andersen, Frances I. "2 (Slavonic Apocalypse of) Enoch." In *The Old Testament Pseudepigrapha*, ed. Charlesworth.

Andrews, Herbert T. "The Letter of Aristeas." In *APOT*, ed. Charles.

Argyle, A. W. "The Greek Apocalypse of Baruch." In *The Apocryphal Old Testament*, ed. Sparks.

Barnett, Richard D. "Bringing God into the Temple." In *Temples and High Places in Biblical Times*, ed. Avraham Biran. Proceedings of the Colloquium in Honor of the Centennial of Hebrew Union College–Jewish Institute of Religion, Jerusalem, 14–16 March 1977. Jerusalem: Hebrew Union College–Jewish Institute of Religion, 1981.

Barr, James. Review of *Books of Enoch*, by J. T. Milik. In *JTS*, n.s., 29 (1978): 517–30.

Barton, J. M. T. Introduction to "The Ascension of Isaiah." In *The Apocryphal Old Testament*, ed. Sparks.

Bauckham, Richard. "Early Jewish Visions of Hell." *JTS*, n.s., 41 (1990): 355–85.

Becker, Jürgen. *Untersuchungen zur Entstehungsgeschichte der Testamente der Zwölf Patriarchen*. Arbeiten zur Geschichte des antiken Judentums und des Urchristentums 8. Leiden: Brill, 1970.

Betz, Hans Dieter, ed. *The Greek Magical Papyri in Translation Including the Demotic Spells*. Chicago: University of Chicago Press, 1986.

Bickerman, Elias. *From Ezra to the Last of the Maccabees*. 1947; rpt. New York: Schocken, 1962.

Bietenhard, Hans. *Die himmlische Welt im Urchristentum und Spätjudentum.* Tübingen: Mohr (Siebeck), 1951.

Black, Matthew. *The Book of Enoch or I Enoch: A New English Translation.* In consultation with James C. VanderKam, with an appendix by Otto Neugebauer. SVTP 7. Leiden: Brill, 1985.

Blenkinsopp, Joseph. *A History of Prophecy in Israel.* Philadelphia: Westminster, 1983.

———. "Prophecy and Priesthood in Josephus." *JJS* 25 (1974): 239–62.

Bousset, Wilhelm. "Die Himmelsreise der Seele," *Archiv für Religionswissenschaft* 4 (1901): 136–69, 229–73 (rpt. as separate booklet, Darmstadt: Wissenschaftliche Buchgesellschaft, 1960).

Box, G. H., with J. I. Landsman. *The Apocalypse of Abraham.* London: SPCK, 1918.

Bright, John. *A History of Israel.* 3d ed. Philadelphia: Westminster, 1981.

———. *Jeremiah.* Anchor Bible 21. Garden City, N.Y.: Doubleday, 1965.

van den Broek, R. *The Myth of the Phoenix According to Classical and Early Christian Traditions.* Leiden: Brill, 1972.

Charles, R. H. "The Ascension of Isaiah." Rev. J. M. T. Barton. In *The Apocryphal Old Testament,* ed. Sparks.

———. "The Book of the Secrets of Enoch." In *APOT,* ed. Charles.

———. "The Date and Place of Writing of the Slavonic Book of Enoch." *JTS* 22 (1921): 161–63.

———. "Jubilees." Rev. C. Rabin. In *The Apocryphal Old Testament,* ed. Sparks.

———. "The Syriac Apocalypse of Baruch." Rev. L. H. Brockington. In *The Apocryphal Old Testament,* ed. Sparks.

———. "The Testaments of the Twelve Patriarchs." In *APOT,* ed. Charles.

———, ed. *Apocrypha and Pseudepigrapha of the Old Testament.* 2 vols. Oxford: Oxford University Press, 1913.

Charlesworth, James H., ed. *The Old Testament Pseudepigrapha.* 2 vols. Garden City, N.Y.: Doubleday, 1983, 1985.

Childs, Brevard. *Isaiah and the Assyrian Crisis.* Studies in Biblical Theology, second series, 3. London: SCM, 1967.

Clements, R. E. *God and Temple.* Oxford: Basil Blackwell, 1965.

Clifford, Richard J. *The Cosmic Mountain in Canaan and the Old Testament.* Harvard Semitic Monographs 4. Cambridge, Mass.: Harvard University Press, 1972.

Collins, John J. "Apocalyptic Eschatology as the Transcendence of Death." *CBQ* 36 (1974): 21–43.

———. *The Apocalyptic Imagination: An Introduction to the Jewish Matrix of Christianity.* New York: Crossroad, 1984.

———. *The Apocalyptic Vision of the Book of Daniel.* Harvard Semitic Monographs 16. Missoula, Mont.: Scholars, 1977.

———. "The Genre Apocalypse in Hellenistic Judaism." In *Apocalypticism in the Mediterranean World and the Near East: Proceedings of the International Colloquium in Apocalypticism, Uppsala, Aug. 12–17, 1979,* ed. David Hellholm. Tübingen: Mohr (Siebeck), 1983.

———. "A Throne in the Heavens: Apotheosis in pre-Christian Judaism." In *Essays in Memory of Ioan P. Culianu,* ed. Collins and Fishbane.

———, ed. *Apocalypse: The Morphology of a Genre. Semeia* 14 (1979).

Collins, John J., and James H. Charlesworth, eds. *Mysteries and Revelations: Apocalyptic Studies Since the Uppsala Colloquium.* Journal for the Study of the Pseudepigrapha Supplement Series 9. Sheffield: JSOT Press, 1991.

Collins, John J., and Michael Fishbane, eds. *Essays in Memory of Ioan P. Culianu.* Albany: SUNY Press. Forthcoming.

Cross, Frank Moore. *Canaanite Myth and Hebrew Epic.* Cambridge, Mass.: Harvard University Press, 1973.

Culianu, Ioan Petru. *Psychanodia I: A Survey of the Evidence Concerning the Ascension of the Soul and Its Relevance.* Leiden: Brill, 1983.

Daniel, Suzanne. *Recherches sur le vocabulaire du culte dans la Septante.* Études et commentaires 61. Paris: Klincksieck, 1966.

Davis, Ellen. *Swallowing the Scroll: Textuality and the Dynamics of Discourse in Ezekiel's Prophecy.* JSOT Supplement Series 78, Bible and Literature Series 21. Sheffield: Almond, 1989.

Dean-Otting, Mary. *Heavenly Journeys: A Study of the Motif in Hellenistic Jewish Literature.* Judentum und Umwelt. Frankfurt: Peter Lang, 1984.

Di Lella, Alexander A. Introduction and commentary to *The Wisdom of Ben Sira,* trans. Patrick W. Skehan. Anchor Bible 39. Garden City, N.Y.: Doubleday, 1987.

Dimant, Devorah. "1 Enoch 6–11: A Methodological Perspective." *SBL Seminar Papers 1978,* 1:323–39.

Eichrodt, Walther. *Ezekiel: A Commentary.* Tr. Cosslett Quin. London: SCM, 1970.

Elior, Rachel. Review of *Faces of the Chariot,* by David Halperin. In *Numen* 37 (1990): 241–47.

Emerton, J. A. "The Origin of the Son of Man Imagery." *JTS,* n.s., 9 (1958): 225–42.

Eshkoly, Aaron Ze'ev. "Some notes to the history of the Messianic movements" (in Hebrew). *Sinai* 12 (1942): 84–89.

Fishbane, Michael. *Biblical Interpretation in Ancient Israel.* Oxford: Oxford University Press, 1985.

———. "From Scribalism to Rabbinism: Perspectives on the Emergence of Classical Judaism." In *The Garments of Torah: Essays in Biblical Hermeneutics.* Bloomington: University of Indiana Press, 1989.

Fischer, Ulrich. *Eschatologie und Jenseitserwartung im hellenistischen Diasporajudentum.* Berlin: de Gruyter, 1978.

Flusser, David. "Melchizedek and the Son of Man." *Christian News from Israel* (April 1966): 23–29.

Fossum, Jarl E. *The Name of God and the Angel of the Lord: Samaritan and Jewish Concepts of Intermediation and the Origin of Gnosticism.* Wissenschaftliche Untersuchungen zum Neuen Testament. Tübingen: Mohr (Siebeck), 1985.

Fraade, Steven. "'They Shall Teach Your Statutes to Jacob': Priest, Scribe, and Sage in Second Temple Times." *JBL,* forthcoming.

Freedman, David N. "Temples Without Hands." In *Temples and High Places in Biblical Times,* ed. Avraham Biran. Proceedings of the Colloquium in Honor of the Centennial of Hebrew Union College–Jewish Institute of Religion, Jerusalem, 14–16 March 1977. Jerusalem: Hebrew Union College–Jewish Institute of Religion, 1981.

von Fritz, Kurt, ed. *Pseudepigrapha I*. Entretiens sur l'Antiquité Classique 18. Geneva: Vandoeuvres, 1972.

Gaylord, H. E., Jr. "3 (Greek Apocalypse of) Baruch." In *The Old Testament Pseudepigrapha*, ed. Charlesworth.

Goodenough, E. R. *By Light, Light: The Mystic Gospel of Hellenistic Judaism*. New Haven, Conn.: Yale University Press, 1935.

Grafton, Anthony. *Forgers and Critics: Creativity and Duplicity in Western Scholarship*. Princeton: Princeton University Press, 1990.

Greenberg, Moshe. "The Design and Themes of Ezekiel's Program of Restoration." *Interpretation* 38 (1984): 181–208.

———. *Ezekiel 1–20*. Anchor Bible 22. Garden City, N.Y.: Doubleday, 1983.

Greenfield, Jonas C., and Michael E. Stone. "Remarks on the Aramaic Testament of Levi from the Geniza." *RB* 86 (1979): 214–31.

Grelot, Pierre. "La géographie mythique d'Hénoch et ses sources orientales." *RB* 65 (1958): 33–69.

Gruenwald, Ithamar. *Apocalyptic and Merkavah Mysticism*. Arbeiten zur Geschichte des antiken Judentums und des Urchristentums 14. Leiden: Brill, 1980.

Gry, L. "Quelques noms d'anges ou d'êtres mystérieux en II Hénoch." *RB* 49 (1940): 195–204.

Hall, Robert G. "*The Ascension of Isaiah*: Community Situation, Date, and Place in Early Christianity." *JBL* 109 (1990): 289–306.

Halperin, David. "The Exegetical Character of Ezek. X 9–17." *VT* 26 (1976): 129–41.

———. *The Faces of the Chariot: Early Jewish Responses to Ezekiel's Vision*. Texte und Studien zum antiken Judentum 16. Tübingen: Mohr (Siebeck), 1988.

———. *The Merkabah in Rabbinic Literature*. American Oriental Series 62. New Haven, Conn.: American Oriental Society, 1980.

———. "A New Edition of the Hekhalot Literature." *JAOS* 104 (1984): 543–52.

Hanson, Paul D. *The Dawn of Apocalyptic: The Historical and Sociological Roots of Jewish Apocalyptic Eschatology*. Rev. ed. Philadelphia: Fortress, 1979.

———. "Rebellion in Heaven, Azazel, and Euhemeristic Heroes in 1 Enoch 6–11." *JBL* 96 (1977): 195–233.

Haran, Menahem. "The Law-Code of Ezekiel XL–XLVIII and Its Relation to the Priestly School." *HUCA* 50 (1979): 45–71.

———. *Temples and Temple Service in Ancient Israel*. Oxford: Oxford University Press, 1978.

Hartman, Louis F., and Alexander A. DiLella. *The Book of Daniel*. Anchor Bible 23. Garden City, N.Y.: Doubleday, 1978.

Hartmann, Lars. *Asking for a Meaning: A Study of 1 Enoch 1–5*. Lund: Gleerup, 1979.

Hayes, John H. "The Tradition of Zion's Inviolability." *JBL* 82 (1963): 419–26.

Helmbold, Andrew K. "Gnostic Elements in the 'Ascension of Isaiah.'" *New Testament Studies* 18 (1972): 222–27.

Hengel, Martin. "Anonymität, Pseudepigraphie und 'Literarische Fälschung' in der jüdisch-hellenistischen Literatur." In *Pseudepigrapha I*, ed. von Fritz.

———. *Judaism and Hellenism: Studies in their Encounter in Palestine During the Early Hellenistic Age*. 2 vols. Tr. John Bowden. Philadelphia: Fortress, 1974.

Himmelfarb, Martha. "The Experience of the Visionary and Genre in the Ascension of Isaiah 6–11 and the Apocalypse of Paul." In *Early Christian Apocalypticism: Genre and Social Setting*, ed. Adela Yarbro Collins. *Semeia* 36 (1986): 97–111.

———. "Heavenly Ascent and the Relationship of the Apocalypses and the *Hekhalot* Literature." *HUCA* 59 (1988): 73–100.

———. "The Practice of Ascent in the Ancient Mediterranean World?" In *Essays in Memory of Ioan P. Culianu*, ed. Collins and Fishbane.

———. "Revelation and Rapture: The Transformation of the Visionary in the Ascent Apocalypses." In *Mysteries and Revelations*, ed. Collins and Charlesworth.

———. Review of *Faces of the Chariot*, by David Halperin. In *Critical Review of Books in Religion* 3 (1990): 340–42.

———. Review of *Heavenly Journeys: A Study of the Motif in Hellenistic Jewish Literature*, by Mary Dean-Otting. In *JBL* 106 (1987): 126–28.

———. "Sefer Zerubbabel." In *Rabbinic Fantasies: Imaginative Narratives from Classical Hebrew Literature*, ed. David Stern and Mark Jay Mirsky. Philadelphia: Jewish Publication Society, 1990.

———. "The Temple and the Garden of Eden in Ezekiel, the Book of the Watchers, and the Wisdom of Ben Sira." In *Sacred Places and Profane Spaces: Essays in the Geographics of Judaism, Christianity and Islam*, ed. Jamie S. Scott and Paul Simpson-Horsley. Westport, Conn.: Greenwood, 1991.

———. *Tours of Hell: An Apocalyptic Form in Jewish and Christian Literature.* Philadelphia: University of Pennsylvania Press, 1983.

Holladay, Carl R. *Theios Aner in Hellenistic Judaism: A Critique of the Use of This Category in New Testament Christology.* SBL Dissertation Series 40. Missoula, Mont.: Scholars, 1977.

Hollander, H. W., and M. de Jonge. *The Testaments of the Twelve Patriarchs: A Commentary.* Leiden: Brill, 1985.

Horsley, Richard A. "'Like One of the Prophets of Old': Two Types of Popular Prophets at the Time of Jesus." *CBQ* 47 (1985): 435–63.

Horsley, Richard A., and John S. Hanson. *Bandits, Prophets, and Messiahs: Popular Movements at the Time of Jesus.* Minneapolis: Winston, 1985.

Houk, C. B. "The Final Redaction of Ezekiel 10." *JBL* 90 (1971): 42–54.

Hughes, H. M. "The Greek Apocalypse of Baruch or III Baruch." In *APOT*, ed. Charles.

Hultgård, Anders. *L'eschatologie des Testaments des Douze Patriarches.* 2 vols. Uppsala: Almqvist & Wisksell, 1977, 1982.

Hurtado, Larry W. *One God, One Lord: Early Christian Devotion and Ancient Jewish Monotheism.* Philadelphia: Fortress, 1988.

Idel, Moshe. *Kabbalah: New Perspectives.* New Haven, Conn.: Yale University Press, 1988.

James, M. R. *Apocrypha Anecdota II.* Texts and Studies 5:1. Cambridge: Cambridge University Press, 1897.

de Jonge, Marinus. *Jewish Eschatology, Early Christian Christology and the Testaments of the Twelve Patriarchs: Collected Essays of Marinus de Jonge.* Leiden: Brill, 1991.

———. "Levi, the Sons of Levi and the Law in *Testament Levi* X, XIV–XV, and XVI." In *Jewish Eschatology*.

———. "Notes on Testament of Levi II–VII." In *Studies on the Testaments*.

————. *Studies on the Testaments of the Twelve Patriarchs: Text and Interpretation.* SVTP 3. Leiden: Brill, 1975.

————. "The Testament of Levi and 'Aramaic Levi.'" In *Jewish Eschatology.*

————. "The Testaments of the Twelve Patriarchs." In *The Apocryphal Old Testament,* ed. Sparks.

————. *The Testaments of the Twelve Patriarchs: A Study of Their Text, Composition, and Origin.* Assen, Netherlands: Van Gorcum, 1953.

de Jonge, Marinus et al. *The Testaments of the Twelve Patriarchs: A Critical Edition of the Greek Text.* Leiden: Brill, 1978.

Josephus. *Jewish War.* Tr. H. St. J. Thackeray. Loeb Classical Library. Cambridge, Mass.: Harvard University Press, 1928.

Junod, Éric. "La formation et la composition de l'Ancien Testament dans l'Église grecque des quatre premiers siècles." In *Le canon de l'Ancien Testament: sa formation et son histoire,* ed. Jean-Daniel Kaestli and Otto Wermelinger. Geneva: Labor et Fides, 1984.

Kapelrud, Arvid S. "Temple Building, a Task for Gods and Kings." *Orientalia,* n.s., 32 (1963): 56–62.

Katz, Steven T. "The 'Conservative' Character of Mystical Experience." In *Mysticism and Religious Traditions,* ed. Steven T. Katz. New York: Oxford University Press, 1983.

Kaufmann, Yehezkel. *The Religion of Israel* (abridged). Tr. Moshe Greenberg. Chicago: University of Chicago Press, 1960.

Kobelski, Paul J. *Melchizedek and Melchireša'.* Catholic Biblical Quarterly Monograph Series 10. Washington: Catholic Biblical Association, 1981.

Koenen, Ludwig, and Claudia Römer, eds. *Der Kölner Mani-Kodex: Über das Werden seines Leibes.* Abhandlungen der rheinisch-westfälischen Akademie der Wissenschaften, Papyrologica Coloniensia 14. Opladen: Westdeutscher, 1988.

Kuhn, K. H. "The Apocalypse of Zephaniah and an Anonymous Apocalypse." In *The Apocryphal Old Testament,* ed. Sparks.

Lacocque, André. *The Book of Daniel.* Tr. David Pellauer, with a foreword by Paul Ricoeur. Atlanta, Ga.: John Knox, 1979.

Landsberger, B., and J. V. Kinnier Wilson. "The Fifth Tablet of *Enuma Eliš.*" *JNES* 20 (1961): 154–79.

Levenson, Jon D. *Sinai and Zion: An Entry into the Jewish Bible.* Minneapolis: Winston-Seabury, 1985.

————. *Theology of the Program of Restoration of Ezekiel 40–48.* Harvard Semitic Monographs 10. Missoula, Mont.: Scholars, 1976.

Lewy, Hans. *Chaldean Oracles and Theurgy: Mysticism, Magic, and Platonism in the Later Roman Empire.* Cairo: L'Institut Français d'Archéologie Orientale, 1956.

Lieberman, Saul. *Hellenism in Jewish Palestine.* New York: Jewish Theological Seminary, 1950.

————. "Metatron, the Meaning of His Name and His Functions," in Gruenwald, *Apocalyptic and Merkavah Mysticism.*

Lightstone, Jack. "Sadducees versus Pharisees: The Tannaitic Sources." In *Christianity, Judaism, and Other Greco-Roman Cults: Studies for Morton Smith at Sixty,* ed. Jacob Neusner. 4 vols. Leiden: Brill, 1975.

Lindblom, J. *Prophecy in Ancient Israel.* Oxford: Basil Blackwell, 1962.

Mach, Michael. *Die Entstehung des jüdischen Engelglaubens. Entwicklungsphasen des jüdischen Engelglaubens in vorrabbinischer Zeit.* Texte und Studien zum antiken Judentum 34. Tübingen: Mohr (Siebeck), 1992.

Mack, Burton. *Wisdom and the Hebrew Epic: Ben Sira's Hymn in Praise of the Fathers.* Chicago: University of Chicago Press, 1986.

Maier, Johann. "Das Gefährdungsmotiv bei der Himmelsreise in der jüdischen Apokalyptik und 'Gnosis.'" *Kairos* 5 (1963): 18–40.

———. *Vom Kultus zur Gnosis. Kairos.* Religionswissenschaftliche Studien 1. Salzburg: Otto Mueller, 1964.

Maunders, A. S. D. "The Date and Place of Writing of the Slavonic Book of Enoch." *The Observatory* 41 (1918): 309–16.

Meade, David G. *Pseudonymity and Canon: An Investigation into the Relationship of Authorship and Authority in Jewish and Earliest Christian Tradition.* Wissenschaftliche Untersuchungen zum Neuen Testament 39. Tübingen: Mohr (Siebeck), 1986.

Merkur, Daniel. "The Visionary Practices of Jewish Apocalyptists." In *The Psychoanalytic Study of Society* 14, ed. L. Bryce Boyer and Simon A. Grolnick. Hillsdale, N.J.: The Analytic Press, 1989.

Milik, J. T. *The Books of Enoch: Aramaic Fragments of Qumrân Cave 4.* With the collaboration of Matthew Black. Oxford: Oxford University Press, 1976.

———. "Le Testament de Lévi en Araméen." *RB* 62 (1955): 398–406.

Morfill, W. R., tr., and R. H. Charles, ed. *The Book of the Secrets of Enoch.* Oxford: Oxford University Press, 1896.

Morray-Jones, C. R. A. "Transformational Mysticism in the Apocalyptic-Merkabah Tradition." *JJS* 43 (1992): 1–31.

Mullen, E. Theodore, Jr. *The Assembly of the Gods.* Harvard Semitic Monographs 24. Chico, Calif.: Scholars, 1980.

Musurillo, Herbert. *Acts of the Christian Martyrs.* Oxford: Oxford University Press, 1972.

Newman, Carey. *Paul's Glory-Christology: Tradition and Rhetoric.* Leiden: Brill, 1992.

Newsom, Carol. "A Maker of Metaphors—Ezekiel's Oracles Against Tyre." *Interpretation* 38 (1984): 151–64.

———. *Songs of the Sabbath Sacrifice: A Critical Edition.* Harvard Semitic Studies. Atlanta, Ga.: Scholars, 1985.

Newton, Michael. *The Concept of Purity at Qumran and in the Letters of Paul.* SNTS Monograph Series 53. Cambridge: Cambridge University Press, 1985.

Nickelsburg, George W. E. "The Apocalyptic Construction of Reality in *1 Enoch.*" In *Mysteries and Revelations,* ed. Collins and Charlesworth.

———. "Enoch, Levi, and Peter: Recipients of Revelation in Upper Galilee." *JBL* 100 (1981): 575–600.

———. *Jewish Literature Between the Bible and the Mishnah.* Philadelphia: Fortress, 1981.

———. *Resurrection, Immortality, and Eternal Life in Intertestamental Judaism.* Cambridge, Mass.: Harvard University Press, 1972.

———. Review of *Books of Enoch,* by J. T. Milik. In *CBQ* 40 (1978): 411–19.

———. "Two Enochic Manuscripts: Unstudied Evidence for Egyptian Christianity." In *Of Scribes and Scrolls: Studies on the Hebrew Bible, Intertestamental Judaism, and Christian Origins Presented to John Strugnell on the Occasion of His Sixtieth Birthday,* ed. Harold W. Attridge, John J. Collins, and Thomas

H. Tobin. Lanham, Md.: The College Theology Society and University Press of America, 1990.

Niditch, Susan. "Ezekiel 40–48 in a Visionary Context." *CBQ* 48 (1986): 208–24.

Ó Fearghail, Fearghas. "Sir 50, 5–21: Yom Kippur or the Daily Whole Offering?" *Biblica* 59 (1978): 301–16.

Odeberg, Hugo. *3 Enoch, or The Hebrew Book of Enoch.* Cambridge: Cambridge University Press, 1928.

Otto, Rudolf. *Reich Gottes und Menschensohn.* Munich: Beck, 1934.

Pennington, A. "2 Enoch." In *The Apocryphal Old Testament,* ed. Sparks.

———. "The Apocalypse of Abraham." In *The Apocryphal Old Testament,* ed. Sparks.

Philo. *Philo* vol. 6. Tr. F. H. Colson. Loeb Classical Library. Cambridge, Mass.: Harvard University Press, 1935.

Philonenko, Marc. "La cosmologie du 'Livre des secrets d'Hénoch.'" In *Religions en Égypte hellénistique et romaine.* Colloque de Strasbourg, 16–18 mai 1967. Paris: Presses universitaires de France, 1969.

Picard, Jean-Claude. "Observations sur l'Apocalypse grecque de Baruch." *Semitica* 20 (1970): 77–103.

Pines, Shlomo. "Eschatology and the Concept of Time in the Slavonic Book of Enoch." In *Types of Redemption,* ed. R. J. Zwi Werblowsky and C. Jouco Bleeker. Supplements to *Numen* 18. Leiden: Brill, 1970.

Plöger, Otto. *Theocracy and Eschatology.* Tr. S. Rudman. Richmond, Va.: John Knox, 1968.

Pope, Marvin H. *El in the Ugaritic Texts.* Leiden: Brill, 1955.

von Rad, Gerhard. *Wisdom in Israel.* Tr. James D. Martin. Nashville, Tenn.: Abingdon, 1972.

Robinson, H. Wheeler. "The Hebrew Conception of Corporate Personality." In *Werden und Wesen des Alten Testaments,* ed. Paul Volz, Friedrich Stummer, and Jonathan Hempel. Beihefte zur Zeitschrift für die altestamentliche Wissenschaft 66. Berlin: Töpelmann, 1936 (rpt. in Robinson, *Corporate Personality in Ancient Israel.* Philadelphia: Fortress, 1964).

Rogerson, J. W. "The Hebrew Conception of Corporate Personality: A Re-Examination." *JTS,* n.s., 21 (1970): 1–16.

Rowland, Christopher. *The Open Heaven: A Study of Apocalyptic in Judaism and Early Christianity.* New York: Crossroad, 1982.

———. "The Visions of God in Apocalyptic Literature." *JSJ* 10 (1979): 137–54.

Rubinkiewicz, R. "Apocalypse of Abraham." In *The Old Testament Pseudepigrapha,* ed. Charlesworth.

Rubinstein, Arie. "Observations on the Slavonic Book of Enoch." *JJS* 13 (1962): 1–21.

Russell, D. S. *The Method and Message of Jewish Apocalyptic.* London: SCM, 1964; rpt. Philadelphia: Westminster, n.d.

Satran, David. *Biblical Prophets in Byzantine Palestine: Reassessing the Lives of the Prophets.* SVTP. Leiden: Brill, forthcoming.

———. "The Lives of the Prophets." In *Jewish Writings of the Second Temple Period,* ed. Michael E. Stone. Compendia Rerum Iudaicarum ad Novum Testamentum, 2.2. Assen: Van Gorcum, 1984.

Schäfer, Peter. "The Aim and Purpose of Early Jewish Mysticism." In *Hekhalot-Studien.*

————. *Geniza-Fragmente zur Hekhalot-Literatur.* Texte und Studien zum antiken Judentum 19. Tübingen: Mohr (Siebeck), 1988.

————. *Hekhalot-Studien.* Texte und Studien zum antiken Judentum 19. Tübingen: Mohr (Siebeck), 1988.

————. *Rivalität zwischen Engeln und Menschen.* Studia Judaica. Berlin: de Gruyter, 1975.

————. *Synopse zur Hekhalot-Literatur.* Texte und Studien zum antiken Judentum 2. With the collaboration of Margarete Schlüter and Hans Georg von Mutius. Tübingen: Mohr (Siebeck), 1981.

————. "Tradition and Redaction in Hekhalot Literature." *JSJ* 14 (1983): 172–181 (rpt. in *Hekhalot-Studien*).

————. *Übersetzung der Hekhalot-Literatur,* vol. 3. With Klaus Herrmann, Lucie Renner, Claudia Rohrbacher-Sticker, and Stefan Siebers. Texte und Studien zum antiken Judentum 22. Tübingen: Mohr (Siebeck), 1989.

Schaeffer, C. F. A. *The Cuneiform Texts of Ras Shamra-Ugarit.* London: Oxford University Press, 1939.

Schlüter, Margarete. "Die Erzählung von der Rückholung des R. Neḥunya ben Haqana aus der *Merkava*-Schau in ihrem redaktionellen Rahmen." *FJB* 10 (1982): 65–109.

Scholem, Gershom G. *Jewish Gnosticism, Merkabah Mysticism, and Talmudic Tradition.* 2d rev. ed. New York: Jewish Theological Seminary, 1965.

————. "Die Lehre vom 'Gerechten' in der jüdischen Mystik." *Eranos-Jahrbuch* 27 (1958): 237–97.

————. *Major Trends in Jewish Mysticism.* Paperback ed. New York: Schocken, 1961.

————. *Origins of the Kabbalah.* Tr. Allan Arkush. Philadelphia and Princeton: Jewish Publication Society and Princeton University Press, 1987.

Segal, Alan F. "Heavenly Ascent in Hellenistic Judaism, Early Christianity and Their Environment," *ANRW* II.23.2 (1980), 1333–94.

————. *Paul the Convert: The Apostolate and Apostasy of Saul the Pharisee.* New Haven, Conn.: Yale University Press, 1990.

Slingerland, H. Dixon. *The Testaments of the Twelve Patriarchs: A Critical History of Research.* Missoula, Mont.: Scholars, 1977.

Smith, Jonathan Z. *To Take Place: Toward Theory in Ritual.* Chicago: University of Chicago Press, 1987.

————. "Wisdom and Apocalyptic." In *Religious Syncretism in Antiquity,* ed. Birger A. Pearson. Missoula, Mont.: Scholars, 1975 (rpt. in Smith, *Map Is Not Territory: Studies in the History of Religions.* Leiden: Brill, 1978).

Smith, Morton. "Ascent to the Heavens and the Beginning of Christianity." *Eranos-Jahrbuch* 50 (1981): 403–29.

————. "Ascent to the Heavens and Deification in 4QMᵃ." In *Archeology and History: The New York University Conference in Memory of Yigael Yadin,* ed. Lawrence H. Schiffman. Journal for the Study of the Pseudepigrapha Series 8, JSOT/ASOR Monographs 2. Sheffield: JSOT, 1990.

————. *Jesus the Magician.* San Francisco: Harper & Row, 1978.

————. "Palestinian Judaism in the First Century." In *Israel: Its Role in Civilization,* ed. Moshe Davis. New York: Jewish Theological Seminary, 1956.

————. *Palestinian Parties and Politics That Shaped the Old Testament.* New York: Columbia University Press, 1971.

————. "Pseudepigraphy in the Israelite Tradition." In *Pseudepigrapha I,* ed. von Fritz.

Sparks, H. F. D., ed. *The Apocryphal Old Testament*. Oxford: Oxford University Press, 1984.

Speyer, Wolfgang. *Die literarische Fälschung im heidnischen und christlichen Altertum*. Handbuch des Altertumswissenschaft 1.2. Munich: Beck, 1971.

Stone, Michael E. "Apocalyptic Literature." In *Jewish Writings of the Second Temple Period*, ed. Michael E. Stone. Compendia Rerum Iudaicarum ad Novum Testamentum, 2.2. Philadelphia: Fortress, 1984.

———. "Apocalyptic—Vision or Hallucination?" *Milla wa-Milla* 14 (1974): 47–56.

———. "The Book of Enoch and Judaism in the Third Century B.C.E." *CBQ* 40 (1978): 479–92.

———. "Enoch, Aramaic Levi and Sectarian Origins." *JSJ* 19 (1988): 159–70.

———. *Fourth Ezra*. Ed. Frank Moore Cross. Hermeneia. Minneapolis: Fortress, 1990.

———. "Lists of Revealed Things in Apocalyptic Literature." In *Magnalia Dei: The Mighty Acts of God (Essays on the Bible and Archeology in Memory of G. Ernest Wright)*, ed. Frank M. Cross, Warner Lemke, and Patrick D. Miller. Garden City, N.Y.: Doubleday, 1976.

———. "On Reading an Apocalypse." In *Mysteries and Revelations*, ed. Collins and Charlesworth.

———. "The Parabolic Use of Natural Order in Judaism of the Second Temple Age." In *Gilgul: Werblowsky Festschrift*, ed. Shaul Shaked, David Shulman, and Gedaliahu G. Stroumsa. Numen Supplement 50. Leiden: Brill, 1987.

Suter, David. "Fallen Angel, Fallen Priest: The Problem of Family Purity in 1 Enoch 6–16." *HUCA* 50 (1979): 115–135.

———. "Mašal in the Similitudes of Enoch." *JBL* 100 (1981): 193–212.

———. *Tradition and Composition in the Parables of Enoch*. SBL Dissertation Series 47. Missoula, Mont.: Scholars, 1979.

Tcherikover, Victor. *Hellenistic Civilization and the Jews*. 1959; rpt. New York: Athanaeum, 1974.

Tcherikover, Victor, Alexander Fuks, and Menahem Stern, eds. *Corpus Papyrorum Judaicarum*. 3 vols. Cambridge, Mass.: Harvard University Press, 1957–64.

Theodor, J., and Ch. Albeck. *Midrash Bereshit Rabba*. 2d corrected printing. Jerusalem: Wahrmann, 1965.

Tiede, David Lenz. *The Charismatic Figure as Miracle Worker*. SBL Dissertation Series 1. Missoula, Mont.: Society of Biblical Literature, 1972.

Torrey, Charles Cutler. *The Lives of the Prophets: Greek Text and Translation*. Journal of Biblical Literature Monograph Series 1. Philadelphia: Society of Biblical Literature and Exegesis, 1946.

Turdeanu, Émile. "Apocryphes bogomiles et apocryphes pseudo-bogomiles." In *Apocryphes slaves et roumains de l'Ancien Testament*. SVTP 5. Leiden: Brill, 1981.

Vaillant, A. *Le livre des secrets d'Hénoch*. Textes publis par l'Institut d'études slaves 4. Paris: Institut d'études slaves, 1952.

VanderKam, James C. *Enoch and the Growth of an Apocalyptic Tradition*. Catholic Biblical Quarterly Monograph Series 16. Washington: Catholic Biblical Association of America, 1984.

Vermes, Geza. *The Dead Sea Scrolls in English*. 3d ed. London: Penguin, 1987.

Vital, Hayyim. *Sepher haHezyonot*, ed. Aaron Ze'ev Eshkoly. Jerusalem: Mosad haRav Kook, 1954.

Weinfeld, Moshe. *Deuteronomy and the Deuteronomic School.* Oxford: Oxford University Press, 1972.

Wintermute, O. S. "Apocalypse of Zephaniah." In *The Old Testament Pseudepigrapha*, ed. Charlesworth.

Yarbro Collins, Adela. "The Seven Heavens in Jewish and Christian Apocalypses." In *Essays in Memory of Ioan P. Culianu*, ed. Collins and Fishbane.

Zimmerli, Walther. *Ezekiel 1.* Hermeneia. Tr. Ronald E. Clements. Philadelphia: Fortress, 1979 (German original, 1969).

Index